PALESTINIAN WOMEN AND MUSLIM FAMILY LAW
IN THE MANDATE PERIOD

Gender, Culture, and Politics in the Middle East
miriam cooke, Simona Sharoni, and Suad Joseph, *Series Editors*

For a full list of titles in this series,
visit https://press.syr.edu/supressbook-series
/gender-culture-and-politics-in-the-middle-east

Palestinian Women and Muslim Family Law in the Mandate Period

❧

Elizabeth Brownson

Syracuse University Press

∞ The paper used in this publication meets the minimum requirements of the American National Standard for Information Sciences—Permanence of Paper for Printed Library Materials, ANSI Z39.48-1992.

For a listing of books published and distributed by Syracuse University Press, visit https://press.syr.edu.

ISBN: 978-0-8156-3628-1 (hardcover)   978-0-8156-3646-5 (paperback)
978-0-8156-5474-2 (e-book)

Library of Congress Cataloging-in-Publication Data
Names: Brownson, Elizabeth, author.
Title: Palestinian women and Muslim family law in the mandate period / Elizabeth Brownson.
Description: First Edition. | Syracuse, NY : Syracuse University Press, [2019] | Series: Gender, culture, and politics in the Middle East | Includes bibliographical references and index.
Identifiers: LCCN 2019004979 (print) | LCCN 2019020369 (ebook) | ISBN 9780815654742 (E-book) | ISBN 9780815636281 (hardcover : alk. paper) | ISBN 9780815636465 (pbk. : alk. paper)
Subjects: LCSH: Women, Palestinian Arab. | Women (Islamic law) | Islamic courts. | Justice, Administration of (Islamic law) | Women—Palestine—History—20th century. | Sex discrimination against women.
Classification: LCC HQ1728.5 (ebook) | LCC HQ1728.5 .B76 2019 (print) | DDC 305.409469405—dc23
LC record available at https://lccn.loc.gov/2019004979

Manufactured in the United States of America

For Kevin, Emma, and Bryan

Contents

Acknowledgments

MANY COLLEAGUES, family members, and friends helped me in the process of researching and writing this book. First, I am very grateful for the ongoing support and guidance of my former graduate school adviser, Nancy Gallagher. She continues to be my go-to person to consult, as she always has wise, pithy advice. Steve Humphreys was also invaluable to my development both as a scholar and a teacher. I learned a great deal in both respects, particularly when I was his teaching assistant for several courses, and I very much appreciated his kind encouragement. Both offered crucial feedback on my manuscript in its early stages, as did Adrienne Edgar and Lisa Hajjar. Other University of California, Santa Barbara (UC Santa Barbara) folks I must thank include Sandra Campbell, Magda Campo, Meryle Gaston, Garay Menicucci, and Dwight Reynolds. At the University of Wisconsin–Parkside (UW-Parkside), my colleagues Jeff Alexander, David Bruce, Seif Da'na, Peggy James, Laura Khoury, Sandy Moats, Ed Schmitt, and all of my colleagues on the Committee for International Studies have been very supportive since my arrival.

I have several people to thank for helping me during the course of my research in Palestine, Israel, and in the United Kingdom. At Birzeit University, Wael Abdeen graciously found students for me to interview, Rema Hammami kindly shared her recent research findings, and Penny Johnson and Eileen Kuttab provided several helpful contacts. The late Nazmi Da'na generously arranged and assisted with an interview with the mufti of Hebron and gave me an enlightening tour of the city. Wafa al-Arj, legal adviser for Palestine's Ministry of Women's Affairs, kindly took the time to outline the draft unified family law for me. A lawyer at the Women's Centre for Legal Action and Counselling in Ramallah, who wishes to remain anonymous, discussed its legal outreach programs and family law reform efforts with me, and the Centre provided a great deal of literature as well. I am also extremely grateful to Adel Manna at the Van Leer Institute and to Khaire Nagamey for securing permission to use the Al Aqsa Library. My delightful research assistant, Salwa Alenat, was not only very competent but she also became a dear friend in the course of my research. I am also very much indebted to Khader Salameh and his associates at the Al-Aqsa Library, all of whom were very kind and helpful, for giving me access to their copies of the *sijillat* (court registers). The staff at the Israel State Archives was also accommodating, as were those at the Middle East Centre Archive in Oxford and the Public Records Office in London. John and Tatiana Knight generously welcomed me into their home while I used the Oxford archive. And I am most grateful to Judith Tucker for answering my endless questions at the 2006 World Congress for Middle Eastern Studies (WOCMES) Conference in Amman.

I especially would like to thank all of my wonderful interviewees for their participation in my project. Both the Palestinian senior ladies and the college-aged women gave this book a much-needed personal perspective on Muslim family law. I also am very indebted to Shaykh Tamimi, Judge Kholoud al-Faqih, Judge Somoud Damiri, and Mufti Muhammad Mahar Aswadi.

The editorial team at Syracuse University Press has been wonderful to work with, and I am particularly grateful to Suzanne Guiod for her patient guidance from the beginning of the process.

A number of institutions enabled me to complete this book. The Center for Middle East Studies at UC Santa Barbara awarded me two year-long and two summer Foreign Language and Area Studies fellowships for Arabic study. The Center also provided a number of travel grants for the Middle East Studies Association annual conference, allowing me to receive feedback on several chapters of my manuscript. The History Department at UC Santa Barbara provided me with several travel grants, and Jenny Sheffield at the Graduate Division worked a great deal to secure my Fulbright-Hays Doctoral Dissertation fellowship. At UW-Parkside, I received several Committee on Research and Creative Activity awards for conferences and university start-up funds that allowed me to do further research in Palestine, as well as a College of Social Sciences and Professional Studies teaching load reduction.

Finally, I thank my husband, Kevin Lung, for being incredibly supportive throughout this whole process, particularly when we were blessed with our children, Emma and Bryan. I am also grateful for my parents, Sandy and Holly, and my sister, Laura, who have always believed in me. My parents-in-law, Jette and Emmet, and the rest of my family have been very encouraging as well, and I thank them all.

Palestinian Women and Muslim Family Law
in the Mandate Period

Introduction

The Court, the Law, and the Colonial Context

IN THE JERUSALEM *SHARI'A* COURT in 1936, Na'ma began her suit by informing the judge that she and Sahi, her ex-husband, had one daughter together, who was in her care. Then Na'ma stated that she had initially volunteered to pay her child's living expenses but now was asking her husband to pay child support, along with her court fees. Sahi confirmed the divorce and that his daughter was living with his former wife, but refused to offer an amount of child support that he would pay. At that point, he and Na'ma disagreed on the selection of respected men from their community who were to decide the amount of support, so the judge appointed them. These men concluded that the daughter's support should be thirty mils per day, which the judge ordered Sahi to pay, along with the court fees.[1]

It is quite likely that Na'ma had initially volunteered to pay her daughter's child support as leverage in persuading her husband to consent to a divorce. Then, after the divorce, she had nothing to lose in returning to court to request her forfeited financial rights. As Na'ma's case well demonstrates, it was, and is, common for Palestinian and other Muslim women to use creative strategies as they maneuvered within family law courts, enabling them to benefit from a male-dominated, and largely male-privileged, system.[2] To do so, they conformed to patriarchal constructions of gender and tacitly accepted a male-controlled structure but were often able to advance their interests or otherwise gain from the process. This way of conceptualizing women's dealings within the court was inspired loosely by Deniz Kandiyoti's influential article on patriarchal bargains, which she defines as "the existence of set rules and scripts regulating gender relations, to which both genders accommodate and acquiesce, yet which may nonetheless be contested, redefined, and renegotiated."[3] Although Kandiyoti focuses on women's tactical choices within family structures of male dominance and their implications for women's autonomy and access to resources, I found her theoretical framework useful for explaining how women both resisted and accepted the court system and its application of Muslim family law as well.

A major theme of this book emphasizes Palestinian women's innovative maneuvers in such negotiations within the Jerusalem (*al-Quds*) court, focusing on the British Mandate period (1920–1948). Thus, this study builds on previous scholarship examining women's strategies used in *shari'a* courts.[4] But I have also found new tactics used by women, such as in Na'ma's case discussed here; another approach women used was requesting maintenance in court as a means of obtaining another goal, such as a wife-initiated divorce. This study highlights several other maneuvers used by women in *shari'a* court, none of which have been published to my knowledge. The book also analyzes gendered interactions and negotiations in maintenance (*nafaqa*), wife-initiated divorce (*khul'*), and child custody (*hadana*) proceedings, the vast majority of which were initiated and argued by female plaintiffs. In addition, the study includes interviews with Palestinian senior citizens (rather, most of them are noncitizens living under occupation). The cases and interviews together offer new insight on Palestinian gender roles and expectations, as well as women's perceptions of Muslim family law and their legal status, today and in the past.

This book also assesses change and continuity in the *shari'a* court system from the Ottoman Empire to the Mandate period. It examines the respects in which Mandate-period judges followed either the classical Hanafi law of the Ottomans or the 1917 Ottoman Law of Family Rights (OLFR), the new family law code that British administrators instructed *shari'a* courts to apply in Palestine. Specifically, this study analyzes judges' rulings in cases in which they actually had to choose between the Ottoman family code and classical Hanafi law. While the new law code relied on Hanafi law a great deal, it also included reforms that benefited women, such as encouraging monogamy. This book demonstrates certain changes in the judges' application of family law compared to the Ottoman era in all three types of court cases. But overall, it finds that there was more continuity between the two periods because neither party that could have effected meaningful reform was interested in doing so.

A number of studies have analyzed the processes and effects of colonial powers or centralizing states adopting European (or European-esque) law codes and legal institutions.[5] Some scholars have also examined how these changes affected women's status; most of them demonstrate that the legal codes resulted in new forms of patriarchy and disadvantages for women. For example, Kenneth Cuno shows how the early Egyptian legal reforms of the mid- to late nineteenth century resulted in considerably less flexibility for judges and were detrimental to women in several respects.[6] My study partly reinforces this trend in the scholarship, as there were several shortcomings for women in the 1917 Ottoman family code, but I also show that it included some gains for women.

In recent decades, there have been a growing number of studies on Muslim women's legal status and interactions within *shari'a* court systems in the Middle East, for which the main source is court registers (*sijillat*). Using gender as a central tool of analysis in examining different types of court records, this research also demonstrates that Muslim women in the region have had considerable agency historically, and presently, as active participants in their legal affairs and families.[7] These gendered *sijillat* studies use various approaches and engage diverse aspects of women's status and constructs of gender. Several analyze women's access to property, focusing on inheritance, dower, or religious endowments.[8] Others examine women's changing status in modern family law codes over time and how judges' application of the law has affected women's lives.[9] Another methodology uses the family as a conceptual framework, which can incorporate a variety of approaches, such as examining gendered access to property or how interactions in court affect relationships within the family.[10] In his most recent book, Beshara Doumani focuses on family-held religious endowments and lawsuits among relatives, demonstrating the vast differences in women's access to property in two parts of the Ottoman Levant. Over two centuries, he found "over ninety-eight per cent of all family waqfs include females consistently" in Tripoli, whereas women were excluded from 90 percent of family waqfs in Nablus.[11] Doumani largely attributes this striking contrast to the cities' distinctive political economies, the emphasis on urban agriculture in Tripoli, and the importance of trade networks in Nablus.[12]

My study contributes to scholarship on gender constructs and women's status in Muslim family law in the Middle East because it provides a gendered analysis of Palestinian court records, highlights women's creative tactics in court, and examines judges' application of the law during the British Mandate period. There are a few important studies examining court records with a gendered lens for Ottoman Palestine,[13] and the post-1948 era,[14] but the only substantial gendered *sijillat* study on Palestine from the Mandate era is *Women, Property and Islam* by Annelies Moors. Her book examines Palestinian women's access to property via inheritance and dower in the Nablus area, as well as paid labor in the post-1948 era, whereas my study focuses on maintenance, wife-initiated divorce, and child custody cases in the Jerusalem area. These cases are particularly useful for analyzing women's interactions in court because they were among the most common types of cases heard, and thus they well characterize women's court experiences. In addition, the cases I examined were nearly all initiated by women, so they are also significant for uncovering women's gendered strategies as they represented themselves in court. As mentioned, this is one of the book's most important themes. In this respect, I emulate *Morality Tales* by Leslie Peirce, who uses a microhistory approach to track three women's dealings in an Anatolian court for one year in the mid-sixteenth century. I build on her emphasis of women's maneuvers in court, although this book examines a great many individuals in the context of Mandate Palestine.

The Colonial Context: Muslim Family Law in Mandate Palestine

For those unfamiliar with Islam and the Middle East, the term *shariʻa* is largely misunderstood, particularly because it has been so obscured in the post-9/11 United States. To begin, "Islamic law" is not an ideal translation for *shariʻa* because it is far too narrow. More accurate is the divinely inspired, dynamic corpus of scholarly debates on guidelines and instructions for religious duties, with an emphasis on guidelines because few actions are forbidden in Islam.[15] Many are not only misinformed about what *shari'a* is but also uninformed as to why it is still the basis of family law for Muslims in most of the region. After all, following the Ottoman Empire's precedent in the late nineteenth century, most of the Middle East has introduced secular codes for civil, commercial, penal, and other laws, thus secularizing the law in every significant respect except one.[16] Then why, with a few exceptions, does *shari'a* remain the dominant source of Muslim family law, which deals with matters such as marriage, divorce, child custody, and inheritance?[17]

We can trace much of the reason to the era of European colonialism and state-centralizing efforts in the region, and beyond, which tended to have a deleterious impact on women, constructs of gender, and family law as officials imposed new forms of patriarchal cultures and legal systems.[18] For the most part, British and French colonial authorities tended to favor the so-called hands-off approach when it came to family law. They not only realized that their interference would exacerbate local resentment of foreign rule but also were rather uninterested in effecting reforms that could actually improve women's status. When British administrators in Palestine did address women specifically, they either conflated women's and children's issues or focused on regulating and disciplining working-class and marginalized women such as prostitutes or prisoners (most of whom were imprisoned for petty crimes).[19] Also, when colonial powers did enact change affecting women, or when they attempted to do so, the policies often curtailed women's rights. One notorious example was Lord Cromer in Egypt, who was quick to criticize the custom of veiling, but his policies greatly disadvantaged Egyptian women. In particular, he drastically curbed Egyptians' access to education by raising tuition fees in primary schools and restricting women's medical training to midwifery.[20] Prior to British rule, Egyptian midwifery students were trained in additional medical fields and received the same number of years of training as men.[21]

In contrast, as I show in chapter 1, the first official codification and major reform of Muslim family law, the Ottoman family code of 1917, included both disadvantages and benefits concerning women's status. While patriarchal to be sure, it did include important reforms for women, such as discouraging polygamy and allowing women to collect back-payments of maintenance. Perhaps this was partly because it was constructed from within, as opposed to being imposed by colonial rulers, and it did not incorporate western-inspired codes. For example, as Amira Sonbol notes, significant laws addressing rape and so-called honor crimes in Jordan's family code are actually based on French laws rather than *shari'a*.[22] Rather, the architects of the Ottoman family code based it within the four main Sunni schools of thought (*madhahib*) of *shari'a*. But for Mustafa Kemal Ataturk, the first president of the Turkish Republic, the Ottoman family code did not go nearly far enough. Ataturk quickly abolished the *shari'a*-based family code after gaining power. Most instructive for our purposes, Nermin Abadan-Unat points to the "absence of colonial rule" in Anatolia as one of the major factors that contributed to Ataturk's success in secularizing Muslim family law in modern Turkey.[23]

But in the colonized Middle East, including Palestine, family law and the *shari'a* court system were virtually the only institutions that European rulers permitted their male subjects to control during this period. These circumstances tended to entrench the perception among the colonized that upholding established interpretations of Muslim family law, with all of its male privileges, provided the foundations of community and family honor.[24] Thus, cultural heritage, religious tradition, and group identity became intertwined with the sustaining of Muslim family law and the *shari'a* courts in the context of colonial rule. Extensive reform of personal status law was hardly realistic under these conditions, as colonized peoples had more pressing matters at hand. This trend manifested itself in the face of European colonialism across the Middle East and beyond.[25]

The situation was even more complex for Palestinian Arabs under British control (1917–1948) because of the dual threat they encountered from British and Zionist colonialisms. British rule in Palestine was a new form of imperial control in that it was sanctioned by the League of Nations and included a to-be-determined expiration date, as was true of the other Mandates that the European powers established post–World War I. The Permanent Mandates Commission, however, endorsed settler colonialism only in the Palestine Mandate.[26] Thus, British rule in Palestine was also very much linked to Zionist settler colonialism; indeed, the Mandate's founding document specifically promised to facilitate the establishment of a Jewish so-called national home (read: eventual state) in Palestine. Zionist colonialism was a permanent, European settler encroachment, and it involved the self-rule of a state-within-a-state that strove for independence. In accordance with the terms of the Mandate, the British not only supported the Zionists in promoting Jewish immigration and land purchases but also allowed Zionists to form autonomous proto-state institutions.[27] It is important to recognize that these circumstances made Palestine an exceptional case among the Mandates that the European powers created.[28]

The vast majority of the population, the indigenous Palestinian community consisting of Muslims and Christians, was given no such rights. Palestinian Muslims were only allowed control over their population's religious foundations (*awqaf*) and the *shari'a* court system, and their Christian counterparts were similarly constrained. Palestinians were not permitted to form elected assemblies unless they explicitly accepted terms of the Mandate, which they opposed because of its unequivocal support for the Zionist endeavor.[29] Palestinians were also given little say in their own education system, and they had few funds for establishing an independent one after the devastation of World War I. Providing education and other social services for the Palestinians was in any case not a priority for the colonial government. The British Mandate administration spent more resources on disciplining government teachers than on expanding education, and similarly, the government was so focused on regulating midwives that it limited rural Palestinians' access to health care.[30] While the Zionists' independent education system, supported by philanthropic efforts from abroad, was able to provide education for "77 percent of the Jewish school-age population (ages five to nineteen)," by the end of the Mandate period only 44.5 percent of Palestinian children were in school, the vast majority of whom attended primary school only.[31] In addition, Palestinians lacked the resources to develop economically anywhere near the scale of the internationally funded European Zionist movement. Furthermore, the Jewish Agency, which functioned as the *Yishuv*'s proto-government, was entitled to diplomatic representation before the League of Nations, in London, and beyond.[32] Additionally, the British forbid Palestinians to arm or form paramilitary groups, while they were unable or unwilling to prevent such Zionist organizations from smuggling in enough weapons to arm 10,000 fighters by the mid-1930s.[33]

Despite exerting their authority in numerous respects that affected Palestinians, the British generally avoided the realm of family law. Rather, family law, along with the religious courts that applied it, was perhaps the sole legal sphere in which the British were hesitant to involve themselves. Declining to improve Palestinian women's position in family law, and on occasion passing misogynist secular laws, played a role in hindering the overall development of the Palestinian community.[34] Whether or not it was an intentional British policy, these sorts of actions, and inactions, had the effect of undermining the establishment of an eventual Palestinian state. Keeping Palestinian women in their place dovetailed with the Mandate's general policy of assisting the establishment of a Jewish state, at least until 1939.

Evoking images of their encounter with British rule, Palestinians under Israeli occupation today also wield very little control over their own destinies, whether in the form of the national self-determination they have long sought, the right of return to their homes in what is now Israel, or their freedom of movement within post-1948 Palestine (the West Bank, Gaza, and East Jerusalem). Thus it is not surprising that Palestinians have been slow to achieve genuine Muslim family law reform in the face of occupation, whether under the Ottomans, the British, the Jordanians, the Egyptians, or the Israelis. By contrast, other countries in the region have adopted far wider family law reforms, such as Tunisia's 1956 Code of Personal Status, Morocco's 2004 Mudawana, and Egypt's Law No. 1 of 2000; Turkey eliminated religious family law altogether in its 1926 Civil Code.[35] In another striking similarity to the Mandate period, the *shari'a* court system is nearly the extent of genuine Palestinian control over their present reality. Why would they be motivated to radically reform the one institution representing their cultural heritage that is still in their hands today? Despite the unlikely odds, Palestinian women's rights groups, human rights groups, the Palestinian Authority's Ministry of Women's Affairs, the *shari'a* judiciary, and others are making efforts to reform Muslim family law and draft a unified code for the West Bank and Gaza. Chapter 1 examines the changes they hope to achieve as well as Palestinians' largely progressive views on reform.

Shari'a, Muslim Family Law, and the Court

In certain ways, the Jerusalem Shari'a Court served to protect women's interests within the context of the family and shari'a during this period, while in others it restricted women's power in their family relationships. When I use the term shari'a, I am referring to the body of Muslim family law as it existed in this period. This is partly because, as mentioned, other spheres of law had been largely secularized, but also because the scope of this book is limited to the family law aspects of shari'a. For practicing Muslims, shari'a is a far more comprehensive concept and also includes guidelines for observing one's religion, such as how to pray, how to perform the hajj, and so on. When referring to shari'a, I include the divinely established laws and guidelines, jurisprudence (fiqh) or the process by which jurists have established law, and other less-than-divine influences that have encroached through the years, namely customary law (sometimes termed "traditional law") that has its origins in local practices (urf).[36] Rather than shari'a, I will more often use the term "Muslim family law" because it specifically refers to the laws dealing with marriage, divorce, child custody, and inheritance. In the context of the British Mandate period, shari'a courts applied Muslim family law by following some combination of classical Hanafi law, the Ottoman family code, and customary law.[37]

Many Muslims consider shari'a a divine creation, or at least divinely inspired, in its entirety, and they also view it as based on the Qur'an and sunna (the Prophet's custom, or his sayings and doings).[38] There is, therefore, a tendency to think that shari'a has remained unchanged over the centuries, when in fact it has continually evolved since the founding of the four Sunni systems of law over a millennium ago.[39] Shari'a has also absorbed many external and other nondivine influences, most notably customary law and aspects of the legal reforms in the late Ottoman period.[40] In the twentieth century, states in the Middle East have developed personal status, or family law, codes; while ostensibly based on shari'a, they are actually based on a variety of sources in addition to the classical schools, including aspects of western law codes.[41] And of course most modern states have continued to introduce new procedures and legislation responding to modern realities.[42]

Popular western culture today continues to generalize and stereotype Islam, and by extension *shari'a* court systems, as an unchanging patriarchal institution through which men consolidate control over the women within their family, and especially over their oppressed wives. Scholars have conclusively refuted the dated perception of *shari'a* being stagnant and have shown that the gates of interpretation (*bab al-ijtihad*) were never actually "closed" in the late ninth century.[43] As for the other charge, it is undeniable that in many respects the *shari'a* court did, and does, function as a patriarchal system. In cases I researched, it was not unusual for a man to ask the judge for an order (*hukm*) compelling his wife to return to his home. If a husband had a house meeting *shari'a* conditions (*meskin shar'i*), which meant that he was providing sufficiently for her, the judge usually ruled for her to return to her husband and to obey him.[44] As we will see in chapter 2, however, jurists' conception of obedience was restricted to the wife returning to and living in the marital home.[45] In terms of divorce in Hanafi law, the Ottomans' orthodox system of law, men were at an unambiguous advantage because a man could divorce his wife without providing any reason and without even registering it in court. Likewise, after the mother's caretaking period, which lasts from birth until approximately the age of seven for boys and nine years for girls in Hanafi law (*hadana*), the father retained legal custody of the children.

To only mention the privileged male position in the *shari'a* court is an incomplete picture, however. In fact, in cases beyond the realm of family law, such as property disputes, historically the *shari'a* courts treated women no differently than men.[46] Furthermore, men's advantages came with a substantial price, as husbands exclusively bore the economic burden of supporting their wives and other family members. There were also significant financial consequences to divorcing one's wife. The court records that I examined from 1920s–1930s Palestine demonstrate that the *shari'a* court was far more complex and nuanced than simply a manifestation of a patriarchal social order. Muslim women often demanded their rights in accordance with Muslim family law, and sometimes they did so in conflict with it. It was common for women in Mandate Palestine to appear in court claiming their right to maintenance, which included the housing, food, clothing, and other sorts of provisions that the husband was required to give her each month in order to support the family. Women also came to court to claim the custody of their children, to divorce their husbands, and to claim their inheritances (*irth*). Another common reason they went to court was to demand the advanced dower (*mahr mu'ajjal*), which the husband is supposed to give his wife when they sign the marriage contract. Simply the fact that Palestinian women were appearing in court regularly as plaintiffs is important in itself; indeed, they were the vast majority of plaintiffs in this study. But we will also see how the cases, supplemented with interviews, demonstrate a sense of Palestinian women's perceptions of the law, as well as their legal rights and obligations.

The judges implementing the law on a day-to-day basis were central in shaping the extent to which the law actually privileged men. The very idea that judges were the instruments of applying what was often a male-privileged law is complicated by the fact that they have long been considered, and many continue to consider themselves, as the protectors of women, which often translates to their rulings.[47] In some respects, judges adhered to the tenets of *shari'a* quite rigidly, such as Mandate-era interpretations of Hanafi custody ages and the father's absolute custody of the children if the mother remarries. Judges, however, were more flexible in other respects, and a number of variables could influence the outcome of any case, including the husband's sympathy—or lack thereof—for his wife's situation, the socioeconomic status of both parties, the disposition of the judge, the involvement and competence of lawyers (*muhamun*), the prominence of either family in the community, or the support of the wife's family for her decision to initiate a lawsuit. We will deconstruct all of these variables in the course of this book, but let us note here the particular relevance of the last one. The woman's support of her family is critical in this study because the vast majority of cases I analyzed were those in which the woman was the plaintiff and the man was the defendant. Most women would have been unwilling to settle their marital issues in court unless they had obtained their families' support for doing so. This was particularly true for wife-initiated divorce cases; not only did a woman's father generally act as her witness when she initiated divorce, but she would usually return to his house after the divorce. If a woman's family did not approve of her decision, they would probably also be reluctant to welcome her home.

While at a glance the main actors in the *shari'a* court appear to have been the two parties, the judge, and any lawyers or guardians involved, the court also functioned, and continues to function, as a mechanism through which families could interact and try to resolve their problems with outside help. In so doing, the courts serve as a way of maintaining customary ways of dealing with interfamily disputes as well as those with in-laws. One of the most common interventions that still takes place is when arbitrators from each family, and sometimes close friends, sit down with the couple, seeking to remedy their differences rather than divorcing immediately. This can happen before either side resorts to going to court, or it can help resolve cases that have already begun. Judges often encourage further arbitration from the families, which can help the parties come to an agreement. Thus the courts continue to operate in a way that provides a similar structure to the family-based model for people to work out their problems, but with the involvement of court actors, namely judges and often lawyers, as well. It is worth noting that the entire concept of a revocable, or minor, divorce hinges on the hope that the couple will reconsider the divorce, and this often takes place by means of arbitration.

My interviewees for this book confirmed the major role that arbitration continues to play in Palestinian society and its family law systems. When I asked Layla, one of my interviewees from a West Bank village near Ramallah, if she knew any women who had gone to court to resolve problems with their husbands, she said sometimes neighbors and friends help the family solve the problem, and sometimes they go to court.[48] In addition, Layla's son, a school teacher, mentioned how the court system is set up to encourage reconciliation. A divorce is usually not granted in the first court session, and arbitrators are often involved at some point in an attempt to resolve the couple's differences and avoid divorce. As Richard Antoun's ethnographies in Jordan from the 1970s and 1980s and Ziba Mir-Hosseini's work in postrevolutionary Iran demonstrate, arbitration continues to play an important role prior to and during the court proceedings of family disputes.[49]

Sources and Approach

My main source for this book is approximately 370 court cases from the Jerusalem *Shari'a* Court dating from 1925 to 1939. The bulk of the cases in the registers I examined included maintenance, wife-initiated divorce, child custody, dowers, husbands registering divorces, and inheritance. I chose to focus on maintenance, wife-initiated divorce, and child custody cases for this study because these types of cases had not been analyzed for this period in Palestine and they nearly all feature women as the plaintiffs. The Jerusalem court saw cases for Palestinian Muslims of all classes, both from surrounding villages and Jerusalem residents. Most of the proceedings cited in this book are exemplary of the larger sampling, but at times I also discuss unusual cases to demonstrate the range of ways in which proceedings could transpire. The court records are microfilm copies located in the Al-Aqsa Library in Jerusalem, which is directly next to the Al-Aqsa Mosque on the Haram al-Sharif/Temple Mount.[50] The records were not indexed but merely copied, presumably in the order that they were recorded in the court.

I also conducted interviews with thirty-two Palestinians, the first fifteen during my dissertation research. For the initial research, nine interviewees were older Palestinian women, two were women divorcées in their thirties, and three were Palestinian men. I also interviewed Shaykh Tamimi, who was the Chief Islamic Justice (*Qadi al-Quda*), the head of the *shari'a* court system in Palestine, at the time. These interviews helped contextualize and inform my findings from the court registers; in particular, they helped my understanding of how women perceived and felt about the *shari'a* court and family law and how both influence their lives. In chapter 5, I discuss issues of methodology, the women interviewees themselves, and my findings from the interviews. The interviews were especially helpful for understanding Palestinians' views and experiences related to wife-initiated divorce, which I discuss in chapter 3.

I completed the remaining interviews while doing follow-up research in January 2014, this time focusing on how interviewees thought and felt about Muslim family law reform. I interviewed two of Palestine's first women *shari'a* court judges, Judge Kholoud Al-Faqih, who then presided over the Birzeit court (as of 2018, she presides over the Tulkarm court), and Judge Somoud Al-Damiri, Chief Prosecutor for the *shari'a* courts. As of 2018, there are three women serving as *shari'a* court judges (Al-Faqih, Asmahan Al-Wahidi, and Sireen Anabousi), a woman chief prosecutor (Al-Damiri), and one woman marriage officiant (Tahreer Hammad) in Palestine.[51] It is unprecedented for women to be appointed as *shari'a* court judges in the Middle East and, to my knowledge, as chief prosecutors or marriage officiants as well.[52] I asked Al-Faqih and Al-Damiri about their views on particular family law reforms and explored the impact of women judges presiding, particularly whether or not they are likely to encourage progressive change. Other interviewees included those involved in family law reform efforts, including a lawyer from the Women's Centre for Legal Aid and Counseling (WCLAC), a lawyer from Al-Haq (a human rights organization), and a legal adviser for the Palestinian Authority's Ministry of Women's Affairs. Also, I interviewed the mufti of al-Khalil (Hebron), which is considered a more conservative part of Palestine, to help gauge how more traditional parts of society may respond to reforms. The rest of my interviewees were female Birzeit University students, all of whom were around twenty years old, and I inquired about both their knowledge of current family law and their views on potential reforms.

I also explored three other archives in Jerusalem, while waiting for permission to use the Al-Aqsa Library in 2006, and a few archives in the United Kingdom. The archives in Jerusalem included the Central Zionist Archives and the Israel State Archives. I examined any record groups that could even tangentially deal with Palestinian women during this period, such as education files, health files, police reports, and personnel records. In the United Kingdom, I made use of the National Archive and the Public Records Office in London, as well as the Middle East Center Archive at St. Antony's College at Oxford University. I similarly combed through collections that could address any aspect of Palestinian women's history. The articles I published in the *Journal of Palestine Studies*, cited earlier, were the primary fruits of my research findings from these archives. This research also informed and contributed to the larger arguments in this book, however, particularly that Palestinians had little incentive to overhaul the one indigenous institution that they still controlled in the context of British rule, given colonial policies that controlled their education systems and health care providers. Also, Palestinian women were unlikely to contest the patriarchal *shari'a* court system while socioeconomic opportunities were minimal for most of them. While there were new job and educational opportunities for a few, the vast majority of Palestinian women did not benefit from them.

The layout of this book includes a chapter that contextualizes this study, three chapters on court records, and one chapter focusing on the interviews. Chapter 1 provides an overview of the historical context and legal structures during the British Mandate period, the fundamentals of Muslim family law, and Palestinians' practices relating to marriage and divorce during this period. It also addresses changes in Muslim family law in the post-1948 period in Palestine and Israel. To help determine in what respects Palestinians were following or disregarding the law, I draw on Hilma Granqvist's Mandate-era ethnographies of a Palestinian Muslim village throughout the book. The rest of the study is organized by type of court case, as chapters 2, 3, and 4 analyze maintenance, wife-initiated divorce, and child custody records, respectively. In each of these chapters, I use a gendered lens to analyze the cases with several objectives in mind. First, I try to determine which factors most contributed to women being successful in their claims and what women were ultimately trying to obtain, along with the gendered strategies that they used in court. Also, I assess whether there was more change or continuity in court rulings from the Ottoman period to the Mandate era, focusing on judges' adherence or departure from the OLFR when there was a discrepancy between classical Hanafi law and the Ottoman code. Finally, I draw on interviews to examine Palestinian women's perceptions of the *shari'a* court system, Muslim family law, and their legal status in family law, which I mostly use in chapter 3 on wife-initiated divorce, and in chapter 5, where I explain my methodology in the interviewing process and further insights from the initial group of interviewees. But first, to understand the context in which the court cases took place, we need to explore the setting of Palestine under British rule and an overview of changes in Muslim family law during and since this period. Also, we will see how several social practices diverged from the law, both from the Ottoman family code and Hanafi law, sometimes to women's benefit and at times to their detriment.

1

The Historical, Legal, and Social Setting

BEFORE DELVING INTO Muslim family law and Palestinian society during the British Mandate period (1920–1948), we need to briefly examine the legal systems of this colonial setting and how they fit into the larger context of British support for Zionism (Jewish nationalism). British authorities established a legal structure that would support Jewish immigration and land purchases, which intentionally enabled the Zionist movement to flourish at the expense of the Palestinian people.[1] Regarding family law, however, British officials largely preserved the status quo because they sought to avoid exacerbating Palestinian and Jewish resentment. Furthermore, improving women's legal status was never a priority for the Colonial Office.

As for Palestinians' views on Muslim family law reform, they were preoccupied with their nationalist cause and mounting vulnerability at the hands of both the British and the Zionists, so they had little opportunity or inclination to bring about significant change in the one indigenous institution that they still controlled. Rather, maintaining family law systems and challenging foreign interference actually became a form of resistance for Palestinians. Muslim women supported their unequal but familiar *shari'a* court system for the same reason, and also because most

Portions of this chapter were published in a similar form as "Reforms of Restrictions? The Ottoman Muslim Family Law Code and Women's Marital Status in Mandate Palestine," in *Middle Eastern and North African Societies in the Interwar Period*, edited by Kate Fleet and Ebru Boyar (Brill, 2018).

Palestinian women's employment and other socioeconomic prospects were limited.[2] However, women did challenge the court system from within, which we will examine in chapters 2, 3, and 4.

This chapter focuses on Muslim family law and Palestinian society during the Mandate period up to the present. First, the chapter provides an overview of the Mandate government's new legal framework. Next, the greater part of the chapter explains the central elements of Muslim family law, including the Ottoman family code of 1917 that the British preserved. It also describes rural Palestinians' marriage- and divorce-related practices and in what ways they followed and disregarded the law. The chapter concludes with a discussion of changes in Muslim family law in Palestine and Israel since 1948.

The Legal Structures of the Mandate Government

Ruling Palestine posed an all but irresolvable dilemma for the British from the outset. When General Allenby occupied Jerusalem in December 1917, Palestine was suffering tremendously from World War I, and relations between indigenous Palestinian Arabs and the immigrant Jewish community were already tenuous. Britain had recently promised to "use [its] best endeavours to facilitate" Zionism per the Balfour Declaration. This policy was particularly aggravating to Palestinians because they comprised some 90 percent of Palestine's population at the beginning of British rule, and Britain had previously committed to help establish an independent Arab state after the war. When a civilian administration took over governance of Palestine from the military in 1920, the first high commissioner hoped to both advance Zionist settlement and mitigate Palestinian grievances, an impossible task because the Zionists wanted the Palestinians' land for a Jewish state.

Herbert Samuel, the head of the Mandate government's first civilian administration from 1920 to 1925, sought to realize two conflicting goals. The high commissioner's first priority was to facilitate Jewish immigration, land purchases, and development in order to establish a Jewish proto-state. Secondly, he hoped to win over the vast majority, the indigenous Palestinian population, to that objective. In his memoirs, Samuel identifies the 1917 Balfour Declaration, in which the British government promised to actively help establish a Jewish "national home" in Palestine, as "our basic problem of the relations between Arabs and Jews."[3] Samuel was first a Zionist Jew, but he also felt a responsibility to reach out to the Palestinian community and to offer what he considered concessions. Any conciliatory gestures Samuel made, however, could not compromise his first priority. Even though his so-called concessions tended to be more superficial than substantive, Samuel thought he would be able to woo the Palestinian leadership into appeasement by offering a limited role in his government.

Initially, Samuel attempted to persuade Palestinian leaders by offering them representation on a legislative council composed of elected members from all three religious communities, Muslim, Jewish, and Christian, as well as appointed British officials. Stipulated in the terms of the Order-in-Council of 1922, a sort of constitution that described the structure of the Mandate government—sans national, political, or any explicit rights for Palestinians—the council was to advise the high commissioner on legislation. Samuel tried on two occasions to establish the council but Palestinian leaders refused to participate for several reasons. The first proposed council greatly underrepresented the Muslim proportion of the population with four Muslims, three Christians, and three Jews.[4] Samuel somewhat remedied the representation issue in his second proposed council, but the main obstacle for Palestinians remained.

The Mandate document itself, which was sanctioned by the League of Nations, was unacceptable to Palestinians because it included the Balfour Declaration verbatim. Also, the Mandate failed to mention Palestinians by name, nor did it address their national aspirations for self-government. If Palestinians were to recognize the legitimacy of a government council, this would also indicate their recognition of the government's pro-Zionist policies. Palestinians were upset by the government's support of Jewish immigration and land purchases, preferential treatment of Jews in general, and the very idea of establishing a Jewish proto-state in Palestine. Most Palestinian leaders felt they could not reconcile their opposition to the Mandate's Zionist goals with participation in the government carrying out those objectives. In the end, the Mandate government did consult Arab leaders about legislation on occasion, but it did so in a superficial capacity only.[5]

Given this impasse, Assaf Likhovski has argued that the British had no choice but to empower the high commissioner to an inordinate extent, in that he was "forced" to control the legislative as well as the executive powers of government.[6] This justification is disingenuous because the British could have opted to recognize Palestinians' national aspirations and rights. After his multicultural legislative council idea failed, Samuel formed an advisory council consisting entirely of Mandate government officials. The attorney general was responsible for drafting legislation, which the high commissioner and the Colonial Office approved before it was enacted. In addition to writing laws and advising the government, the attorney general was the government's representative in court and supervised prosecutions.[7] Clearly, checks and balances were not considered an asset for the structure of the Mandate government. The first and most influential attorney general, Norman Bentwich, a British Jew and committed Zionist, explains the powerful position in his memoirs: "I exercised a general supervision over the administration of the courts, both civil and religious, and over the Land Registration and Survey Departments, as well as being the legal advisor and legal draftsman of the Government."[8] Bentwich's memoirs also describe how he took full advantage of his position to further the Zionist cause.

To some extent the administration's legal system aimed to facilitate the Mandate's objective of fostering a Jewish state, while certain legal structures evolved amorphously or were left nearly alone. The former was particularly true of the new land courts that the Mandate government quickly established, as well as legislation related to land transactions and security. A related priority was commercial law as a means of promoting the Jewish sector of the economy, and consequently Mandate officials replaced Ottoman commercial codes quite early on. As Likhovski remarks, "eager to aid the Zionist cause . . . [Attorney General] Bentwich concentrated his efforts on providing Palestine with a set of modern commercial laws that he believed would facilitate economic development and thus attract more Jewish immigration."[9] Likewise, the Order-in-Council of 1922 abolished the capitulations to which the Ottomans had been subject for centuries. Of course up until its rule of Palestine, Britain had insisted they remain intact. In the late 1920s, the government went further to promote Jewish industry when it enacted protective tariffs and eliminated customs dues on industrial raw materials.[10] It should be noted that certain British officials in Palestine disagreed with Bentwich's overtly Zionist objectives and actions for various reasons; above all they realized that Zionism threatened the stability of British rule. Some of these officials wished to preserve Palestinian culture in accordance with their preconceived notions of all things biblical, and others sympathized with Palestinians, though usually in a paternalistic way. Officials in London, however, tended to support the attorney general's Zionist goals and formulated policy accordingly, particularly up until World War II.[11]

In other respects, the Mandate government gradually changed Palestine's legal system while it initially retained a good deal of Ottoman law. During the *Tanzimat* (lit., "reorganization") reforms of the mid-nineteenth century, the Ottomans had secularized and codified much of the law, which had been based on both state-decreed legal codes (*qanun*) and *shari'a*. The Ottomans also established a four-level civil court system to apply the new codes, which included criminal, commercial, and procedural laws. The reforms largely excluded religious endowments (*awqaf*) and Muslim family law at this point, as *shari'a* courts and other religious communities' family courts operated independently from the new civil courts, but procedural changes did affect how *shari'a* courts functioned.[12] Also, Iris Agmon points out that the *Tanzimat* reforms created orphan funds, a new institution created to oversee orphans' property. This innovation was yet another encroachment on *shari'a* courts' jurisdiction because they had previously enjoyed exclusive control over matters related to orphans and had to comply with new procedures.[13] In this partial secularizing process, the Ottomans drew extensively on French codes while retaining some aspects of *shari'a*, but the Mecelle, the Ottoman civil code, was not without gaps.[14] Thus the Order-in-Council of 1922 instructed judges and government officials to consult English common law when Ottoman codes made no mention of a legal matter.[15] In any case, the Mandate government eventually replaced much of the Ottoman civil code with English common law, especially statutes that were based on French codes.[16]

Legislation and judicial rulings were the main means by which government officials slowly anglicized Ottoman law during the Mandate.[17]

Regarding legislation, the British passed so many laws in the 1920s that the Palestinian press often referred to the government as the "law factory."[18] Palestinians were most concerned about new laws that enabled escalations in Jewish land purchases and immigration. Consequently, British lawmakers initially focused on procedural changes, apart from furthering the virtue of efficiency, because they assumed this would be less controversial than other forms of legislation. Also, by prioritizing procedure and by amending existing laws, the British could claim to be preserving or reforming the law, depending on the audience. Imperial policy played a significant role as well, however. Throughout much of the British Empire, officials tended to prioritize procedural law reforms, uphold existing law, and fill gaps with common law.[19] An example of a procedural change was eliminating Turkish and adopting the new official languages of Arabic, Hebrew, and English. Regarding judicial decisions, British and Jewish judges were often unfamiliar with Ottoman law, and there was apparently little effort to remedy this lack of knowledge. Likhovski notes that there were few copies of the French translations of Ottoman codes, and indeed there was "no authoritative English version" at all.[20] Such limited access to the Mecelle must have ensured that judges frequently used English common law to make their rulings.

For the layout of the civil court system, the British preserved the Ottomans' four-level structure but added new types of courts. The first level consisted of local magistrate courts in smaller towns and municipal courts in larger towns, both of which heard minor civil and criminal cases.[21] The second level was composed of four district courts in Jerusalem, Jaffa, Haifa, and Nablus; the government added a Tel Aviv district court in 1937. The district courts heard appeals from the first-level cases, major cases, and those beyond first-level jurisdiction.[22] The last tier for all practical purposes was the Supreme Court in Jerusalem, which heard appeals from the district courts, although in theory the Privy Council could hear Supreme Court cases if intricate conditions were met.[23] Also, the British established special courts to deal with particular issues, such as the two land courts and military courts. The cases in the land courts largely dealt with land purchase disputes, while the military courts dealt with disorder and security concerns. No type of court in Mandate Palestine employed the jury system because British officials assumed juries would be too susceptible to corruption and political pressure.[24] Rather, the courts used panels of judges; for example, in the district courts, the leading judge was British, while the other two were Palestinian or Jewish.[25]

Muslim Family Law and Palestinian Society during the Mandate

The Mandate government was reluctant to reform existing systems in Palestine when it came to religious family law, which includes matters of marriage, divorce, child custody, and inheritance. Consequently, the administration maintained the status quo in which multiple systems of family law operated, with each religious community controlling its own courts. But upon their arrival in Palestine, the British encountered unusual circumstances regarding Muslim family law. During World War I, the Ottomans had promulgated an unprecedented codification, the Ottoman Law of Family Rights of 1917, which I will refer to as the Ottoman family code. This law code not only was the world's first official codification of Muslim family law but also would become a model for several Middle Eastern states.[26] The Turks, however, had little opportunity to implement the code because Ataturk abolished religious family law with the 1926 Turkish Civil Code.

Why the Ottomans took it upon themselves to codify family law during a multiple-front war is an interesting question in itself. Robert Eisenman suggests it was because many Turkish women "were obliged to emerge from their seclusion to fill the places left by the men."[27] He argues that in the context of decades of expanded girls' education and debates over women's status, it made sense for the government to improve women's rights precisely when women were actively supporting the state in its time of need.[28] These conditions may well have played some role, but the Ottomans likely had less altruistic motivations for issuing the family code as well. Certainly the Ottomans established the new code in the context of the state's broad, ongoing modernization project that included education for women; but doing so was also likely intended to help realize the Empire's longstanding ambition to unify its citizens. The Ottoman family code did not affect all religious communities in the same way, as it included a different set of articles for non-Muslim subjects. But in part, the 1917 Ottoman code harked back to the initial decrees of the Tanzimat promising equal rights and responsibilities, in that it was another attempt to unify the Empire's religious communities by promoting a common Ottoman identity. Although in the guise of a shared family code, it was yet another way of imposing the Ottomanist ideal of the Tanzimat. In short, the new Ottoman code was to provide all citizens with one national family law while accounting for religious differences.

In Palestine, the British occupied the region in 1917 shortly after the promulgation of the Ottoman family code, and they changed remarkably little of it. Rather, British authorities upheld the bulk of the Ottoman code in the Muslim Family Law Ordinance of 1919, only rescinding the articles relating to Jews and Christians.[29] In explaining the Mandate government's hesitance to change Muslim family law, Lynn Welchman suggests that "the existence of the OLFR was presumably the reason why the British felt no need to introduce legislation into the area of family law as they had in India, for example."[30] The Mandate government did not attempt to enforce the new code; rather, it instructed the British-invented Supreme Muslim Council to oversee its application. Led by the office of yet another British innovation, the Grand Mufti of Palestine, the Council managed all matters relating to Muslim religious endowments and family law. While many Zionists saw the Supreme Muslim Council as a concession to Palestinians, it was nearly the extent of Muslims' government-sanctioned authority over their own community. Also, the Council exerted far less power than its Zionist counterparts, given the elaborate proto-state apparatus that the Mandate government allowed the Zionists to establish.

Some Palestinians nevertheless felt that the British interfered in their religious affairs, as illustrated by the following 1941 wire that Palestinian leaders in Cairo sent to the colonial secretary: "We vehemently protest against continued British Government intervention in Moslem religio[u]s affairs and supervision [of the] Moslem Supreme Council and demand termination [of] government control[,] restitution [of] council[,] all powers and privileges and [the] application [of] principles [of] elections [with] councilors according [to the] Moslem Supreme Council [and the] Constitution[.] Palestine Arab Higher Committee."[31] Because they were in exile, these leaders were probably looking for any excuse to chastise the administration, but there was also a legitimate grievance. The British did interfere in family law in 1936 by criminalizing marriage for girls under fifteen, which was considerably younger than what the Supreme Muslim Council had set for its community, as we will see.[32] In any case, it is unlikely that the Supreme Muslim Council took its instruction to ensure the application of the Ottoman family code too seriously, given its anxieties about the British and the Zionists. The extent to which the shari'a courts applied the Ottoman code is a topic in need of further inquiry. In chapters 2, 3, and 4, we will examine this question as it applies to cases of maintenance (nafaqa), wife-initiated divorce (khul'), and the mother's period of child custody (hadana).

In several respects, the Ottoman family code improved women's rights in family law from their status in classical Hanafi law, which was the Ottomans' official school of law. Each of the four Sunni schools had different benefits and detriments for women. For example, the Hanafis permitted an adult woman to contract her own marriage without a guardian present. It also, however, established extremely narrow terms under which women could access judicial dissolution (sometimes termed "annulment"), did not allow women (and other dependents) to sue for delinquent maintenance payments, and restricted the mother's access to child custody compared with the other schools, as we will see. Thus it was astute of the lawyers who constructed the Ottoman family code to use the classical principle of selection (talfiq), which allowed them to select among the Sunni systems. In certain ways, they chose elements from the school that would improve women's legal status, but certainly not in all circumstances. In any case, the architects of the new code did have a general preference for Hanafi law; it was, after all, the Ottoman Empire's official school of law.[33] However, while Ottoman courts had officially favored Hanafi law and judges prior to the code, they had also used judges from other schools, particularly Shafi'i and Hanbali, and had allowed their rulings to stand.[34]

Until recent decades, western scholars of Muslim family law tended to applaud the Ottoman family code with enthusiasm for being an indicator of progress and social change.[35] This characterization is inaccurate for several reasons. First, the code failed to improve women's position in child custody because it left the mother's restricted period of caretaking intact.

Also, many studies have paid little attention to the law's application or the amount of change that it effected. One cannot comprehensively assess a new law code without gauging the extent to which its laws are applied and to what extent social change accompanies them. We will examine both criteria throughout this book. Finally, it should be emphasized that the Ottoman code limited judges' options by condensing a large corpus of legal interpretations and practices into a single code; that is, when judges chose to apply it. Consequently, the code did not always translate into an improvement in women's legal status. Indeed, Judith Tucker argues that because of the lack of genuine reforms in the code and the flexibility in interpretations and applications of the law during prior centuries, "the overall result of codification was not a gain for women."[36] I agree the Ottoman code was fairly conservative and in some ways restricted options for judges. I will also show, however, that it included important benefits for women, such as encouraging monogamy and offering women more agency in their living situations.

The following sections outline the main features of classical Hanafi family law in marriage, divorce, and child custody. They also describe rural Palestinian society in this period, including values and practices that at times conflicted with the courts' application of family law. Finally, the sections examine the ways in which the 1917 Ottoman family code modified Hanafi law, how it attempted to change certain cultural practices, and to what extent Palestinians followed the new code. All of these discussions will provide context for the following three chapters on maintenance, wife-initiated divorce, and the mother's period of child custody.

Gendered Expectations in Marriage and the Social Context

Marriage was, and is, a social and religious expectation of most Palestinian Muslims; those who are financially, physically, and mentally able are generally expected to marry. Historically, it was most common for the bride, particularly in rural Palestine, to leave her family home and live with her husband's family upon marriage. Urban Palestinians tended to live in nuclear households, but the oldest son's family often lived with his parents.[37] Despite its religious connotations, marriage was, and is, not a sacrament in Islam; rather, it is considered a contract with obligations that one should perform and rights that one can expect and claim in court if necessary. This is true for the husband and the wife, both of whom are responsible for fulfilling their gendered roles and duties; both spouses also enjoy gendered rights within the marriage. The husband is considered the provider for the family. He is required to support his wife, children, and other dependent family members with all the food, clothing, shelter, and items they may need for daily life. Collectively, this support is called *nafaqa* and it is a wife's, and any dependent's, fundamental right in Muslim family law to receive it. A married woman is entitled to maintenance regardless of her personal finances; also, her husband is expected to provide for her in the manner to which she was accustomed before marriage. As for her duties, the wife is responsible for maintaining the home, raising her children, and obeying her husband; she is perceived as the nurturer of the family. It is important to note that, historically, jurists' conception of disobedience (*nushuz*) was fairly narrow and usually used to determine a woman's right to receive maintenance. While Ottoman-period legal experts debated the details of circumstances that would merit disobedience, they did concur on a few. For example, they agreed that a wife's abandonment of her husband's home or being sexually unavailable to her husband both constituted disobedience.[38]

The husband must fulfill the sexual needs of his spouse as well. If there is one element of marriage that is equally obligatory on both the husband and the wife, it is the responsibility to provide sexual satisfaction for his or her partner. Either party may seek redress in court if his or her partner fails to meet those needs. In two Jerusalem court cases from 1928 and 1936, the wife sued her husband for divorce because he was sexually incapable. In both cases, the husband ended up paying his wife compensation to persuade her to stay in the marriage.[39] There were no cases in which the husband sought permission to withhold maintenance due to his wife's inability or unwillingness to have sexual relations. Perhaps it is unlikely that a husband would make such an emasculating claim in a public venue. In any case, he did have the option of divorcing her or marrying an additional wife instead of going to court if he could afford it. Also, one should note that marital rape was, and is, not a concept in Muslim family law, nor did it exist in much of the world until the late twentieth century. Thus it would seem unlikely for the wife to contest her sexual duty under these circumstances. One last point regarding the husband's sexual responsibility is that his inability to perform sexually was grounds for his wife to acquire a judicial dissolution, which she could initiate unilaterally and retain her financial divorce rights.

A perhaps more significant aspect to a couples' sexual relationship, particularly in rural areas, concerned the wife's status in her marriage. As Hilma Granqvist notes in her late 1920s study of marriage-related topics in Artas, a Muslim village a little south of Bethlehem, "the whole village knows whether a man has intercourse with his wife or not. Although a woman may be little inclined sexually, just this intercourse has great value and importance for her as the sign of the husband's favor and goodwill towards her personally and in public opinion; for she is in this way stamped as a 'beloved' or 'hated' wife."[40] Going to court could have been a way for a wife, especially from a rural area, to reclaim her social status by publicly declaring there was a medical reason that she was not "beloved." It is perhaps not a coincidence that in both impotence cases discussed previously, each party was from a village.

In the context of interwar Palestine, as in much of the world, the first priority for selecting a marriage partner was meeting the family's needs and concerns. The cultural descriptions provided here will focus on Palestinian society in rural areas, where some 75 five percent of Palestinians lived in the 1930s. For the Muslim community, the agrarian percentage of the population was even higher. Granqvist demonstrates that major considerations for rural Muslim families included keeping property within the family and obtaining lower dower costs for the groom's family.[41] The dower (*mahr*) is sometimes termed the "bride's marriage gift"; it consists of the gold, cash, or other gifts agreed upon in the marriage contract that the groom gives to the bride's father on her behalf. By the Mandate era in Palestine, the dower was usually paid in cash, but it could also consist of some combination of land, olive trees, animals, other forms of property, or even service.[42] The amount of the dower depended on whether or not the bride's and groom's families were related (the closer the relationship, the smaller the dower) and the bride's family's social status, her character, and her beauty.[43] Despite proverbs and villagers' assertions claiming that widows' dowers were worth half the amount of maidens, Granqvist found there was actually "no difference worth mentioning" during this period, although the marriage ceremonies were less elaborate.[44] The bride's parents usually spent part of the dower on gold and household items for their daughter. Annelies Moors's ethnographic and court record–based study of women's access to property in the Nablus region found that women typically received about a third of their dowers in this period.[45] Despite the Qur'an's affirmation that the entire dower belongs to the bride, which was among its many new protections for women, the dower was often controlled by the bride's father in practice.[46]

Because agrarian families wished to retain property and curb dower costs when selecting spouses for younger members, they tended to prefer cousins who were the children of uncles on the father's side. Rural Palestinians favored cousins to the extent that a man had the "right" to his cousin, "even if she is already sitting on the bridal camel."[47] Preference for cousin marriages, followed by clan marriages, and finally by village marriages was also because of the bride's family's concerns about her well-being in her new home. Granqvist cites a common adage that fathers and brothers said to the bride as she left her family: "We have not given [you] to [just] any sort of people. We have given [you] to people upon whom we can depend."[48] Also, if a woman married within her extended family, or at least within her village, it was a great deal easier for her family to ensure that she was well treated. Simply the wife's family's proximity would have likely encouraged her in-laws to treat her well. A man who married within the village was more likely to be considerate of his wife than one who married outside the village, knowing that his in-laws could descend at any time.[49] Furthermore, it was critical for women to maintain strong relationships with their families in order to protect themselves in the event of difficulties with their in-laws, as we will see. The bond with a woman's family could be upheld more easily if she married within the family or the village.[50] Interestingly, even though Artas residents preferred cousin marriages, marriages to "strangers," people from outside the village, were actually far more common. Granqvist explains that for grooms' families, there were simply not enough women within Artas to allow additional cousin marriages; another major factor affecting brides' families was that "stranger" wives received considerably more expensive dowers.[51] Finally, for both sides, families had greater options for a match when they looked beyond the village.

Marriage certainly was momentous for the two individuals involved, but it was just as much about the bonding of two families. Granqvist illustrates the significance that rural Palestinians ascribed to the connection of two families in many respects. She explains that the common practice of villagers marrying several family members into another family simultaneously indicates "how anxious people are to bind families firmly together by marriage."[52] While it was certainly more cost-effective for families to hold more than one wedding at once, the bond created between families was also important and enduring. Granqvist cites the example of an Artas man who, after his engagement, began seeking his future in-laws socially and in everyday work; she also references two families who still worked together on both families' fields during the harvest, even though the marriage that connected them had taken place "long ago."[53] The village's practices of levirate and sororate marriages were other means of strengthening the bonds of in-laws. Levirate marriage, a pre-Islamic practice dating at least to the Hebrew Bible and forbidden in the Qur'an, is the term for a man marrying his deceased brother's widow. Granqvist describes levirate marriage in Artas as "indeed a right but not a duty" but a somewhat rare practice, accounting for less than 3 percent of marriages in the village.[54] Sororate marriage refers to the custom when a woman dies and her husband requests a replacement bride from her family, usually a sister. Granqvist asserts that "such an appeal is not and scarcely can be rejected," indicating the importance of the two families' relationship.[55]

Rural families initiated marriages for adolescent and teenage members for a variety of reasons, very often because they required an additional worker. It is worth noting that one was considered married when the parties signed the marriage contract, which could take place years before the marriage was actually consummated. Social expectations of marriage shortly after reaching puberty along with the strong preference for cousin, clan, and village marriages were significant reasons for early marriages.[56] These factors were closely connected. Because families usually desired a cousin or a clan marriage, they had to seize the opportunity to marry a relation before she or he married another candidate. However, practical considerations

were also important in determining when the marriage would be negotiated. Granqvist emphasizes that while a man could have personal incentives for pursuing marriage or a particular woman's hand, it was just as likely
that his family, particularly his mother, needed a female laborer.

> It may be that his [family] require someone to carry out those duties
> which are specifically a woman's and cannot with propriety be done by
> a man, or there is not enough woman's help in the house; often it is a
> question of replacing a sister or a daughter who has [wed]; or the man's
> mother declares that she can no longer manage the work and must have
> help. . . . One notices that, as soon as she has a daughter-in-law in the
> house, a woman no longer needs to grind the corn, which used to be
> one of the heaviest of the women's tasks and necessitated their sitting at
> the mill half the night. But the wives of her sons also fetch water, gather
> wood and manure, etc., so that a woman with daughters-in-law is said
> to be a "lady" who keeps servants, and a woman herself looks upon this
> position with joy, as an ideal one.[57]

It is important to note that the gender-specific work a new wife performed
eased her mother-in-law's and other women family members' workload
considerably more than her husband's. As the passage above indicates,
rural women's work was very labor-intensive in this period. In addition to
the tasks mentioned of grinding corn, transporting water, and gathering
firewood and manure, women were also responsible for caring for their
children, tending and gathering grasses for the livestock, baking bread,
weeding the fields, planting certain crops, carrying crops to market, making *leben* (a thick, delicious yogurt) and cheese, mending clothes, and
cleaning the home.[58] Also, during the harvest, women worked alongside
the entire family to complete the harvesting chores, including threshing,
sorting, and picking olives and fruit.[59] Apart from ploughing, which Palestinians generally considered men's work, men and women (and children)
performed most of the same harvesting jobs together.

This description of rural women's responsibilities also illustrates why
they usually did not practice seclusion. With so much of their work being out-
doors, including taking produce to market, seclusion was hardly practical.[60]
Rural women typically did not veil, either, and they were often perceived

as being very influential members of their households and as having few restrictions compared to urban elite and middle-class Palestinian women, who often veiled.[61] It is worth noting that urban areas saw some middle-class women start to remove the veil in the 1920s, with veiling "gradually diminishing by the 1930s."[62] The practice fluctuated a great deal by town or city, however, and some sources contended it was still a common practice.[63]

The Ottoman Law of Family Rights' Marriage Reforms and Reality

The 1917 Ottoman family code preserved the basic patriarchal structure of marriage and its gendered rights and obligations, but it also improved women's legal status from classical Hanafi doctrines in several respects. First, the new code followed the more flexible position of the classical Shafiʿi and Hanbali schools regarding lapsed maintenance payments, as opposed to the rigid Hanafi stance.[64] Shafiʿi law and Hanbali law both allowed a woman to sue her husband for delinquent payments, even in circumstances of divorce or the husband's death.[65] Classical Hanafi law did not permit suing for back payments of support; rather, a wife must demand a missed payment immediately for her claim to be admissible in court. This aspect of the code was clearly an important reform for women. We will examine to what extent the code's provisions for support were actually implemented in Palestine in chapter 2.

Another reform regarding marriage in the Ottoman family code was increasing the age of legal majority from the beginning of puberty to age seventeen for girls and age eighteen for boys and by requiring a judge's consent to marriage under these ages.[66] This was a significant change given that the majority opinion among classical schools viewed the age range for puberty, which also indicated one's legal majority, from nine to fifteen years for girls and from twelve to fifteen years for boys.[67] Ottoman-period muftis (legal experts), however, agreed that marriage should not be consummated until the girl was physically mature for a sexual relationship.[68] Hanafi judges usually understood this to mean the development of the girl's body, as opposed to the beginning of menstruation.[69] Along with the ages of legal majority, the Ottoman code established seventeen for females and eighteen for males as the minimum ages at which one could marry without a judge's consent. It is important to note that an adolescent (*murahiq*) could be allowed to marry if she or he was physically mature and the parents had obtained a judge's permission; but in no circumstances could a judge marry a girl under the age of nine years or a boy under twelve years.[70]

There is little consensus on the average marriage ages for Palestinians in this period. Granqvist maintains that the "marriageable age" for boys and girls was "shortly after puberty" in the village of Artas, and her research shows "very few unmarried males of marriageable age."[71] This was likely because of a shortage of women in the village—if a potential groom's family wanted a local bride, they could not wait around. Also, Granqvist cites a number of contemporary observers whose estimates of marriage ages ranged from twelve to seventeen for girls.[72] It is important to note that if a wedding took place before a girl had completed puberty, consummation of the marriage would not occur until after she had started menstruating. Thus several years could transpire from the signing of the marriage contract, when one was considered "married," to the consummation of the marriage. Moors found that many women who grew up in Al-Balad, a village near Nablus, during the Mandate period recalled they had married just after puberty, and 30 percent of them were younger than fourteen.[73] In 1923, a Palestinian government doctor in Ramallah asserted that judges in *shari'a* courts throughout Palestine were refusing to register marriages for girls who were under sixteen years old.[74] While his assertion could have been more accurate for urban areas, Moors and Granqvist both show that this was not the case in at least parts of the countryside. In contrast, Sarah Graham-Brown cites the 1931 census and its purported average marriage age for Muslim women of twenty years, maintaining that this challenges the common perception that fourteen to fifteen was the standard marriage age for women.[75] A British-conducted census is, however, an unreliable source on this issue. Not only did Palestinians detest British rule, but the British were also attempting to crack down on child marriage; consequently, Palestinians would have had very little incentive to submit accurate ages on their marriage contracts.

There are several other reasons for discrepancies on the age of marriage during this period. Much of it arises from a great deal of ambiguity about peoples' ages in general. As C. T. Wilson, an English missionary and observer of rural Palestine, noted in 1906, "People have but little idea of their children's ages, or, of their own . . . if parents know, even approximately, their children's ages, it arises from . . . their [birth occurring] in a year when some event of special interest took place."[76] Even among urban Palestinians in the Mandate era, during which the government attempted to register birth records, remembering precise birth dates and years was likely not common. Fadwa Tuqan, the famous poet from Nablus, recalls her mother's response when she inquired about her birth: "The day I was cooking *akkub* [globe thistle]. That's the only birth certificate I have for you." Tuqan goes on to explain, "Like all our people Mother dated events by relating them to outstanding occurrences. She would say: 'That happened in the year of the grasshoppers, or the year of the earthquake,' etc."[77] Tuqan's mother eventually remembered her daughter's birth was in 1917 because her cousin died in the war the previous year.[78]

Moors mentions another reason for the lack of consensus on marriage ages, which is the remarkable inconsistency between her oral histories and the *shari'a* court marriage registers. Fifty-five percent of her interviewees from the village of Al-Balad said they had married under sixteen, yet Moors found no contracts in which the bride's age was recorded as younger than seventeen.[79] Moors concludes that families must have either reported incorrect ages or waited until the girls were seventeen to register the marriages.[80] But if it was the former, did the courts knowingly record erroneous ages? It is impossible to say. It is also likely that many women had difficulty recalling their specific ages at marriage, but undoubtedly there is a considerable discrepancy between seventeen years, according to the court records, and the age of menstruation, soon after which a majority of women told Moors they had married.

Despite the ambiguity of marriage ages, there are indications that Palestinian leaders were working and perhaps succeeding to promote older marriages in this period. Ruth Woodsmall, a Young Women's Christian Association researcher, reported in 1936 that the Supreme Muslim Council actively encouraged its own minimum marriage age of eighteen years for girls, which "was regarded by the common people as practically a law, and hence, was followed to a large degree."[81] She went on to describe "the Grand Mufti and SMC as an effective instrument for reform . . . creating a public opinion against early marriage, and is, thus, effectively pushing up the marriage age."[82] Certainly, the Supreme Muslim Council was more progressive on minimum marriage ages than the Mandate government with the council's recommendation of eighteen years for girls. British authorities decided upon fifteen years for girls in the 1936 criminal code. There was, however, a proviso in the code that permitted younger marriages, allowing a girl under fifteen to marry if her parents consented, she had reached puberty, and a doctor verified that consummation would cause her "no physical ill effects."[83]

Ela Greenberg reveals a few strategies with which the Supreme Muslim Council encouraged its minimum marriage age. First, the council issued a pamphlet "attack[ing] the practice of giving expensive dowries" because this often meant a younger bride. The council's pamphlet asserted that "the honor of the girls is dependent upon morals and manners and not upon the price of the dowry and the ostentatious dress. She should adorn herself with good character."[84] Greenberg acknowledges the pamphlet did not directly confront early marriage, but she also points out the council's message was that a girl's "education was far more important than her age and the wealth fetched with her dow[er]."[85] Second, Greenberg shows how the council used its Islamic Girls School in Jerusalem to encourage later marriages by "creat[ing] two ways for girls to remain in school after having finished the school's curriculum, [both] tactics for delaying marriage."[86] Girls could either remain in the highest class or they could take a sewing course to continue their education and delay marriage for several years. Schools run by one Protestant organization encouraged later marriage as well, but by using contracts with financial penalties if parents took their daughters out of school before a certain age, typically at ages fifteen or sixteen years.[87] Also, as mentioned, a Palestinian government doctor maintained in 1923 that shari'a court judges throughout Palestine would not register marriages for underage girls.[88] Families could misrepresent a girl's age of course, but judges seemed to be trying to encourage change. Finally, Granqvist mentions a rural shaykh who refused to marry underage youth out of fear of the government's punishment.[89]

The third important marriage reform in the 1917 Ottoman family code concerns a woman's right to live separately from her husband's family. According to classical Hanafi law, the Ottoman Empire's official school, the only situations in which a wife could demand a discrete living space were (a) if she were sharing accommodations with her husband's older children from another marriage or (b) if she were living with a cowife. Otherwise, a wife could be compelled to live with members of her husband's family, including his younger children from another marriage, his concubine, and his mother.[90] The Ottoman code significantly reformed this Hanafi interpretation and greatly improved the conditions under which a wife could be expected to live. Article 72 of the code specifies that a husband must obtain his wife's permission before housing her with any of his family members, with the exception of his younger children from another marriage. Tucker notes this was a "clear advance" for women but also points out that "we may wonder whether many women were in a position to assert this right, but the potential advantages are manifest."[91] This new right—for women to live separately from one's husband's concubine, older children from another marriage, and mother-in-law—is particularly significant because under classical Hanafi law, a wife and her mother-in-law (and her husband, and his concubine!) could be required to share a "house" that could amount to a lockable room with private toilet and cooking facilities.[92]

There are indications that Palestinians in rural areas were aware of this improvement in women's legal status; however, it was more common for wives to live with their husbands' relatives in village settings. In a general description of rural married life, Granqvist notes that after the wedding week, "the husband is allotted only his little corner for his and his wife's bed. . . . In one single room live a man and his wife, his unmarried sons and daughters, but also his married sons with their wives and children."[93] She goes on to discuss the economic advantages of a family living together, and then explains that was why a woman in Artas "was blamed" when she "insisted on having a room for [she and her husband] and was not content to live with his relatives."[94] Also, it is worth noting that this woman gained the support of her uncle and mother, which was central to obtaining her goal. Finally, her status as a "stranger wife," from outside the village, likely did not help her reputation.[95]

Granqvist gives another example in which a woman's father welcomed her kindly when her husband sent her home, but "not only due to love for her but chiefly because he wished . . . to annoy her husband's relatives.

They all live in the same place, a cave . . . and he thought that it was the husband's relatives who were to blame . . . and disturbed the harmony between her and her husband. So he reminded them that a wife has a legal right to a separate room."[96] The woman ended up back with her husband's family, where she still had to perform hard labor; however she had done so in her father's house as well. In this anecdote the woman's father was likely using her as a pawn against his rivals, rather than endeavoring to improve his daughter's situation. Both accounts involved monogamous marriages, and therefore the demand for a separate room was in accordance with the 1917 Ottoman family code, not classical Hanafi law. Also, both examples, along with Granqvist's description of typical married life, suggest that, in rural Palestine, separate housing from the husband's relatives was a right that women, or their families, claimed rarely. When they did so, it likely indicated a problem in the marriage, within the family, or a larger rivalry between families.

The Ottoman Code, Marriage Contract Conditions,
and Reasons for Polygyny

The last significant marriage-related reform in the 1917 Ottoman family code was its explicit recognition of a woman's right to add a stipulation (*shurut*) to the marriage contract (*'aqd*) that her husband will not marry another wife; of course the groom had to agree to these terms.[97] If a husband contravened such a contract, his wife would have the right to divorce him.[98] This article was clearly intended to encourage monogamous marriages. While indirectly giving women, or their families, more control over their marriages was important, the article only included one type of marriage contract stipulation. This did not nullify other sorts of stipulations; however, it also did not encourage them. Historically, marriage contract conditions could be included on a wide variety of issues, so long as they did not contravene principles in *shari'a*. Hanbali legal experts wrote most extensively on appropriate stipulations in the medieval period. In addition to conditions allowing the wife to divorce if the husband married a second wife or acquired a concubine, Tucker shows that Hanbali muftis accepted stipulations requiring the couple to live in the wife's hometown and for the husband to accommodate and support his wife's children from a prior marriage.[99] Medieval Maliki and Hanafi muftis, of the Ottoman Empire's official school, allowed various stipulations as well, such as promising not to harm the wife, providing particular clothing, and exempting the wife from performing hard labor.[100]

Mamluk courts (1250–1517) in Cairo and Damascus permitted litigants to use any orthodox school they wished, and they also saw a variety of marriage contract stipulations. Many were similar to the Hanbali conditions already discussed, including the wife's right to divorce if the husband married another wife and the husband's promise to house and support his wife's prior children. Yossef Rapoport demonstrates that Mamluk judges also allowed conditions that transformed the deferred dower from a payment upon death or divorce into a "payment on demand."[101] Doing so gave the wife considerable financial leverage over her husband within the marriage. It is important to emphasize that this newly defined dower was not a rare occurrence in the registers; in fact, it had become "standard practice" in Damascus by the mid-fourteenth century.[102] It is logical to infer that changing the dower in this respect not only enhanced the wife's economic power but also empowered her in other ways. Rapoport argues that it facilitated the inclusion of additional advantageous conditions in the marriage contract and enabled women to make new demands during their marriages because the new dower gave them increased financial leverage and, therefore, greater protection for their interests.[103]

In the Ottoman period, Hanafi, Maliki, and Shafi'i law dominated in different regions of Egypt, and marriage contract conditions were common among all three schools. Nelly Hanna found stipulations in roughly a third of the seventeenth-century Cairo marriage documents that she examined. Merchants or artisans were the most common socioeconomic group of urban Egyptians that employed conditions in her records. Judges allowed stipulations including the usual discouraging of polygyny; the husband agreeing to an atypical type of household, such as a separate residence from his family; and guaranteeing divorce in the event the husband failed to provide maintenance.[104] Hanna explains that the reason for the latter condition was a woman could have difficulty acquiring a divorce even if her husband was not supporting her. There was little agreement among the schools on the appropriate consequence for this dereliction of responsibility. Hanafi judges did not permit judicial dissolutions on grounds of the husband's failure to provide for his wife, but Shafiʻi, Maliki, and Hanbali judges were willing to annul marriages for this reason.[105] Regardless of the school, if a woman had this condition in her contract, she could obtain a divorce without the risk of a legal challenge. In addition to the typical monogamy requirement and the husband's support of the wife's children, the most common conditions used in marriage contracts throughout Ottoman Egypt included specifying the location of residence, usually to reside reasonably near the wife's family; the husband's promise not to harm his wife; and the husband's pledge not to be absent for a specified lengthy period.[106] If any of these conditions were not fulfilled, the wife could obtain a divorce without losing her financial divorce rights.

In Ottoman Palestine and Syria, however, women appear to have had fewer legal protections in their marriages via stipulations. Tucker's seventeenth- and eighteenth-century research on marriage registers in Palestine and Syria indicates that women, or their families, added conditions to their marriage contracts rarely. This change in Syria is rather mystifying, given the frequent use of stipulations transforming the deferred dower into a payment on demand in Damascus during the Mamluk period. Because Ottoman Egypt, Palestine, and Syria all enjoyed a diversity of legal traditions and Sunni schools, Tucker speculates that "local customs rather than doctrinal difference" explains the infrequency of including stipulations, compared to their commonplace use in Egypt.[107] Further research over additional periods is needed to provide a broader representation of marriages in Ottoman Palestine and Syria.

In discussing the Ottoman family code's explicit recognition of marriage contract stipulations discouraging additional wives, we should also recognize that there were many reasons for Palestinians to choose polygynous marriages within their families. Socially acceptable reasons for polygyny could include a first wife's inability to conceive, the high rate of child mortality, and a family's need for more workers. A man's personal reasons for marrying a second wife could also include his first wife being older or not of his choosing; it could even be a punishment to his first wife if they had a disagreeable relationship.[108] In rural Palestine, a marriage becoming polygynous could actually be in response to the first wife's needs. Granqvist references two women's examples: "One of them had a co-wife because the home required female labour and it is not the custom to keep women servants; another because in case of the husband's death his relatives would take possession of his home, and she would have to leave it because she had no son. . . . She had therefore, in order to ensure her position, insisted on his marriage with another woman in spite of his first objections to the proposal."[109] We can likely assume that these examples, particularly the latter one, occurred in urban areas as well. In her second book, Granqvist further explains that it was unusual to employ female servants in rural areas and that in situations where it was the first wife requesting a cowife, the new wife often "easily falls into the position of a servant to the first wife."[110] Clearly there were numerous motivations for a family to choose polygyny, which could enhance the first wife's quality of life by decreasing her workload.

Furthermore, polygyny was an indicator of enhanced social status because it was expensive for a man and his family to finance an additional dower. Another reason it was and is a costly proposition is because the Qur'an instructs men to provide separate households for each wife. Tucker shows that Ottoman-era legal experts interpreted this to mean a separate room with kitchen and bathroom accommodations for each wife.[111] It seems that rural Palestinians circa 1900, however, often disregarded both the Qur'an's and the muftis' directions. According to one longtime resident of Palestine, P. J. Baldensperger, despite the Qur'an's command and that "the parents of the wife also try their utmost to have a separate house, or at least room, for their daughter . . . only in very rare cases have I known this to be done. They usually live in one room."[112] Baldensperger expressed this observation in an article about rural Palestinians. Unfortunately, Granqvist does not state absolutely whether or not this sort of living situation was common practice in agrarian areas during the Mandate period. Her description of common living arrangements, mentioned previously, suggests that most rural families lived together in one room, but she does not specify that this happened in polygynous marriages.[113] She does discuss one polygynous marriage in which the first wife lived in the "front part of the house and the others in the back."[114] Granqvist may have meant separate rooms, but the description is not entirely clear. It is evident, however, that when a shaykh or other legal authority became involved in a family dispute, the cowives did receive separate rooms.[115] In any case, the great expense of polygyny rendered it a relatively uncommon practice, especially in rural areas where Palestinians were less likely to be able to afford an additional dower and, ideally, separate housing. Also, rural areas had fewer local women available for any type of marriage. Granqvist notes that for Artas, the polygyny rate was 10.7 percent in 1935, down from 13 percent when she included men who were deceased.[116] Also, a few decades before the Mandate, Wilson mentions that polygyny was far less common in rural areas than in urban areas.[117]

It appears that Palestinians employed marriage contract stipulations of any kind only on occasion during the Mandate era. It was usually the bride's father who served as her representative and negotiated her marriage contract, particularly for a first marriage. A father may well have been willing to grant his daughter's wishes in the contract, but a Palestinian girl was typically in her teens when she married. The Mandate government fell extremely short when it came to educating Palestinians and improving literacy rates, particularly among rural women.[118] Consequently, many Palestinians were unlikely to be fully knowledgeable about women's rights in Muslim family law and changes in the Ottoman code. Likewise, it was unusual for fathers or other guardians to include written stipulations in their daughters' contracts. Moors's research on women's access to property in the Nablus area shows that including stipulations was "virtually done only in the city" during the Mandate period.[119] She found that urban conditions most often pertained to housing arrangements, usually to guarantee that a couple would live apart from the husband's family. Another common stipulation required the husband to equip the household with certain items.[120] Moors does not provide statistics for the Mandate era, but she estimates that only 2 percent of Nablus-area contracts in the 1970s to 1980s contained conditions.[121] We can most likely assume the numbers were at best similar during the Mandate, given her observation about stipulations discussed above and that a small minority of Palestinians lived in cities. Today, however, it is more common for well-educated Palestinian women to use marriage contract stipulations, which I discuss later in this chapter and in chapter 4.

Finally, other marriage reforms in the Ottoman family code include the requirement to register marriage contracts in court, the ban on forced marriages, and the emphasis on a woman's right to her dower. Before the twentieth century, unregistered marriages were not unusual, and marriages were also conducted orally at times. Registering marriage contracts ensured that the terms of marriage were binding and followed the law; it also enabled judges to apply the prohibition on forced marriages. Regarding the dower, the Ottoman code prohibited parents from keeping any part of their daughter's dower, and it forbade them from compelling her to spend it on her trousseau and other items for her new life (*jihaz*).[122] The bride's exclusive right to her dower had always been a woman's fundamental right in the Qur'an, but often this was ignored by local custom. Granqvist maintains that "the woman herself in many cases receives part of the [dower], at times the whole of it . . . it is said in Palestine that only an avaricious father would not give the [dower] to his daughter or an outfit or other gifts bought with it."[123] Moors's research in Al-Balad shows that women tended to receive about a third of the prompt dower in this period. It was not uncommon for women to sue in court when a guardian other than the father withheld part of the dower; however, it was rare for a woman to take her own father to court.[124] A bride's father taking part of the dower was expected, and a woman needed to maintain their relationship in the event she encountered problems with her husband or in-laws and wished to return home.[125]

Granqvist makes the same point in explaining why women tended to let their brothers keep their shares of the inheritance. When Granqvist posed the question to one of her main sources in the village, the woman exclaimed, "But then she would have no more rights to her father's house!"[126] Thus not claiming her rights enabled a woman to reinforce the bond with her father or brothers, which gave her more protection from her in-laws. Similarly, when a brother was able to marry by means of a sister's dower, via an exchange marriage, he felt more strongly "in the obligation to protect her and give her presents as long as she lives."[127] Likewise, a woman who decided to gift part or all of her dower to a male family member often did so for strategic reasons. Considering men's ability to marry an additional wife and their lack of legal restrictions to divorce, it made a great deal of sense for women to invest in protection for themselves vis-à-vis their close male relatives.

Divorce Islamic Style

Divorce in classical Hanafi law, the official Ottoman school of law, was for the husband a straightforward course of action with few legal constraints. A husband could divorce his wife without stating a reason and without registering the divorce. But despite the legal ease with which men could divorce, there were also considerable financial incentives to remain married. Upon divorcing his wife, a husband was required to give his wife the deferred dower and any remaining balance of the advanced dower. A bride was supposed to receive at least part of the advanced dower at the signing of her wedding contract, and she was entitled to the deferred dower if her husband divorced her or died. The husband also had to support his former wife during her three-month waiting period (*'idda*) following the divorce. In the event she was pregnant, his former wife was to receive maintenance payments until the end of her pregnancy.[128] Finally, the husband was responsible for child support during the mother's temporary custody, or caretaking, period.[129] We will examine to what extent judges adhered to this element of classical Hanafi law in Mandate Palestine in chapter 4.

Men may have encountered no legal obstacles to divorce, apart from their financial responsibilities, but many faced social pressure from their own families, their spouses' families, and their communities to remain married. In most cases, a man's family would have been reluctant to support his wish for divorce unless the wife was truly an appalling woman, because then they would need to help fund another dower. It was expected that Palestinians would remarry following divorce in this period; one did not remain single unless she, or he, was elderly or unable to remarry. Indeed, women divorcées in Artas had no problems getting remarried in the mid-nineteenth and early twentieth centuries. Out of eleven divorced women in this period, all remarried except two: one was "taken back as a sister," and one died while in her father's house in extenuating circumstances during World War I.[130] Also, a man had to contend with his wife's family: a woman's father, brothers, mother, and other relatives could exert a great deal of pressure on her husband to treat their family member well, which included staying married to her. As Granqvist notes: "The woman represents a far too high value for it not to be a man's interest to esteem and take care of her; one can after all not so easily get a new wife. Even the women themselves would resent bad treatment from their husband and not permit it. If she has a father or a brother she will never submit to the whims of a despotic man . . . a woman with the support of her father's family knows how to carry out her own will in opposition to her husband and his family."[131] Of course, a woman's success in doing so must have depended on her family's socioeconomic status to some extent. Granqvist goes on to explain, "There are women in Artas who, far from being at all submissive in spirit, are really dominating personalities, with an imposing dignity, to whom their husbands must certainly very often give way."[132] The women Granqvist describes here not only were unlikely to ever face the prospect of divorce, but they were also the stronger partners in their marriages. Although the economic obligations that came with divorce certainly played a role in preserving marriages, family pressure, in-laws' demands, and a wife's strength of character were also incentives for many men to stay in their marriages. These factors taken together added up to a low divorce rate. Granqvist reports that only 4 percent of marriages in Artas from the mid-nineteenth century up to 1927 ended in divorce.[133] Interestingly, there seemed to be little stigma associated with divorced women, as we will see in chapter 3. Rather, it was the husband who felt "shame and humiliation that his wife [went] to another man," which was another reason for few divorces.[134]

A woman encountered a very different legal situation if she wished to divorce her husband under the classical Hanafi school. Wife-initiated divorce (*khul'* or *mukhal'a* in my cases) was possible, but she could not simply divorce her husband unilaterally, outside of court, or for her own reasons. Rather, a woman had to convince her husband to consent to the divorce, and this included giving up her rights to the deferred dower and maintenance during the waiting period. If he was opposed to divorce, she often had to add more financial incentives. A far better option for women was divorce via judicial dissolution (*tafriq*), which a woman requested in court unilaterally. If the judge granted it, she retained her financial divorce rights of the deferred dower and maintenance during the waiting period.

The acceptable grounds for this type of divorce in classical Hanafi law were rather unusual circumstances, however, such as the husband's impotence or insanity. The most absurd of the ostensible possibilities for a Hanafi court-ordered divorce was the requirement for the husband's disappearance (often termed "desertion"). A woman had to wait ninety-nine years from the time of her husband's birth before she could obtain the divorce on these grounds![135] Tucker shows that in practice, however, Ottoman-period Hanafi courts regularly allowed Shafi'i and Hanbali judges to rule according to their schools. These judges often accepted the husband's infectious disease, disappearance, and occasionally a present husband's nonsupport as grounds for judicial divorce.[136]

A wife usually had the alternative of returning to her father's house, however, if she was ill-treated by or incensed with her husband or her in-laws. There was even a term for it—a woman who was "offended and angry" (hardana)—to which Granqvist devotes an entire chapter of her second book. As she explains, "a woman is hardana when, considering herself unjustly treated in her husband's house, or in order to procure a better position therein, she goes away from her husband's house to her father's house."[137] Whether or not being hardana actually improved a woman's position vis-à-vis her in-laws depended on her family's full support, her competence in dealing with the situation, and how her community perceived her actions.[138] It seems whether or not the woman was considered justified in leaving her husband's home was an issue on which the whole village made a judgment: "If the daughter is at fault, it is shameful for [her family]."[139] Also, a woman's return home necessitated a strong relationship with her family because when her husband arrived to negotiate her return, her family had to provide a feast for him and his entourage.[140] A woman's state of anger in her father's house could even be a near-continuous state lasting several years. One woman related to Granqvist that out of fifteen years of marriage, she was hardana "most of the time"![141] This practice is significant because it was effectively a way in which a woman could live as if she had obtained a khul' divorce, but without needing the consent of her husband. Of course, she could not remarry in these circumstances. Also, sometimes this return to the father's house was in fact a woman's initial move in obtaining a divorce.[142]

If, however, the woman was pregnant or already had a child, it was usually more difficult for her to continue living with her family. Pregnancy transformed the situation a great deal because the woman needed to ensure that her husband acknowledged the child as his. After a public announcement that she was carrying her husband's child, the woman usually returned to him at that point or after the birth. Also, a *hardana* woman had no caretaking rights as she did in a legal divorce. Artas women who left their husbands in anger often took their children with them, but their husbands soon came to claim them. Society perceived children as belonging to the father and that a mother did not have the right to take them away from him.[143] This practice, of a *hardana* woman leaving her husband and returning to her family, does not appear to depart much from divorce practices in rural Palestine during this period. Granqvist maintains that a divorced woman was only able to keep her child until she had finished nursing.[144] As we will see, this was not consistent with Hanafi law, which granted mothers temporary custody until approximately age nine for girls and age seven for boys.

The Ottoman family code of 1917 evidently had much ground to cover in improving women's legal status in divorce. The code did nothing to restrict men's right to unilateral irrevocable divorce (*talaq*), so a man could still divorce his wife at any time and for any reason. But it did introduce a handful of reforms. Classical Hanafi law recognized a divorce even if the husband had divorced his wife while drunk or under coercion, both of which the Ottoman code eliminated by declaring such divorces invalid.[145] Another reform was the registration requirement, which was eventually meaningful for several reasons. A husband could no longer verbally divorce his wife and retract it without facing consequences, because a woman would have proof of the divorce in writing. She would then be able to sue for maintenance and her deferred dower if necessary. Also, it confirmed the fact of her freedom to remarry after the three-month waiting period. This reform could not have been widely effective, however, because the code failed to invalidate divorces that were not registered in court.[146] The long-term significance of this reform has been that compulsory registration of divorces and marriages was later incorporated into Arab states' modern family codes.

The Ottoman family code also expanded the conditions under which a woman could obtain a judicial dissolution (*tafriq*) unilaterally and without losing her financial divorce rights. This type of divorce had significant advantages for women over wife-initiated divorce, in which the wife needed her husband's consent and relinquished her divorce rights. In classical Hanafi law, the conditions for judicial dissolution were extremely narrow and would have applied rarely, such as the ninety-nine years wait (since the husband's birth) for desertion in classical Hanafi law. Article 127 of the code modified the maximum wait for desertion to four years. This appears to be a revolutionary change until noting actual practice in eighteenth-century Palestine. Because Ottoman courts allowed non-Hanafi judges to rule in desertion cases, a woman typically waited only one year for her divorce.[147] But the 1917 code also clarified how judges should rule in various circumstances. Articles 126–127 provide three situations under which a woman could obtain a judicial dissolution because of desertion. If there are no means for the wife to collect maintenance and she has attempted to locate her husband, she is granted a divorce immediately. If there is a designated person to support her, the wife must wait four years after being unable to find her husband. If she has a maintenance provider, but her husband is absent in the context of war, the woman must wait one year after the war has ended. A handful of desertion cases emerged in my research, which we will examine in chapter 3 to help assess the extent to which the Jerusalem court applied the Ottoman code.

The lawyers who wrote the Ottoman family code likely did not consider a present husband's failure to support as legitimate grounds for divorce because women could, and often did, sue for maintenance. As we will see, when a judge ruled in a wife's favor in a maintenance case, he always gave her the right to borrow the amount owed in her husband's name. Because women had this option, along with their preferences for Hanafi law and keeping marriages together, the authors of the code must have seen no reason to allow divorce on these grounds. This appears to be consistent with Ottoman practices because, as mentioned previously, judges in Ottoman courts rarely granted annulment for a present husband's failure to provide maintenance.[148]

There were several other circumstances in which women could obtain a judicial dissolution per the Ottoman family code, including the husband's inability to consummate the marriage or impotence in Articles 119–121. If the condition is incurable, the divorce is granted immediately. If the disease or problem has a possibility of healing, the husband is given a year to improve his performance. If he is not cured after a year, the wife may have her court-ordered divorce. This was not a major reform because impotence had long been an acceptable term for annulment in Ottoman courts. But, as with desertion, it did specify the ways in which judges should apply these grounds in judicial dissolutions. Other conditions in the code included the husband's affliction with a dangerous disease or insanity; however, as mentioned previously, these were grounds for annulment from the wife's petition that Ottoman courts regularly accepted.[149]

The most important long-term divorce reform in the Ottoman family code was that cruelty, physical abuse, or other intolerable treatment were now grounds for judicial dissolution, the proceedings of which were to be entirely run and determined by arbitrators.[150] This Maliki school–inspired reform allowed either spouse to initiate a court-ordered divorce for this reason, termed "discord and incompatibility." Tucker does not mention this reform in her piece on the Ottoman family code, and her broader argument is that the code did little to improve women's overall status in practice.[151] It does seem that the short-term effects of this particular reform were negligible, as my research suggests that judges did not allow these grounds or the procedure required during the Mandate period.[152] But the reform has been used in the post-1948 period, as we will see.

The procedure for this type of divorce calls for two mandatory arbitrators, usually one from each family, who are designated to resolve the couple's differences. If reconciliation is not possible, they determine which spouse is responsible for the failure of the marriage. Indeed, Anderson describes the arbitrators' role as conducting an "investigation" to confirm the charges.[153] If the wife is at fault, the divorce is treated as wife-initiated (*khul'*) and she does not receive her deferred dower or support during the waiting period. If the husband is at fault, the wife receives her divorce rights as in a unilateral husband-initiated divorce (*talaq*). The arbitrators' decision is final, regardless of which spouse they find responsible for the break-up.

This new type of judicial dissolution on grounds of "discord and incompatibility" was at once innovative and traditional. It was innovative in that it has empowered arbitrators with authority that had previously been reserved for judges in Hanafi courts. In fact, judges can only contest arbitrators' rulings if there has been a breach of procedure. This sort of judicial divorce has the potential to increase options for women because it expanded grounds for divorce in which a wife could keep her financial rights, but this depends on the finesse of her arbitrator. Thus it also had the effect of legalizing arbitration practices that had long been customary. While no plaintiffs in my survey of cases from the Mandate period attempted to use discord and incompatibility as grounds for annulment, the reform did become significant after the British Mandate. It has been adopted in several modern family codes and it has been used in Palestine and Israel since 1948. Indeed, in Israel today, shari'a courts employ this article of the Ottoman family code to the letter, as Hoda Rouhana's study of "discord and incompatibility" divorce cases shows.[154] We will examine her findings in the section on Muslim family law post-1948.

Child Custody According to Abu Hanifa

Classical Hanafi law gave the father considerable legal advantages over the mother in child custody. Upon the divorce or separation of a couple, a girl resided with her mother until nine years, and a son stayed in his mother's care until the age of seven.[155] The father was required to provide child support for the duration of the mother's caretaking or temporary custody period (hadana). At the end, the child went to live with his or her father, who had permanent custody. The child also went to the father's family even if the father was not present, had died, or was incapable of supporting her. If the mother remarried at any time during her caretaking period, she would lose temporary custody immediately. Despite that Hanafi jurisprudence restricted the mother's custody period to the child's age of seven or nine, it was not always followed. Tucker demonstrates that both Ottoman legal experts and sitting judges referenced a child's age in years infrequently, as they instead favored the child's physical developmental stages to determine the end of the mother's caretaking period.[156] She also shows how the stage in which a child should be in his mother's care differed for boys and girls; for boys, it was from birth until he could dress and feed himself, and for girls, the stage lasted until she began puberty.[157] As we will see in chapter 4, Mandate-era judges departed from this Ottoman practice because they decided cases according to the child's age rather than childhood stages.

While the paternal extended family was clearly privileged over the maternal family, the mother's family did have limited custody rights during the mother's caretaking period in the event the mother was unable to care for her child. In such circumstances, the court gave the child to her maternal grandmother for the duration of the mother's custody. The central rationale for the father's preferential status in child custody matters comes down to the father's ultimate role as the provider and protector of his family in Muslim family law; the father is thus further considered the natural and sole guardian of his children. The status of the father as his child's natural guardian was apparently one that the drafters of the new Ottoman family code did not wish to disrupt, because the Ottoman code made no improvements in women's position in child custody. We will see that the application of child custody law diverged somewhat from the tenets of classical Hanafi law in chapter 4.

Social Practices Inconsistent with Family Law

Many rural social practices relating to marriage and divorce departed from both classical Hanafi law and the Ottoman code, some of which could elevate women's status. Perhaps the most significant way in which Palestinian society favored custom over the law was in arbitration practices. A contemporary source fittingly describes the significance of the local men's coffeehouse: "Disputes of every kind should be presented before the chiefs and *mukhtars* to be settled here. These decisions are more acceptable than those of the law of the courts."[158] The author does not indicate a net gain for or detriment to women, but the passage does explain a great deal about rural Palestinians' preferred methods for settling disputes and the tendency to seek local arbitrators rather than urban courtroom judges. There are other social practices that do suggest benefits for women, compared with their legal status. We have already discussed how a woman could leave her husband in anger, which, if executed strategically, could improve her position within his family or be an initial step toward divorce. This practice was in contradiction to family law, which dictated that a woman should live in her husband's home. Also, Granqvist discusses how a woman's "brothers can, under certain circumstances, compel the husband to divorce her," including situations in which the husband suffered from leprosy, someone in his family cursed her family, the husband was unjust to her, or the husband was impotent.[159]

There were several other customs and mores that had no basis in the law, and many departed from the patriarchal underpinnings of the law. First, a family's social standing could be an important factor influencing which party was most empowered in a marriage. The significance of marriage partners' social status is evident in Granqvist's account of a man who was deceived by his in-laws when they switched brides on him, swapping his betrothed for her aunt. There was very little he could do about it because he had already paid the dower and the father of his intended bride was the civil leader (*mukhtar*) of the village, whereas his own father was dead and his family impoverished.[160] Another important factor in determining a rural woman's status in the family was the extent of her assertiveness, which Baldensperger well describes:

> The [peasant] woman is just as often—virtually—the head of the family, and differs in nothing from woman in the rest of Creation. She at least influences her husband, in most cases for all things, not only in the house, but in all matters affecting their common weal. She is interested in the agricultural business—looks after the herds and herdsmen, animals and servants. I have known many [peasant] women to manage everything a good deal better than the husband, and even scolding him to some degree for any mismanagement, or teaching him what to say in the men's assembly. But, notwithstanding this, she did not escape a good flogging occasionally. Yet it does not follow that the [peasant] woman is to be pitied in being considered an inferior being. She enjoys her life and liberty to a certain extent, at least in many instances.[161]

This account from circa 1900 was still accurate during the Mandate era. As observed here, rural women were critical to their families' livelihoods and participated extensively in agricultural and economic activities alongside their husbands. Baldensperger even notes that they were "just as often virtually the head of family" and greatly influenced their husbands' political participation as well. Clearly, Palestinian women often had a great deal of agency in practice, which conflicted with their disadvantaged legal status in many ways.

The status of widows was another respect in which law and practice were often inconsistent. In Muslim family law, a widow is entitled to receive her deferred dower, the amount of which is determined in her marriage contract, but she inherits a great deal less than her sons. The amounts of dower and inheritance are poor ways of gauging a widow's status vis-à-vis her husband's family during this period, however. As Granqvist demonstrates in several examples from Artas, having sons was a far more significant indicator, in which case a widow could enjoy considerable autonomy and exert extensive authority. Her insight on the potentially high status of widows is instructive: "A widow can have great power when she is the head of the house, has money at her disposal and is the guardian of her children. If the latter have become used to their mother's authority, it may continue long after the sons are grown up and she remains the central and most important person in the family. The sons take her into their confidence, they listen to her advice and when they marry, often by her arrangement their wives come under her control, become her servants carrying out her commands."[162] Thus a widow's power largely depended on whether or not she had sons. Of course, the extent of a widow's influence depended on the strength of the relationship with her sons, as they must have been accustomed to their mother's authority. Additionally, being a mature woman past childbearing years was important because it precluded questions about her respectability and efforts to find another husband. In Moors's analysis of factors affecting rural widows' status in more recent decades, she also discusses the importance of sons, a woman's maturity, and the compatibility of the relationship between the widow and her husband's family.[163]

But sometimes social practices contravened the law in ways that reduced women's status as well. We have already seen how the paternal extended family usually shared a single room, rather than providing separate rooms for sons and their families per the Ottoman code. Of course, this was not only a conventional practice but also an economic reality; rural Palestinians were unlikely to have been able to afford multiroom accommodations in this period. Second, Granqvist mentions an incident in which a woman was married to an impotent man for ten years, and in order to obtain a divorce, her brothers had to pay him 10 pounds.[164] According to both Hanafi law and the 1917 Ottoman family code, as well as prior Ottoman practice, she should have been entitled to a judicial divorce in which she kept her financial divorce rights. Rather, her brothers had to pay an additional sum. Most significantly, it appears that in rural Palestine, the approximate ages of the mother's temporary caretaking period, established in classical Hanafi law, were often not followed in practice. Rather, a divorced woman was only able to nurse her children, and once weaned, they had to return to their father.[165] This, however, departs from the way judges applied the law in the courts during the Mandate period. As we will see in chapter 4, judges interpreted classical custody law quite narrowly in this study compared to the more flexible Ottoman practices. Also, unlike during the Ottoman period, judges ruled according to the child's age in years, rather than per developmental stages.

Muslim Family Law in Palestine and Israel since 1948

After the creation of Israel in 1948, the state upheld the 1917 Ottoman family code for the minority Muslim Palestinian population within its borders. Israeli forces had expelled, both directly and indirectly, approximately 85 percent of Palestinians from what became Israel during the 1948 war, after which Israel refused to allow their return, disregarding United Nations resolutions.[166] The Israelis preserved the Ottoman family code intact for its Muslim population, while other states in the Middle East have tended to use it as a foundation for family law codes. In Jordan, the family codes of 1951 and 1976 were based on the Ottoman code in several respects, as we will see. In the West Bank, Palestinians came under Jordanian rule from 1948 to 1967, and shari'a courts still apply much of Jordan's 1976 family law. Egypt governed Gaza during the same period; thus Gaza courts still largely employ the 1954 Law of Family Rights that was based on Egyptian family laws.[167] Since the Oslo Accords, shari'a courts in the West Bank have been under the jurisdiction of the Palestinian Authority (PA), as were Gazan courts until 2007. But after the split between Hamas-governed Gaza and the PA-governed West Bank, Gaza and the West Bank have maintained separate legislative and judicial systems. This political rift has increased the critical need for a unified family law code. Despite women's groups' and other nongovernmental organizations' (NGOs) ongoing efforts since the 1980s to reform Muslim family law by establishing a unified code, and more recently involving the PA, the Occupied Territories still lack a unified family law code. In the absence of a sitting legislature because of Israeli restrictions, human rights and women's NGOs, the PA's Ministry of Women's Affairs, and the Chief Islamic Justice's office have been negotiating a new draft law that includes important reforms. Also, since Oslo, Chief Justices have introduced several procedural changes that have improved women's status, which we will examine. The last discrete group of Palestinians in Palestine/Israel that are subject to yet another set of laws are so-called permanent residents of Jerusalem, which is how the Israeli government categorizes Palestinians who live in East Jerusalem. They are not Israeli citizens but they have the option of using *shari'a* courts in Israel or those in East Jerusalem, and they are ostensibly subject to Israeli civil laws.

Muslim Family Law for Palestinian Citizens of Israel

Israel has effected reform by passing civil legislation that seemingly trumps religious law, which the family courts of each religious community are supposed to uphold. The first of these civil laws is the Marriage Age Law (1950), which raised the minimum marriage age for girls to seventeen years. Next, the Women's Equal Rights Law (1951) banned polygyny, equalized inheritance, and required a woman's consent for her husband to divorce unless he has obtained a court-ordered divorce. The Penal Law of 1977 went further than the 1951 law and criminalized polygyny, stating that offenders must serve a five-year sentence.[168] Another significant civil law is the Maintenance Law (1972), in which the state took up the responsibility of delinquent maintenance payments; the husband then owes the amount of the missed payments to the state. In addition, the Spouses or Property Relations Law (1973) declares that all property accumulated during marriage is equally owned by both spouses.[169]

While these civil laws may appear to indicate progressive reform for Palestinian and other citizens of Israel, studies have shown that the enforcement of these laws is often quite haphazard, and many laws contain major loopholes. The Working Group on the Status of Palestinian Women in Israel, an umbrella group of women's and human rights NGOs that has submitted reports to the Convention on the Elimination of Discrimination against Women (CEDAW) Committee in 1997, 2005, and 2010, argues that polygyny, forced marriage (particularly among Bedouins), unilateral divorce, child custody, and child marriage remain significant problems for Palestinian-Israeli (Arab-Israeli) women.[170] Also, the Working Group points to a considerable gap in the Women's Equal Rights Law (1951) in that it "contains a proviso which states that the law does not apply to matters relating to marriage and divorce."[171] Another major loophole in the law concerns the 1973 property law. If the marriage contract contains a stipulation that a divorce will follow Muslim family law and the couple's property is only registered in the husband's name, a woman has no recourse in *shari'a* court.[172] One last example is the minimum marriage age, which the Knesset raised from seventeen to eighteen years in 2013, much to the chagrin of many in the ultra-Orthodox (Jewish) community. However, the state allows numerous exceptions, and the law is regularly contravened because Israel recognizes underage marriages that are performed or certified by religious courts.[173]

The Working Group's reports to CEDAW also address major disparities between the Muslim community and other religious communities in Israel. Whereas Jews, Druze, and Christians have been able to choose between state family or religious courts regarding matters of "child custody and support, alimony, and property rights," Muslims were required to use religious courts until 2001.[174] Since the Knesset passed a law permitting Muslims to access state family courts that year, Palestinian-Muslim Israelis may now choose between state courts and traditional *shari'a* courts for the family law matters listed above. However, all Israelis must still use an appropriate religious court for marriage and divorce.[175] Also, most Palestinian-Muslim citizens of Israel are likely to continue using the *shari'a* courts even when they have a choice, given the political implications of opting for an Israeli family court. Rouhana points out that Palestinian-Israelis harbor considerable suspicion and resentment toward the state because of numerous grievances, including the Knesset's prior interferences in Muslim family law; thus this law is unlikely to have meaningful impact on their communities.[176] But it is important to recognize that the Knesset passed this law largely because of Palestinian-Israeli women's activism.[177]

Rather than eliminating gender inequality, as the name of Israel's Women's Equal Rights Law suggests, male litigants and other actors within the *shari'a* court system have found new ways of perpetuating patriarchy. Rouhana makes a compelling case for this argument in her examination of 1997 arbitration-determined divorce cases from the Court of First Instance and the *Shari'a* Court of Appeal in Israel, focusing on cases in which the plaintiff seeks a judicial dissolution on grounds of "discord and strife," sanctioned by the 1917 Ottoman family code.[178] In this type of divorce, arbitrators determine which party is responsible for the marital discord and, accordingly, whether or not the wife will receive her financial divorce rights as in a husband-initiated divorce. Analyzing their gendered arguments and the circumstances in which men and women were able to secure judicial dissolutions on these grounds, Rouhana concludes that rulings were not consistent, largely because arbitrators play an extraordinarily decisive role in these cases.[179] In fact, the judges accepted their recommendations in all but one case. Arbitrators' beliefs and views, which typically include the presumption of innate male superiority, were usually prioritized over legal precedents.[180] This further indicates the enduring role of custom with all of its patriarchal manifestations in the court system. In addition, most of the critical actors in the *shari'a* court system are still male, and they enter both court proceedings and arbitrations with ingrained patriarchal assumptions. They continue to construct gender accordingly but with new mechanisms that contravene or minimize Israel's civil laws. Rouhana also shows, however, that the *Shari'a* Court of Appeal did protect women's dower rights in most of the cases, particularly when the arbitrators breached procedure; often they neglected to give a reason for the wife's guilt.[181] One should bear in mind that the authors of the Ottoman code empowered arbitrators with this very judicial authority, which is another indication of the law's overall patriarchal nature. Further, it is useful to

note that the so-called progressive Israeli state chose to uphold the Ottoman family code in its entirety rather than to reform it, as other states in
the Middle East have done.

Muslim Family Law Applied in the Palestinian West Bank and Gaza

The Jordanian Law of Personal Status (JLPS) of 1976, which replaced the
1951 family code and is still used in the West Bank, along with Gaza's
1954 Law of Family Rights (LFR) that was issued by Egypt retained several continuities from the Ottoman family code of 1917. There have also
been important reforms in both family codes concerning women's rights
in maintenance, wife-initiated divorce, child custody, and the minimum
marriage age. The following section will highlight the most significant of
these reforms and address the major differences between the family codes
applied in the West Bank and Gaza.

   Maintenance (nafaqa). The 1951 Jordanian code expanded maintenance
to include medical expenses for a husband's wife and children, as well as
educational costs for a man's adult sons.[182] The 1951 law also stipulated that
a woman may leave the marital home if she is being mistreated without
losing her right to maintenance, which has made it harder for men to withhold maintenance by asserting that one's wife left without permission.[183]
One disadvantage to women in the 1951 code was its new enforcement of
an obedience ruling; that is, a wife could be physically compelled to return
to the marital home.[184] The JLPS of 1976 remedied this provision, however.
It mentions the wife's duty of obedience, meaning residing in the marital
home, but excludes any reference to compulsion, thus "the only result the
husband may obtain in the very rare cases where an award of [obedience] is
made in his favor is ending the wife's right to maintenance."[185] In Gaza, the
LFR of 1954 states that a wife "is obliged" to live in her husband's home, but
a 1967 Egyptian decree forbids forcing a woman to return to it.[186]

   One distinction among the maintenance laws applied in the Occupied
Territories is that the Gaza code does not include medical expenses in
the definition of maintenance, as does the Jordanian code applied in the
West Bank.[187] The laws applied in both areas are similar, however, in that
they follow the Hanafi precedent of basing maintenance on the husband's
circumstances without considering those of the wife.[188] Also, both Gaza's

code and the JLPS conform to Hanafi law, and depart from the 1917 Ottoman family code, in that they do not allow the wife to sue for back payments of maintenance owed by the husband.[189]

Judicial dissolution (tafriq). Both the 1976 Jordanian family code used
in the West Bank and the 1954 family code applied in Gaza expanded the
grounds on which women could obtain a judicial divorce and retain their
financial divorce rights. These new grounds included a husband's failure
to provide maintenance, an absent husband of a year or more—even if he
continues to provide maintenance—and a long prison sentence.[190] Also,
the grounds of "discord and strife" from the Ottoman family code were
upheld in both the Gazan and Jordanian codes but seem to only be implemented by West Bank courts, as I explain below.[191] The 1976 Jordanian
code added more divorce-related benefits for women, such as compensating
women for arbitrary divorce. If a husband divorces his wife "without legitimate cause," she can receive maintenance for one year; this innovation
was modeled on the 1953 Syrian family code.[192]

There is no such provision in the Gazan code. However, the "discord
and strife" grounds for *tafriq* in Gaza's LFR are more advantageous for
women compared to the JLPS. If a wife demonstrates her husband has
injured her, the judge can grant a *tafriq* divorce in Gaza; but in the West
Bank under the JLPS, the wife must also go through an arbitration process
after establishing the injury.[193] It must be noted, however, that Welchman's
early 1990s research found no instances out of 102 *tafriq* cases in which
Gazan women sued for divorce on this basis, and only 8 percent of the
West Bank *tafriq* claims used these grounds.[194] Perhaps the most important
change from the 1917 Ottoman family code for both the Gaza and Jordanian codes was that women can obtain a judicial dissolution for nonpay-
ment of maintenance; in fact, it was the basis for 59 percent of *tafriq* claims
in the West Bank and 39 percent in Gaza in Welchman's study.[195]

Wife-initiated divorce (khul'). Wife-initiated divorce in which the
wife gives up her rights to maintenance during the waiting period and
her deferred dower, to which the husband must consent, is not addressed
in either the 1917 Ottoman family code or Gaza's 1954 code; thus classical Hanafi rules apply in Gaza.[196] There were few *khul'*-related changes
in the 1976 Jordanian law, and none in the 1951 code; therefore Hanafi

law largely dictates *khul'* in the West Bank as well. One reform in the 1976 Jordanian code concerns maintenance for the waiting period. It must be "explicitly included" in the wife's renunciation of her financial rights in order for this right to cease.[197] However, this was part of the standard renunciation statement spoken in court in the majority of West Bank *khul'* cases in Welchman's 1985 study.[198] It should also be noted that West Bank *shari'a* courts have not applied amendments to Jordan's family code since the establishment of the Palestinian Authority in the 1990s, such as the 2001 Jordanian law allowing women to obtain a *khul'* divorce without the husband's consent.

Child custody. The 1951 Jordanian Law of Family Rights raised the end of the mother's caretaking period (*hadana*) from the classical Hanafi position of seven to nine years for boys and from nine to eleven years for girls.[199] The 1976 Jordanian family code, the current law applied in the West Bank, raised the end of the mother's custody period further to the beginning of puberty for both girls and boys.[200] This gives judges considerable leeway in determining custody, as "puberty" is a rather subjective term. In her 1999 study, Welchman maintains that "the practice followed" in the West Bank is to let the minor choose with whom she wishes to live upon reaching puberty.[201] My interviews with a legal adviser for the PA's Ministry of Women's Affairs and a lawyer for the Women's Centre for Legal Aid and Counselling (WCLAC) suggest, however, that some judges will ask a girl, but not all of them, while they do generally ask a boy.[202] For Gaza, only one article in the LFR of 1954 addresses child custody; thus Gaza courts largely follow classical Hanafi law. Article 118 of the Gaza code states that a mother may retain custody of boys until ages seven to nine and of girls until ages nine to eleven, which preserved the Hanafi standard ages but also included an "extension allowed for by the Hanafis."[203]

Marriage age. The 1976 Jordanian family code established fourteen-and-a-half years for females and fifteen-and-a-half years for males as the ages of both minimum marriage and legal majority.[204] Previously, in both the Ottoman family code and the 1951 JLFR, judges had the discretion to approve marriages between the minimum age of puberty (nine and twelve in the Ottoman code and fifteen for both sexes in the 1951 JLFR) and the age of legal majority (seventeen for females and eighteen for males in both codes).[205] Therefore, the JLPS raised the minimum age for males but also ended the judge's role in authorizing marriages between ages fifteen and eighteen years (age seventeen for females).[206] However, as in Israeli law, the 1976 Jordanian code contains a loophole for contravening the minimum age requirement—in the JLPS, it is if the wife is pregnant, has a child, or if both the husband and the wife have reached the minimum age at the time a lawsuit is filed.[207] As in the Mecelle, the Ottoman civil code, Jordan's penal code of 1960 punishes all parties involved in contracting an underage marriage, but Welchman points out this was not implemented in the West Bank until 1995 because there was no liaison between the Israeli-controlled civil courts and *shari'a* courts.[208] Since Palestinians have gained control over their civil courts since the Oslo Accords, Jordan's penal code has been enforced in the West Bank.[209] There are, however, no studies examining the application of that particular article to my knowledge. In Gaza, the 1954 LFR retained the Ottoman family code's provisions on marriage ages, with the ages of legal majority at seventeen for females and eighteen for males, the minimum marriage age set at the minimum age of puberty at nine for girls and twelve for boys, and judges' permission required for marriages between those ages.[210] The next section will describe how this was raised in 1995.

Changes in Muslim Family Law since Oslo

Since the Oslo Accords, the Palestinian legal system has consisted of several overlapping, "competing legal frameworks," including statutory law, Muslim family law, and customary law.[211] Regular (*nizami*) courts apply statutory law and *shari'a* courts largely apply the family codes discussed. Customary law is not recognized in the written law explicitly but the statutes do allow extrajudicial settlements and reconciliation processes.[212] The presence of intersecting systems of law is a historical and present reality in many countries in the region. Palestine's situation, however, is further complicated by discrete family codes, rival political forces, and the ongoing Israeli military occupation.[213] Welchman suggests that Palestine's weak central government, "embryonic 'national' legislation, and prospective statehood" have fueled competition among the legal frameworks. Furthermore, it appears that these forces have contributed to customary law having been "arguably . . . strengthened during the period of PA rule."[214] Among these many challenges to Palestinians' development of legal institutions, the lack of a national family law is the most relevant to this study.

In the absence of a unified family code, Chief Islamic Justices have used procedural changes to institute certain family law reforms since Oslo. First, in 1995, Chief Justice (*Qadi al-Quda*) Shaykh Abu Sardane raised the minimum marriage age for girls in Gaza to fourteen-and-a-half years, as it is in the West Bank.[215] This law unfortunately falls short of international human rights standards advocating eighteen years. But there is reason for optimism because studies since 2000 show that Palestinian society overwhelmingly supports a minimum marriage age law of eighteen years.[216] Likewise, in recent discussions on, or rather, negotiations over, a unified Muslim family law, in which the Chief Justice's office, human rights groups, and the Ministry of Women's Affairs have participated, the consensus is eighteen years for both males and females.[217] Also, actual marriage ages continue to increase for Palestinians in the West Bank and Gaza. The median marriage age in 2011 was 20.0 for women and 24.6 for men, up from 18.0 and 23.0 in 1997. For Palestinians with university degrees in 2011, the age was 23.8 for women and 26.7 for men.[218]

In 2006, Chief Justice Shaykh Tamimi supported an important change in child custody in a draft law that would enable the judge to determine which parent is best suited to gain custody after the mother's caretaking period, which stated the judge could extend the mother's custody until eighteen years if he deemed it the best option for the child.[219] The new draft law contains a similar article. If enacted, these reforms would be important for Palestinian families. Currently, child custody reverts to the father when the child reaches physical maturity because judges apply the 1976 Jordanian law in the absence of a Palestinian code, according to *shari'a* court judge Kholoud Al-Faqih.[220] A *shari'a* court lawyer for the Women's Centre for Legal Aid and Counselling maintains that maturity often translates to ages eleven or twelve for boys and age nine for girls, although lawyers can argue that the girl is not physically mature to prolong the mother's custody.[221] Once the child reaches maturity, some judges will ask the boy with which parent he would like to live, but it is less common for them to ask a girl.[222] Remarkably, in 2009 Gaza legislators raised the end of the mother's custody for unmarried widows to age fifteen for boys and until marriage for girls, "presumably in response to the situation of Gaza war widows after Israel's 2008–2009 incursions."[223]

Shaykh Tamimi also appointed three women judges to the *shari'a* courts in 2009, which was unprecedented for any religious court in the Middle East, including Israel's rabbinical courts. The first judge, Kholoud Al-Faqih, was thirty-two when Shaykh Tamimi appointed her. One of twelve children, Al-Faqih was born in Jerusalem to parents who had only attended elementary school. She graduated from Al-Quds University in law with honors, and proceeded to earn a master's degree in international law. After graduation, Al-Faqih worked for the Women's Centre for Legal Aid and Counselling for seven years, practicing law in both the civil and *shari'a* court systems. She soon noticed there were many female judges in the civil courts but none in the *shari'a* courts. This surprised her because so many family law cases concerned women and sensitive topics. Al-Faqih was determined to rectify the status quo and become a *shari'a* court judge herself. She wrote an extensive legal argument in order to persuade the shaykh to let her sit for the difficult exam. Al-Faqih studied diligently for four months, taking a break from work and sending her three children (now she has four) to her mother's, and proceeded to do very well on the test.[224] What really makes her achievement a significant development in Palestine is Al-Faqih's role as a driver for Muslim family law reform and her participation in the groups negotiating the new draft law. Her profession as a judge, as well as her background as a lawyer providing representation for abused and other disadvantaged women for the Women's Centre for Legal Aid and Counselling, has given her considerable insight regarding which laws are in most critical need of reform. She supports family law changes that would uphold justice for women and men. For child custody law, Al-Faqih supports prioritizing the best interest of the child. She even advocates bringing in social workers to determine which parent should receive custody.[225] Al-Faqih has also been instrumental in the appointments of two women judges and a marriage officiant to the *shari'a* judiciary, as described in the documentary *The Judge*. As of 2018, there are five women working in significant positions in Palestine's *shari'a* courts: three judges, the chief prosecutor, and a marriage officiant.[226] To my knowledge, it is unprecedented for women to hold all three professions, not only in Palestine but also in the Middle East.[227] Clearly Al-Faqih's breakthrough into Palestine's *shari'a* judiciary has been an important milestone, given her views on gender equality and legal reform.[228]

In 2012, Chief Justice Shaykh Yousef announced several additional reforms in an unusual press conference in Ramallah. First, in judicial dissolution (*tafriq*), judges now have the authority to determine if the marriage is harmful to the wife, rather than requiring her to provide evidence of harm, and divorce proceedings are not to last longer than three months. These changes are important because often cases involving harm or divorce would drag on for years as women struggled to procure evidence. As judges supporting the reforms have pointed out, situations involving domestic violence can be "almost impossible to prove."[229] Second, women are able to initiate divorce (*khul'*) without the husband's consent if the marriage has not been consummated. Additionally, husbands are prohibited from demanding extra financial incentives, beyond the usual dower and wedding gifts, in wife-initiated divorce cases.[230] These reforms clearly increase women's access to divorce and ease their financial burden. What is particularly interesting about these decrees is that they emanated from the former Chief Justice Shaykh Yousef, who reportedly has connections with Hamas, a religious political party that is often perceived as conservative and reluctant to alter family law. This suggests the impetus for reform has permeated into many segments of Palestinian society, as does Gaza's 2009 reform extending the mother's custody period for unmarried widows to fifteen years for boys and until marriage for girls.[231]

Applying the Law

Judges' application of the law is another important factor to consider in analyzing women's status in Muslim family law. Welchman's research of Palestinian West Bank court proceedings from the 1960s–1980s shows that certain judges have implemented the Jordanian Law of Personal Status (1976) with considerably more concern for women and respect for changes in society than the code stipulates.[232] For example, whereas the Jordanian code categorically states that "no maintenance is due the wife who works outside the house without the consent of her husband," as this constitutes disobedience, Welchman argues that husbands are rarely able to success-fully exploit this article.[233] She cites a case from 1975 where the judge told the husband that he knew his wife was a teacher before he married her, so he should have stipulated his objection to her working in the marriage contract.[234] In addition, a former judge in Ramallah told her that a hus-band must "establish a 'good reason' if he wishes to forbid his wife" from working.[235] Welchman's study suggests that judges are flexible and reason-able in their rulings, taking social change into consideration in their appli-cation of the law.

Nahda Shehada conducted ethnographic research in Gaza during the early 2000s that also supports this finding. She highlights several cases in which a judge had used creative interpretations and flexibility to apply the law "by emphasizing the text of [Muslim family law] in some cases, and recalling broader principles derived from his religious education" in others.[236] Shehada shows how judges' "concern for protecting the rights of the weak, while maintaining social harmony," as well as preserving fam-ily unity, can trump the letter of the law in judges' rulings.[237] While she demonstrates that this flexibility can mean rulings to women's advantage, it is not always the case. For example, she cites a lawsuit in which a judge concluded that social harmony or family cohesion would be best served by denying a woman maintenance.[238]

Marriage Contract Stipulations

One respect in which the 1917 Ottoman family code has had a positive long-term effect concerns marriage contract stipulations. Although the Ottoman code only explicitly recognized women's stipulations discourag-ing one's husband from taking an additional wife (but did not ban other stipulations), it helped pave the way for women to include a range of condi-tions in their contracts. The first Jordanian family code (1951) went further than the Ottoman code by embracing a "general acceptance of all lawful stipulations" and permitted either spouse to use them.[239] The Jordanian Law of Personal Status (1976), enforced in the West Bank today, provided "unprecedented detail" on specific stipulations, giving several legitimate and invalid examples.[240] The 1954 family law used in Gaza, however, fol-lows the Ottoman family code in this respect and simply states the right of a woman to stipulate that her husband will not marry another wife.[241] While this does not invalidate other types of stipulations, it does not encourage them either. Indeed, the application of the Gazan code regarding stipulations has reflected this lack of encouragement, evidenced by Welchman's research. She found no use of stipulations in her study of Gaza and Rafah marriage contracts from 1989 to 1994, compared to 2 percent of those for Nablus for the same period.[242] Welchman also notes that this finding "suggests strong customary and possible judicial disapproval of stipulations in contracts" in Gaza.[243] For Palestinian citizens of Israel, there have likewise been no changes to the Ottoman law regarding stipulations because Israel upheld the OLFR virtually intact.

Today, Palestinian Muslim women, particularly well-educated, urban women in the West Bank, sometimes include all sorts of stipulations in their marriage contracts. The most common stipulation that emerged in Welchman's study of contracts from Nablus and Ramallah was to specify the couple's place of residence.[244] Also typical are conditions guaranteeing that the wife may continue her education or work.[245] Judges allow women to add almost any type of stipulation, so long as the groom agrees and it does not contravene *shari'a*. Some women even specify the location of the wedding hall. It must be emphasized that this trend was considerably more frequent among well-educated, urban sectors of Palestinian society in the 1970s and 1980s. Moors found stipulations in 13 percent of urban female teachers' contracts in the Nablus court and only 2 percent in all urban contracts; they were included rarely in camp and village contracts for that period.[246]

I would expect there to be higher percentages of stipulations in contracts from the last few decades, as Palestinian women have gained increased access to higher education, but to date no research has been published to my knowledge. From 1995 to 2016, Palestinian women in the West Bank and Gaza who had completed secondary school increased from 12.5 to 23 percent, and those with a bachelor's degree or above increased from 2.4 to 14.2 percent.[247] As in other parts of the Middle East, more Palestinian women than men are obtaining college degrees today, and the same is true of secondary education in Palestine. In 2016, 23 percent of women versus 19.1 percent of men had completed secondary school.[248]

Also, it is worth noting that while most families declined to use written stipulations in Welchman's study, she mentions that many likely sought "oral assurances" from the other family; this may well be the case today also.[249] There is, however, one downside to women including stipulations in their marriage contracts. Today, some educated Palestinian young adults believe that it is the woman's responsibility to add them to the contract.[250] If she does not and wishes to obtain a divorce because her husband prevents her from working, for example, this line of reasoning argues that it is her fault for not having included a stipulation. My research, however, suggests that Palestinians with higher education are well informed of the right to add conditions to the marriage contract today.[251]

Conclusion

Despite its considerable tampering with Palestine's civil legal systems, the British Mandate government was generally hesitant to interfere in the realm of family law. Venturing into Muslim family law reform in any meaningful way would have posed a risk that the British were unwilling to take, and it did not support any of their priorities in Palestine. As for the Palestinian community and its lack of incentive to reform the *shari'a* court system and Muslim family law, they were far more concerned with the dual threat of Zionism and British colonialism. In addition, the *shari'a* court was the one institution that Palestinians still controlled, and defending it against foreign interference became a form of resistance for the Muslim community. For Palestinian women, supporting this indigenous institution with its inherent gender inequalities was not a matter of debate; the context of limited opportunities was not conducive to confronting the family law system. The following chapters on maintenance, wife-initiated divorce, and child custody cases, however, will illustrate how Palestinian women did in fact challenge this patriarchal system from within during the Mandate period.

This chapter has examined Hanafi legal premises of gender roles and duties, the Ottoman family code's limited reforms, and the realities of Palestinian rural society that often complicated the observance and application of laws. Regarding family law constructs, we have seen how a husband's privileged status in marriage came, and comes, along with compulsory responsibilities to provide maintenance for his wife and his family. Likewise, the husband's ability to divorce unilaterally is accompanied by the requirement to give his wife the remainder of the dower and to support her during the waiting period. In the same way, the father has financial obligations in child custody that come with his role as the natural guardian, namely providing child support during the mother's temporary caretaking period. As for the Ottoman family code of 1917, in some respects it aimed to strengthen women in their marital relationships by encouraging them to take advantage of their rights in *shari'a*, such as employing stipulations to discourage polygamy in the marriage contract. Also, the code improved women's rights by allowing access to delinquent maintenance payments and limiting unilateral divorce in particular circumstances. Although the Ottoman code did not have a major impact during the Mandate period, it has been influential in the long term largely because the Israelis and the Jordanians upheld all or much of it, respectively.

It is important to reiterate that inconsistencies between the law and social practice often exist. Sometimes these deviations were to women's benefit, and at other times they disadvantaged women. But Palestinian society faced unprecedented challenges during the Mandate period and as a consequence was little concerned about observing new family laws. This lack of compliance is not unusual, as enforcement has frequently lagged behind reforms when modern states have reformed family laws, including those with improvements for women.[252] In the next chapter on maintenance, we will see how Mandate-period judges were slow to implement aspects of the new Ottoman family code as well. We will also examine the gendered strategies women used in court, the circumstances under which women were most likely to succeed, and how these cases help us understand how Palestinian women may have thought and felt about Muslim family law.

2

He Left Me without Maintenance

AIZA, A PALESTINIAN WOMAN FROM JADIS, a village near Jerusalem, began her 1926 case by claiming that "he [her husband] left me without maintenance, or someone to provide it, and without a house," and she asked the court to determine her monthly maintenance payment (*nafaqa*). Aiza also requested the provision of a house and an enforcer (*kafil*) to ensure "he is a good husband, provides for me, and does not hurt me." Aiza's husband, Muhammad, stated that he was still preparing their house, and he asked the judge (*qadi*) to order her to obey him. In response, Aiza repeated her request for maintenance. The judge ordered Muhammad to pay maintenance until he provided her with a house that complied with *shari'a* and to pay the court fees.[1] Challenging the popular western misperception that a Muslim man is absolutely entitled to his wife's obedience, the Jerusalem *Shari'a* Court did not privilege a woman's obligation to obey her husband over her entitlements in Muslim family law. Rather, lawsuits like Aiza's indicate that judges prioritized a wife's right to her husband's support over a husband's right to his wife's obedience.

As in Aiza's claim, "he left me without maintenance" was an appeal that many Palestinian women made in court as they sought to secure their right to a husband's complete financial support. I use the most common translations for *nafaqa*, maintenance and support, while acknowledging both terms are problematic because they are extremely broad. Extending well beyond housing, food, and clothing, *nafaqa* has long encompassed a wide range of other items that a woman requires for herself and her household. A prominent fourteenth-century Maliki definition of *nafaqa* includes "necessities of life, such as supplies of water, oil, wood, salt, the salary of a midwife . . . cosmetics like kohl to line her eyes, and henna and creams for her skin and hair."[2] In thirteenth-century Damascus, husbands in the lower socioeconomic strata were responsible for providing flour, the cost of grinding and baking bread, oil or cheese, and, biannually, specific items of new clothing.[3] Shi'i legal experts also specified that maintenance should include meat two to three times a week or on occasion.[4]

Through the lens of *shari'a* court maintenance cases initiated and mainly argued by women, this chapter examines the ways in which Palestinian women could benefit by exploiting a male-privileged system during the British Mandate period. In so doing, we will explore gendered strategies that women used to claim their rights, and sometimes to obtain further benefits, as they maneuvered through the Jerusalem court. Women who appeared in court to sue for maintenance often had a quite different motivation for doing so, as we will see. Women were successful in their lawsuits more often when they appealed for maintenance on behalf of their children, some gaining cash payments in addition to housing and provisions.

Beyond representing a trend in maintenance claims, Aiza's case highlights the inherent tension between gendered rights and obligations in Muslim family law. Rather than a sacrament, marriage is considered a contract between two parties wherein a woman has the right to receive complete support from her husband, but she forfeits that right if she disobeys him. It is important to recognize, however, that jurists conceptualized disobedience (*nushuz*) in fairly limited terms, usually as a wife's refusal to reside in the marital home or to have sexual relations with her husband.[5] Also, legal experts mostly referred to disobedience when determining a wife's right to maintenance.[6] Of course, men were obliged to fulfill their wives' sexual needs as well, as discussed in chapter 1.

Furthermore, in Sunni schools of law, the husband must actually prove that his wife is disobedient (*nashiza*) in order to deny her maintenance. In these proceedings Aiza's husband, Muhammad, did not attempt to provide corroboration of her behavior. Also, this lawsuit indicates that a husband lost the right of his wife's compliance if he failed to provide for her. Muhammad seemed to cling to his privileged status in *shari'a* even though he was clearly at fault. Aiza brought him to court because he was negligent in providing a house, and he readily acknowledged it was not finished. As a result, the judge ignored Muhammad's request for his wife's obedience (*ta'a*) because he did not order Aiza to obey her husband. Jerusalem court judges usually stated this instruction whether or not the husband requested it. Therefore, this judge effectively suspended Muhammad's entitlement to his wife's obedience until he had obtained housing. That is precisely what makes this type of case so interesting: it demonstrates that if the husband failed to meet his obligations, then he also forfeited his rights, regardless if his wife had fulfilled her duties.

In addition to demonstrating how Palestinian women creatively negotiated in court, my analysis of maintenance records will also illustrate how the application of the law shifted from the late Ottoman era to the British Mandate period. But in many respects Mandate-era judges followed classical Hanafi law more closely than the new Ottoman family code of 1917, which complicates that paradigm of change. Indeed, Palestinians resisted the imposition of changes to Muslim family law because it was one of the few indigenous institutions they still controlled under British rule. This reality entrenched the perception that upholding established interpretations of *shari'a*, which tended to privilege men, was critical to preserving Palestinian Muslims' collective honor and heritage. But in addition to resisting British rule, Palestinians were also anxious about Zionist encroachment onto their homeland. With these dual threats at hand, it is unsurprising that Palestinians thought little about uprooting their indigenous *shari'a* court system and reforming Muslim family law.

Although legal reform was not a priority, it is clear from my research that Palestinian women, regardless of background and class, were quite familiar with their fundamental rights during this period. Women were particularly well informed about a wife's right to receive maintenance from her husband, including housing, food, clothing, and any other items a woman may need for herself and her household. No matter what financial resources a woman may have possessed when she entered her marriage, or those she may have accumulated during her marriage, a woman still had, and has, the right to be fully supported by her husband. Additionally, the husband must provide for his wife in the manner to which she had been accustomed before marriage. This doctrine of classical Hanafi law also presumes the marriage of socioeconomic equals, which illustrates the most significant aspect of the principle of compatibility (*kafa'a*). According to Hanafi legal experts, the other factors a woman's family should assess in selecting her partner include ancestry, how long his family has been Muslim, freed or enslaved status, religiosity, and profession.[7] Regarding one's freed or enslaved status, it should be mentioned that while slavery was legal until the end of the Ottoman Empire, "the traffic in slaves decreased dramatically toward the end of the nineteenth century, and the institution itself died out in the first decade of the twentieth."[8] The compatibility doctrine only applies to prospective grooms, who should be of equal or higher status to the bride in all of these respects.

Lawsuits that women initiated to obtain maintenance from their husbands were by far the most common type of proceedings that emerged in my study. I examined approximately 370 cases from the Jerusalem *Shari'a* Court, dating from 1925 to 1939, of which roughly half were maintenance claims. Similarly, in Welchman's study of court records in West Bank towns from 1965 to 1985, maintenance lawsuits made up "well over half" the proceedings.[9] This trend is not unique to Palestine; during the late 1980s, maintenance claims comprised nearly two-thirds of Mir-Hosseini's cases from several Moroccan cities and about one-fifth of those from Tehran.[10] She explains that the phenomenon of far fewer maintenance claims in Iran is because of women's disadvantaged position in maintenance disputes compared to Sunni schools of law. Whereas in Sunni jurisprudence the burden of proof for the wife's disobedience rests on the husband, the wife must prove that she has been obedient in Iran's Shi'i legal system.[11] Simply the fact that women were, and are, appearing in court to demand their rights and sue their husbands in public settings counters many stereotypes about Muslim women. But the court records in this chapter demonstrate far more than this; they illuminate new insights regarding women's perceptions of their gendered *shari'a* rights and family obligations. Many of the maintenance claims were similar in terms of procedure, scope, and outcome, indicating basic trends, while those containing departures tend to highlight some of the more innovative tactics that women used in court. Taken together, we can make some overall conjectures about the ways in which women and men may have perceived their status and gender roles in the context of Muslim family law.

Typical Maintenance Claims

Most maintenance cases transpired in the following way. First, the court recorder (*katib*) noted the names and places of residence for the couple. Then the wife, who was the female plaintiff (*mud'a*) in the proceedings, began by saying, "This man is my husband, we have consummated the marriage, we have a marriage contract that is in accordance with *shari'a* (*'aqd shar'i*), and we have [x] many children of [x] ages. [X] many days ago, he left me without maintenance, without someone designated to provide maintenance (*munfiq*), without a proper house meeting *shari'a* standards (*meskin shar'i*), and without clothing (*kuswa*)."[12] Then the woman often emphasized her own financial need or that of her child. She ended her request by saying, "I ask [the court] to determine an amount of maintenance for me, for permission to borrow the monthly amount in my husband's name if he fails to pay (*istidana*), and for my husband to pay the court fees."

In the majority of claims, the male defendant (*mud' aleh*) maintained that he already had obtained a house that met *shari'a* standards, and frequently he asked the court to order his wife to obey him. For a house to be considered acceptable, it needed a separate living space from the husband's family, respectable neighbors, appropriate furnishings, and access to water. Also, there must be sufficient food and clothing. Some of the cases explicitly stated these conditions as necessary for a house to meet *shari'a* requirements.[13] Essentially, the court's definition of a house meeting *shari'a* criteria corresponded with the classical Hanafi meaning of maintenance, but with one significant change. Tucker demonstrates that Ottoman-period Hanafi muftis (legal experts who issue nonbinding but respected opinions) defined a proper living space as a room in a shared house; the room required its own cooking area, bathroom facilities, and a lock.[14] Most significantly, however, a wife in this era could be compelled to share that room with the members of her husband's family and his small children from other wives.[15] The only instances in which a wife could demand a separate living space under classical Hanafi law were if she was sharing it with either a cowife (*durra*) or her older stepchildren.[16] We will see how Mandate-period Jerusalem judges diverged from this Ottoman definition of proper housing because they expected a husband to provide his wife with separate housing from his family. This expectation was in accordance with the 1917 Ottoman family code, which the British upheld for Palestinian Muslims. Throughout this chapter, we will examine other respects in which Mandate-era judges adhered to either the classical Hanafi law of the Ottoman period or reforms in the 1917 Ottoman code.

Outside the courtroom, it appears there was considerable continuity between Ottoman- and Mandate-era housing practices. In rural areas, it was uncommon for women to live apart from their husbands' families. Hilma Granqvist, the Finnish anthropologist who researched marriage and divorce practices in the Palestinian village of Artas circa 1930, describes it as typical for an extended family to share a single room in Palestinian villages, as we saw in chapter 1.[17] But a rural woman could sometimes gain a discrete living space, apart from her husband's family, if she was fully supported by her own family. Granqvist cites one example in which a woman was not only able to obtain a separate room for her nuclear family but also later convinced her husband to move to her native town.[18] In another example, a father exploited his daughter's right to separate housing for his own purposes, without following through or even caring if it improved her situation.[19] It is important to note that Granqvist discusses these examples as rather unusual ones.

In the event the husband declared he had a house meeting proper conditions, the judge sent an official from the court to check (*kashaf*) the house. In nearly every claim in which the husband had a house, the court ruled it conformed to *shari'a* standards. Therefore, the judge denied the wife's request to receive a cash payment, instructed her to obey her husband, and directed the husband to have an agreeable relationship with his wife. However, in some records, the husband told the judge he was still building the house, and he volunteered a monthly sum. If the wife rejected the husband's offer, or if the couple agreed to let the court decide, the judge asked them to appoint respected members from their community (*ahl khubra* or *mukhbirin*). They determined an affordable payment that was appropriate for the woman's social status in her neighborhood or village. Whatever the amount, the court ordered the sum and the couple had to accept it. Either spouse could resort to appeal (*isti'naf*) and retry the case within thirty days, however. If one party had not appeared in court (known as a *ghiyabi* case, or in absentia), the judge allowed extra time for the absent party to be informed about the outcome of the proceedings.[20]

Ostensible Maintenance Cases

Maintenance claims also served as a way for women to come to court for other reasons. Indeed, the phenomenon of women exploiting their right to maintenance was one of the most common gendered strategies that emerged in my research. A number of records began as maintenance and then ended with quite a different outcome from the plaintiff's initial request. It is not entirely clear in some lawsuits if the plaintiff had actually sought the result of her case, but in a number of proceedings there are factors that allow speculation. The most common alternative outcome was wife-initiated divorce (*mukhal'a*), which required the husband's consent. The proceedings typically began as a standard maintenance claim, with the wife stating, "He left me without maintenance" and requesting it, but then the couple abruptly agreed to a wife-initiated divorce. In this type of divorce, the wife gave up her right to the remainder of her dower (*mahr*) and maintenance during the three-month waiting period following divorce ('*idda*), during which she could not remarry. This type of case points to a continuity between classical Hanafi law and the 1917 Ottoman family code, but it was a departure in actual practice. Despite that the Maliki, Shafi'i, and Hanbali schools, as well as the main Shi'i school, all allowed a woman to obtain a judicial dissolution if her husband neglected his duty to support her, the architects of the Ottoman code failed to include this important provision.[21] Rather, they followed the classical Hanafi school, which refused to grant a woman a judicial dissolution on grounds of non-maintenance if her husband was present. The Ottoman code did allow wife-initiated divorce if an absent husband failed to support his wife. Judicial divorce benefits women a great deal compared to wife-initiated divorce in that it does not necessitate the husband's consent and allows a woman to retain her financial divorce rights.

Despite this continuity between Hanafi law and the 1917 Ottoman family code, judges' application of the law during the Ottoman and Mandate periods was somewhat distinctive. Tucker demonstrates that eighteenth-century Hanafi judges commonly deferred to judges from other schools to gain more flexibility in applying the law, allowing non-Hanafi judges to grant wife-initiated divorces when an absent husband failed to support his wife.[22] On occasion, Hanafi courts also upheld women's judicial divorces because of a present husband's nonsupport.[23] But during the Mandate era, judges appeared to have less flexibility in their application of the law in this respect; indeed, I saw no records in which they granted divorces for nonsupport by a present husband. This may well have been because the 1917 Ottoman family code limited their opportunities for legal maneuvering; but also it appears that the Ottoman practice of courts including non-Hanafi judges on staff was no longer followed during the Mandate period.

The following case demonstrates how claims women initiated as requesting maintenance could take on very different outcomes. This suggests women were able to exploit the court system to some degree even though they were denied access to judicial divorce when deprived of maintenance by a present husband. One way in which a lawsuit could begin as maintenance proceedings and end in wife-initiated divorce is represented in the following 1936 case between a couple from Jerusalem and 'Ayn Siniya, a village northeast of Ramallah. The plaintiff, 'Aisha, said that her husband, Khalil, owed her 30 Egyptian pounds of the advanced dower (*mahr mu'ajjal*).[24] The wife was supposed to receive this dower when the marriage contract is signed. 'Aisha asked the court to determine a monthly sum of maintenance until Khalil paid the remainder of what he owed. Khalil confirmed their marriage and that he owed her the advanced dower but said he could not afford to pay it. Then the couple agreed to wife-initiated divorce, and it proceeded in the usual way.[25]

We can assume that 'Aisha sought the divorce, since she likely would have known if Khalil could afford, and if he was willing, to reimburse her the amount that he owed. But the couple must not have agreed to a wife-initiated divorce beforehand, because 'Aisha would have had no reason to request maintenance in those circumstances. In another 1928 lawsuit in which the wife sued for maintenance until her husband could pay her advanced dower, he agreed and the couple remained married.[26] Perhaps the plaintiff in this second claim was hoping to incite her husband to divorce her, but he was unwilling to compensate her with the entire dower and three months of maintenance in a husband-initiated irrevocable divorce (*talaq*). It is also possible that she wished to divorce via wife-initiated divorce, but he was unwilling to let her go and preferred to pay her what he owed.

The next lawsuit demonstrates yet another way in which women could sue for maintenance in order to achieve a different objective. This 1939 case of a couple from al-Khadar, a village near Bethlehem, also began as a standard maintenance claim, but then the husband declared that he had already divorced his wife. After the plaintiff, Khalila, said the usual statements, "this is my husband, we have consummated the marriage, he left me without maintenance," and ended by requesting maintenance, her husband Hussein claimed he had divorced her three times, an irrevocable divorce, ten days before.[27] Although it is unclear why she began the proceedings by asserting "this is my husband," we can likely assume that Khalila's motivation in compelling him to appear in court was to pressure him to record the irrevocable divorce officially and to begin paying her maintenance during her waiting period. If she had wished to give her husband a chance to retract his decision so they could resume their life together, Khalila probably would not have dragged Hussein to court and sued for maintenance. Securing official documentation of the divorce also gave Khalila indisputable grounds with which to claim her deferred dower. Had Khalila not taken her husband to court, Hussein may not have registered the divorce, or he may have tried to revoke it as in a minor divorce. After a revocable divorce, the couple may reconcile during the woman's waiting period without signing a new contract, but an irrevocable divorce is exactly what the term suggests.

Reconciliation after an irrevocable divorce is not an option unless the woman remarries and divorces another man first. That is, this is how it is viewed according to the law; in practice, the courts may well have promoted reconciliation beyond the law. Granqvist mentions one example in which a judge used a creative tactic to enable the reunion of a man who had divorced his wife irrevocably while angry, only to quickly regret it upon hearing his young daughter cry. In addition to divorcing his wife, the man also forbade her from entering his home or drinking from the water jug for six months. The judge instructed him to relocate for six months and to buy a new water container, allowing them to remain married.[28]

One aspect of women's participation in court that is very significant but absent in the case summaries is the critical role of a woman's family in her decision to go to court. This is particularly relevant to wife-initiated divorce proceedings. It is unlikely that a woman who lacked her family's backing in the event she wished to divorce, or even to settle her marital issues in court, would have been willing to go to court. A woman's father typically acted as her witness in the event of wife-initiated divorce and, more importantly, a divorcée usually returned to her father's home afterward. If a woman's family was unsupportive of her decision to confront her husband in court, they were probably also reluctant to allow her to return home. As we have seen in court records that began as maintenance but ended in wife-initiated divorce, it was more than a remote possibility that a woman requesting maintenance in court could end up with a divorce instead.

Granqvist's findings shed light on a married woman's need for her family's support in this period, which she characterizes as a "vital necessity" even when a woman had no apparent problems with her in-laws. As she explains: "Always after her marriage the father's home remains the deciding factor in her life, a woman in her husband's house is dependent on the esteem she enjoys and the support she can still count upon in her father's house."[29] Not only did a woman's family ensure that she was well treated by her in-laws, but their backing also gave her confidence in her daily interactions with her husband's family. Furthermore, a woman's blood relatives' support gave her protection, and a home, in the event her in-laws or husband did mistreat her or if she was discontent with her position in their house. Granqvist goes on: "This is why a 'cut-off' (qati'a) woman—whose [male] relatives: her father, her brothers and her father's brothers are all dead—is so much to be pitied because she has not one from her own family to set against her husband's family."[30] In this situation a woman lacked the male family members on which she could rely to safeguard her interests

while living with her in-laws in both everyday situations and confronta-
tions with her husband's family.

"He Hasn't Provided a House!" Cases

The most typical situations in which maintenance claims emerged were
(a) those during the woman's waiting period of three months that follows a
unilateral divorce and (b) when the husband had failed to provide a house
for his wife. The former type was fairly straightforward, and as long as the
woman was in her waiting period, she won the case. This is most likely
because the wife was no longer living in her former husband's home. As we
have seen, the husband must then provide cash payments because he was
no longer providing maintenance in the form of the necessities in kind.
Ottoman legal experts in jurisprudence (muftis) considered maintenance
to be a specific amount of money that the husband paid to the wife each
month, and this sum was expected to cover all the necessities that com-
prise maintenance, including housing, food, clothing, and all other household and personal expenses.[31] It is important to note that this definition
would have only affected spouses who actually found themselves in court
with marital disputes. If there were no problems in a marriage, the husband
very well may have provided maintenance in the form of the items in kind.
Similarly, in Palestine during the mid-1920s through the 1930s, the *shari'a*
courts seemed to perceive maintenance in terms of a cash payment only
in the event of marital problems when a wife demanded her maintenance
in court.

There were certain conditions under which judges tended to decide
maintenance claims in the female plaintiff's favor and instructed the husband to pay maintenance in cash. As we saw in the typical maintenance
claims, one of these was the husband's failure to provide a house for his
wife. In such proceedings, the judge ordered the husband to pay maintenance until he had found a house for her, after which he could request
to cancel the payments. A plaintiff awarded maintenance in court began
receiving maintenance from the date on which she won her lawsuit in
court. This practice follows classical Hanafi law, which did not allow the
collection of back-owed maintenance payments as in the Shafʻi and Hanbali schools.[32] Despite that the 1917 Ottoman family code allowed the

collection of back-owed maintenance payments, my cases show that Mandate-era judges disregarded the new code in this respect. The plaintiff who succeeded in her maintenance claim did have a practical means of securing the collection of her future maintenance payments, however, because judges also stipulated permission for a successful plaintiff to borrow the monthly amount in her husband's name if he did not pay it (istidana).

The following case demonstrates that the husband was not responsible for a maintenance cash payment in addition to providing the house and all other necessities, and it also involves the rather unusual component of a second wife in the picture. In this 1928 lawsuit involving a couple from Jerusalem, Jamila, the plaintiff, stated her husband had married a second wife (durra) and left her without maintenance and a house. Jamila requested a separate house from her husband's new family and asked for sufficient maintenance payments. Abd al-Qadir, the defendant, said he did not have money for a separate house for Jamila. The judge ordered Abd al-Qadir to pay one Palestinian pound per month, which respected men from their community had determined as an appropriate maintenance payment, instead of food, clothing, and a house.[33] These proceedings affirm the prevailing view of maintenance in this period: a husband had to provide his wife with a proper house equipped with the usual necessities, or he had to pay her a sufficient sum to cover the same items. Presumably because Abd al-Qadir could not afford a separate home for her, the judge made him pay the maintenance in cash. Hanafi muftis' legal discourse in Ottoman Palestine and Syria shows that, as in the other systems of law, husbands were required to provide a distinct living area for each wife.[34] Therefore, the fact that Abd al-Qadir had taken another wife without providing discrete living spaces for both of them was likely the most compelling factor in Jamila's lawsuit. There were only a handful of records in which a second wife was mentioned, but it is worth noting that the woman plaintiff won her claim in all of them.

"He hasn't provided housing" cases demonstrate that the Jerusalem Shari'a Court did not expect husbands to provide a cash payment of maintenance for their wives in addition to housing, food, clothing, and household items. The court certainly did, however, hold husbands responsible for providing their wives with either maintenance in cash or a house, food, clothing, and household necessities. As discussed previously, the sum of the former and the quality and quantity of the latter depended on a woman's socioeconomic class. It may seem curious that these claims all hinged upon the presence or absence of housing when maintenance actually entails a great deal more than housing. But this is precisely because a house that meets *shari'a* standards denotes the entirety of what a woman is entitled to in her right to receive maintenance.

Canceling Payments of Maintenance

The most common reasons for men's numerous requests to stop paying maintenance (*qat' nafaqa*) included the husband had acquired a house, the couple had reconciled after a separation, or the wife's three-month waiting period after divorce had ended.[35] The following 1926 proceedings concerning a couple from a village near Jerusalem is a typical request to terminate maintenance payments. Ahmed asked the judge to cancel his payments because he had provided his wife, Nasra, with a house and they were living together in it. Nasra confirmed these circumstances and she agreed to his request to end the maintenance payments.[36] An important aspect of this type of case was the wife's presence in the proceedings and her consent to every request, which we will examine shortly. Most court records involving cancellation of maintenance payments were similar to the one just mentioned; however, the cases involving reconciliation between the spouses shed light on a strategy that women used to secure their interests within the court system.

The following canceling-maintenance proceedings mostly followed the format above, except some form of reconciliation also took place. One should note that the previous lawsuit did not constitute reconciliation per se because the only recorded problem between the husband and wife had been lack of housing and the husband had resolved it. In the following 1936 case, Abd al-Qadir stated the following: At his previous session in court, the judge had ordered him to pay 35 mils per day for his wife, Khadra, and 15 mils per day for his daughter. Abd al-Qadir maintained he had resolved the differences with his wife and she had returned to his home. He also told the court that he had been paying the stipulated amounts of maintenance for his wife and for his daughter. Khadra confirmed this, asserted that she was obeying her husband, and asked the court to end Abd al-Qadir's maintenance payments. The judge ordered him to cease the maintenance payments and informed Khadra that she could not ask for it again.[37] The proceedings and outcome for this court record were typical of ending-maintenance cases that involved reconciliation, and again we see that the wife's participation in and consent to the ending of payments were significant components of the proceedings.

But the following 1933 canceling-maintenance proceedings departs from the others in that it began with the husband initiating an obedience (ta'a) case, but the wife initiated the ending of maintenance payments in an unusual way. Mahmood, the plaintiff, told the court that he was married, they had consummated the marriage, he had two children, and he was providing a proper house. Mahmood then asked the court to order his wife, Sakini, to obey him. Sakini, the defendant, stated that Mahmood had been paying her maintenance, and they had reconciled nine days ago when she had returned to his home. Sakini asked her representative, who was usually a woman's father or another close male relative (wakil), to leave the courtroom, and she then told the judge she wanted to give up her maintenance payments.[38] Sakini added that Mahmood owed her nothing else. Accordingly, the judge canceled maintenance payments for Sakini and her sons, and he told Sakini that she could not ask for it again.[39] This is a unique lawsuit because it began as obedience, which was most likely being defined as Sakini's return to her husband's house, and shifted to canceling maintenance.[40] It is particularly distinctive because the wife requested ending the payments after asking her guardian to leave the courtroom. This was not only very unusual, but it also implies that her decision was against her family's wishes and what they perceived as being best for her. The fact that there were children in the marriage likely explains a great deal about Sakini's actions that were ostensibly against her best interests. Her utmost concern must have been to preserve the marriage so she could be with her children. Finally, one should note that Sakini's evident willingness to forfeit her right to maintenance to revive her relationship with her husband is similar to the cases we have already discussed.

In all of the canceling-maintenance cases in my study, except those following divorce, the court asked the woman for her approval of her husband's request. Sometimes the wife made the request herself, particularly when it was implicit that the entire reason for the couple being in court was to end the husband's maintenance payments. In circumstances of divorce, there was no need to consult the former wife because she had no more claim to receive maintenance after the waiting period. In the other situations, the fact that women were consulted and asked to voice their acceptance or refusal indicates a way in which the court ensured that it only changed the form of maintenance women received—from payments to maintenance in kind—with their consent. In gaining the wife's approval, the court also confirmed that reconciliation did indeed take place and that she would be cared for in a house meeting *shari'a* conditions. It may appear that consenting to end maintenance payments would be detrimental to their financial circumstances, and certainly some women may have been bullied into accepting maintenance in kind rather than a monthly sum. This choice could serve as a means of empowerment for a wife in her marital and in-law relationships, however. As Annelies Moors's research on Palestinian women's access to property in the twentieth-century Nablus region demonstrates, giving up certain rights often enhanced a woman's status within her family. Moors's oral histories show that when a Nablusi woman gave up her inheritance in favor of her sons or brothers, it tended to strengthen her standing in her kinship relationships.[41]

Women Winning Maintenance

Apart from cases in which the husband had not provided a house, when women always received a sum of maintenance, most other types of maintenance claims hinged upon the husband's willingness to accommodate his wife's request. Such perpetuation of men's authority over women may appear to be consistent with the patriarchal construct of the *shari'a* court, and certainly in maintenance proceedings in which the man possessed a house he was at a clear advantage. In certain lawsuits, however, women successfully sued to collect maintenance payments even while living in their husbands' homes. The odds shifted to the wife's ability to receive additional, extralegal benefits with one or more of the following factors: a cooperative husband, the existence of a second wife or her children, the wife's children in her care, or having a lawyer representing her.

First, we will examine proceedings in which an accommodating husband has volunteered to pay maintenance. In the following 1936 case, the wife seems to have won her request entirely because of her husband's evident willingness to appease her. Yasra, the plaintiff, told the judge that her husband had left her without maintenance and without someone to provide it, and she requested the court to estimate an amount of maintenance. Her husband, Yusuf, confirmed they were married but he said that he was paying her maintenance and they were living together. Yasra agreed they were living together but she insisted that he had not been paying her. Yusuf offered to pay her 80 mils per day. This was apparently in addition to their house because Yasra did not mention lack of housing. Yasra accepted this and asked for a commitment (*ilzam*) from her husband. The court ordered Yusuf to begin paying the maintenance sum that he had volunteered, referring to it in the context of reconciliation, and approved Yasra's request for a commitment.[42] Yasra was not only able to gain the maintenance, but she also demanded and received a court-sanctioned commitment from her husband obligating him to make the payments. But unless there was a factor that the court recorder did not mention, it appears that her success was completely due to her husband's willingness to pay her. It is unclear if Yusuf volunteered to pay maintenance in addition to providing the house because he had done something wrong, which would explain the reference to a reconciliation, or if he simply wanted to placate his wife, perhaps in hopes of a happier life together. There were only a few other records in this study with a comparable situation in that the husband had provided a house in accordance with *shari'a*, the couple was living together, but the wife was still able to procure maintenance payments from him because he volunteered to pay her.

Why was Yusuf willing to pay Yasra maintenance, in addition to providing her with a properly stocked home, when the court would not have required it? Granqvist's research on stranger wives is instructive in understanding this case. Yasra was from Jerusalem, while her husband was from the nearby village of Lifta; therefore Yasra would have been considered a stranger wife.[43] As such, her dower was probably considerably more expensive than typical dowers in Yusuf's village, and since she was from the big city, the lifestyle that she was entitled to was likely costlier than a typical villager. As noted, a Muslim woman has the right to be supported in the manner to which she was accustomed before her marriage. Yusuf had made an expensive investment in marrying Yasra, that is, in paying her dower; he was likely reluctant to divorce her and throw it all away. Yusuf probably thought it was better to fix the problems in his current marriage rather than starting over with a new wife and dower. But apparently to do this, his wife required compensation. Clearly Yasra was very well-heeled before and after her marriage, because she was able to secure an extremely high sum for her maintenance payment. Compared to maintenance amounts awarded to other women living in villages, hers was by far the highest amount awarded. Yasra received 80 mils, despite that she was living with her husband, whereas women in two other lawsuits received 30 and 35 mils. Even though the woman who received 35 five mils was not living with husband, and therefore had the right to receive maintenance as a payment, Yasra's sum was more than twice as high.

Similarly, the male defendant in the next 1928 case was also attempting to placate his wife, but he faced additional challenges. Shahir, the husband, had children from a prior marriage and he was trying to convince his current wife to return to his home. The plaintiff, Rasmia, told the court that her husband did not have a house meeting *shari'a* standards, and she asked the judge to order him to provide a house and maintenance. Shahir countered that he had a house in compliance with *shari'a*, and he said that Rasmia had left without a legitimate reason. Shahir added that he wanted Rasmia to return to his home and he would then resume her maintenance payments. Rasmia agreed she would return, but he must be a good husband and pay sufficient maintenance. In addition, Rasmia insisted that they must have a separate home from Shahir's mother and his former wife's children. The judge ordered Shahir to be a good husband, to give Rasmia a separate home from his family, and to provide sufficient maintenance for her.[44] It is very likely that Shahir's children by his former wife played a key role in Rasmia's success, because men were required to provide separate living spaces for their cowives and families according to both classical Hanafi law and the 1917 Ottoman family code. Additionally, the Ottoman code requires separate living spaces for the wife from her husband's mother and other family members. Therefore, Rasmia had an excellent case against her husband, whereas Shahir did not have much of a defense on this matter. Also, despite implying that Rasmia was being disobedient when she had left their home, Shahir still volunteered to pay maintenance. Most interestingly, the judge upheld Rasmia's demands of maintenance *and* separate housing. Therefore, he must have considered Shahir's failure to provide a separate home for Rasmia as a far greater infringement than her implied disobedience.

A female plaintiff also tended to have a far better chance of winning her maintenance claim in the event that she was able to hire a lawyer (*muhami*). In the following 1935 lawsuit in which the couple was from Jerusalem, the claimant, Huda, appeared in court with her lawyer. Huda told the judge that she had been for married for seven years, she had two sons, and she was pregnant with a third child. She explained that she lived with her husband's family and they harmed her, so she was requesting her own house. Muhammad, Huda's husband, acknowledged that one son was living with him and the other was with his wife. Huda's attorney asked the judge to order the return of her other son, to determine the amount of maintenance until Muhammad found her a house, and to require the husband to pay the court fees. Muhammad claimed the house was *shari'a* compliant, and he asked the court to check it. In the next session, Muhammad also asked the judge to cancel Huda's request, to order Huda to obey him in his house, and to make her pay the court fees. The respected men from their neighborhood found the house to meet *shari'a* conditions, but the judge said Huda had been right to ask for maintenance and ordered Muhammad to pay the court and lawyer's fees.[45] The judge's decision shows an important change from classical Hanafi law because it would have required Huda to live with her husband's family. She could have received separate housing in classical law only if there was another wife, and we can assume Huda's lawyer would have mentioned a second wife if there was one.[46] Also, the decision indicates an adherence to the 1917 Ottoman family code, which gave a woman the right to separate housing from her husband's family. While having a lawyer and young children could have only helped Huda's lawsuit, she did not seem to actually need those advantages. Rather, the judge applied the Ottoman code's criteria for housing and maintenance, which stipulated separate housing from the husband's family. Thus the wife's right to separate housing from her husband's family was an important respect in which the Mandate-era Jerusalem court diverged from the Ottoman period.

Perhaps the most common circumstance in which a husband volunteered to pay maintenance in addition to housing was when his wife's own children were in need. But even if a husband was uncooperative, it was common for a woman to win her maintenance claim when there were young children in her care. It is important to recognize that in most cases involving children, husbands were quite reasonable about paying maintenance. The following 1935 lawsuit of a couple from the affluent village of al-Walaja is an exception to this norm. In these proceedings, the plaintiff won her maintenance claim despite that her husband provided evidence of a house meeting *shari'a* conditions.[47] To begin her claim, Dahabia told the court that her husband, 'Abdin, had left her son and herself without maintenance and without someone to provide it. She asked the court to assess the amount of payments and requested permission to borrow it in her husband's name if he failed to pay and also for her husband to pay the court costs.[48] In response, 'Abdin showed the judge a document from a prior court session stating that he had a house meeting *shari'a* conditions, and he asked the judge to order Dahabia to obey him. Dahabia reasserted her request for maintenance, and this time she asked for clothing as well. The judge ordered 'Abdin to pay his wife 30 mils per day and for Dahabia to obey her husband.[49] Even though the husband had a court document verifying that his house met *shari'a* standards, the court still ordered 'Abdin to pay maintenance for his wife and child as well as the court expenses. This was quite a victory, considering that women typically lost lawsuits in which the husband had a proper house. Dahabia's success appears to depend upon the fact that she had a child in her care. Likewise, in most maintenance cases in which women were denied maintenance because their husbands had houses, they did not have children who needed support.

In this study, the only maintenance claims that women won when the husband was already providing a house included circumstances in which the wife was compelled to live with her husband's family or another wife (or her children), there were children in need, the wife had a lawyer, or the husband failed to appear in court. But these were generally unusual circumstances in maintenance proceedings. Beyond these conditions, whether or not the wife won her maintenance case largely hinged on the husband's response much of the time, and we will see this trend emerge in other types of lawsuits as well. If he recognized that he was not providing for her and could afford to do so, he usually volunteered an amount to pay. But if the defendant lacked the financial ability or felt that he was already providing sufficiently, he could evade a monetary payment if he was already providing proper housing. Of course, as we have seen, the definition of proper, shari'a-compliant housing included maintenance in kind. That usually ended the woman's chances to secure maintenance payments because the court found the house to meet shari'a standards in almost every case. If he had no house, however, the court ordered the husband to pay support until he was able to find one. But, as we have seen, there were several factors, albeit somewhat unusual, that could turn a claim to a woman's favor, which allowed her to collect maintenance payments in addition to receiving housing and provisions.

Conclusion

Maintenance claims signify the most frequent way that women aired their marital problems in my study of 1925–1939 Jerusalem court records. In addition to their husbands not providing sufficiently, women initiated these suits for a number of reasons. Palestinian women who sought to redress issues with their husbands or in-laws in court during the Mandate period undeniably found themselves in a disadvantaged position. Nevertheless, many women not only took advantage of their rights, but they were also able to exploit the system via innovative techniques. For example, there were several proceedings in which the wife used her maintenance right as leverage to procure a different outcome, from obtaining a wife-initiated divorce to provoking her husband to divorce her. To my knowledge, these are new findings in gendered sijillat studies. Yet another way in which a woman could employ her right to maintenance was to give it up as a means of securing a more influential status within her family structure and vis-à-vis her husband.

But the cases we have examined indicate that women's right to receive maintenance was often not a straightforward affair as it played out in court. Women were certainly entitled to receive support from their husbands in the form of housing, food, clothing, and any necessary household items, as they were under classical schools of law. Perhaps the most important change in the application of maintenance was how Jerusalem judges departed from Hanafi law, and followed the 1917 Ottoman family code, in their interpretation of housing that conformed to *shari'a* standards. That is, a wife had the right to separate housing not only from her cowives and older stepchildren but also from her husband's family and, most critically one would think, her mother-in-law. Judges respected this reform in my cases. If a woman was being housed with her husband's family members, then she received separate housing, period. Other situations in which women could often, but not categorically, procure maintenance payments in addition to housing with provisions included the presence of children in her care, a lawyer, or a compassionate husband. This finding was important, as it was quite surprising that women were even able to receive both maintenance in kind and as a cash payment. In other circumstances women were not usually able to receive food, necessities, and housing in addition to a payment, in accordance with previous conceptions of maintenance.

Despite the major departure from Hanafi law of entitling the wife to separate housing from her husband's family, there were also significant vestiges regarding the court's treatment of maintenance. Most notably, judges did not allow a woman to recover delinquent maintenance payments unless there was a prior agreement. Based on the Shaf'i and Hanbali schools of law, the 1917 Ottoman family code allowed missed payments to be considered an accumulated debt; however, the Jerusalem court did not enforce this reform. But judges did always grant women permission to borrow the monthly amount of maintenance in her husband's name, per both classical Hanafi law and the Ottoman code.

Another theme that emerged in this chapter concerns the husband's position of power in many cases: as long as he provided his wife with a house, the husband often dictated the outcome of the proceedings and controlled his wife's ability to receive maintenance in monetary form. But we have seen how in certain circumstances women had a much better chance of securing maintenance as cash payments in addition to housing, as mentioned above. If a woman had a lawyer, if her husband's family lived with them, or if her husband was not supporting their children sufficiently, her chances of winning the claim increased a great deal, and doing so gave her extralegal benefits. There were also court records, particularly those involving children in need, in which the husband voluntarily agreed to provide maintenance payments in addition to housing. It was not usually clear why he was willing to do so. In one case the husband wanted to convince his wife to return to his home after they had separated, and perhaps in others there was simply a wish to placate one's wife and have a peaceful life at home.[50]

The most common outcome of a maintenance claim was the judge's abrupt refusal of the wife's request because her husband was already providing her with a house. We can assume that the couple would usually continue to live together or, as judges put it, the wife would obey her husband in his house. In theory, that is. As we have seen, jurists conceptualized disobedience quite narrowly, typically as the wife refusing to reside in the marital home or to have sexual relations with her husband. The other possibility was that the woman returned to her father's home, as she would have done in the event of a divorce. If the probability was minimal for a woman to win a maintenance payment when she already had housing and there were no factors to facilitate her success, why did women bother to appear in court? A woman suing her husband certainly indicated that something was not working in the relationship, but what exactly did she hope to accomplish?

It may have been a way for a woman to admonish her husband, which may or may not have been related to his role as a provider. Suing one's husband in court was conducted in a very public venue, and it was a statement that could bring some degree of dishonor to the entire family. People likely knew most others in the urban neighborhoods of Mandate Palestine, and certainly they did in villages. By going to court, and compelling her husband to appear in court, a woman was in effect announcing that her husband was not providing adequately or there was another problem in the marriage. Perhaps in some cases the wife wanted her husband to return home if he had been working elsewhere. Another potentially contentious issue could have been a couple living in close proximity to the husband's family; indeed, we saw several maintenance claims in which the wife requested a separate home. The woman probably demanded maintenance or discrete housing in such proceedings as a means of pressuring her husband to change their living situation, and indeed the court sided with the plaintiff in these circumstances. Alternatively, a woman who requested maintenance might have actually been seeking a divorce. In ideal circumstances, she could provoke her husband into divorcing her, but it was relatively unusual for the husband to do so. It was far more common for a maintenance lawsuit to shift into a wife-initiated divorce case, in which the wife gave up her deferred dower and maintenance during the waiting period.

Finally, these maintenance proceedings convey some ways in which Palestinians may have thought about *shari'a* during the Mandate period. They provide glimpses of how people perceived their roles and obligations within the family and how they viewed their gendered rights. Women were well-informed about their maintenance rights, and indeed they used the right to maintenance as a pretext to come to court for a variety of reasons, although most frequently this was divorce. In addition, these maintenance cases shed light on a male perspective of gendered expectations and obligations to some extent. The most common male response in the standard claim, in which the wife requested maintenance but her husband insisted he had already provided a house, was to ask the judge to make his wife obey him. As we have seen, this effectively was a request to compel the wife to return to the marital home. Even if a husband had to forfeit the privilege of his wife's obedience because he was not fulfilling his duties in *shari'a*, he often still requested it. But this preoccupation with obedience is not limited to men. My research included interviews with several elderly Palestinian women, and one trend in their discussions was to mention, unprompted, that women must obey their husbands under *shari'a*. Most of the women also made it clear that a Muslim woman has the right to be respected, treated well, and supported by her husband. Many further emphasized that Muslim women are "free," that they have the independence to make their own decisions, and that Islam gives women "all of their rights." In the next chapter, we will explore women's access to wife-initiated divorce and strategies used to obtain this type of divorce during the Mandate period, and we will also consider Palestinian women's views and experiences from my interviews.

3

I Give Up All of My Rights before and after the Divorce[1]

FATIMA, A PLAINTIFF FROM A VILLAGE NEAR JERUSALEM, began her 1936 case by stating, "Abd al-Rahman is my husband, we have consummated the marriage, and we have a proper marriage contract in accordance with shari'a." Then she said, "He left me without maintenance and without anyone to provide it." She asked for maintenance as well as permission to borrow the monthly amount in her husband's name if he could not pay. Abd al-Rahman confirmed the facts about their marriage. But ignoring Fatima's request for maintenance, he informed the judge that they had agreed to divorce. Fatima declared, addressing Abd al-Rahman, "I give up all of my rights pertaining to the marriage, before and after the divorce, [including] maintenance during the waiting period." Then Abd al-Rahman declared, addressing her, "Immediately, I divorce you." The judge stated that they had a minor divorce (baynuna sughra; a revocable divorce) and would need a new marriage contract and a new dower (mahr jadid) if they wished to remarry one another after the waiting period ended.[2] Finally, the judge said that Fatima's waiting period was in effect from that day, and he dismissed Fatima's initial request for maintenance.[3]

To a greater extent than in most maintenance proceedings, obtaining a wife-initiated divorce required a woman's proficiency in negotiation. Whereas a woman's right to receive support from her husband was, and is, guaranteed in Muslim family law, a wife had to actually convince her husband to agree to divorce if she requested it. It was even more critical for a woman to be a skillful negotiator when she initiated divorce by requesting maintenance because she was likely appearing in court without her husband's agreement to divorce. Had she obtained his consent beforehand, there would have been no reason to initiate the lawsuit with a maintenance claim nor would she have had any reason to expect to receive support. Thus a woman in this situation needed her husband to consent to the divorce in court, which was an institution that sought to preserve marriages, as we will see.

It seems probable that, in cases like Fatima's, the husband may have agreed to the divorce in part because he was embarrassed to be summoned to court by his wife. There was likely more to the story in the majority of the proceedings, but court recorders seem to have omitted most exchanges between the spouses in court. Indeed, many of the proceedings examined in this study are quite formulaic, particularly in the wife-initiated divorce records. In such tense circumstances as divorce, maintenance, and child custody hearings, one would expect a few outbursts from the participants, or at least greater variations in testimonies. Another possible reason for few recordings of impulsive dialogues was because the outcomes of wife-initiated divorce cases were usually quite fixed, with little room for maneuvering once the husband had agreed to the divorce.

During this period in Palestine, a wife initiating divorce usually gave up the rights she was entitled to receive in a unilateral, husband-initiated divorce (*talaq*). First, she waived the right to receive support during the three-month waiting period (*nafaqat al-ʿidda*) that follows all types of divorce. Throughout this time, a woman is prohibited from remarrying another man to determine if she is pregnant by her former husband. If she is pregnant, he must continue to support her until the child is born. The waiting period also provides an opportunity for reconciliation between the couple, unless it comes after a major, irrevocable divorce (*baynuna kubra*). During the waiting period after a minor, or revocable, divorce, the couple may resume their marriage without signing a new marriage contract. After a major divorce, however, the couple cannot remarry unless the wife first marries and divorces another man.

The second forfeited right was the wife's dower. She was supposed to receive her advanced dower (*mahr muʿajjal*) at the signing of the marriage contract. A deferred dower (*mahr muʾajjal*) would serve as an insurance policy for the wife if her husband divorced her or died. In this study, the wife usually gave up any part of the advanced dower that her husband still owed as well as the deferred dower. But sometimes the wife also paid the husband an agreed-upon amount or relinquished child support to obtain her husband's agreement. Occasionally, women even gave up the right to temporary child custody as well, as we will see in chapter 4.

Granqvist's research of rural marriages and family life in the 1920s indicates that Palestinian villagers' divorce practices differed considerably from both Hanafi family law and *shari'a* court proceedings during the Mandate. In her study, rural Palestinians in Artas used one dower instead of two, and in the event the wife wanted a divorce, her family had to pay it back to her husband.[4] Moors shows a similar trend for rural areas surrounding Nablus, where only a third of marriage contracts included a deferred dower during the Mandate. When a deferred dower was present, it typically amounted to "only thirty per cent of the total dower."[5] Granqvist found if the husband wished for the divorce, the wife kept the dower in accordance with Hanafi law. The wife only received half the dower, however, if she had a child living with her former husband, which was customary after the child was weaned.[6]

It is worth noting that Granqvist discusses these divorce practices in general terms, implying that other villages observed them as well. Also, Moors mentions that "recording a deferred dower was more widespread in larger villages which were close to the city and where agriculture no longer was the only source of livelihood."[7] Thus we can likely infer that the deferred dower was not used widely among Palestinians in this period, especially in rural areas where the vast majority lived. These customs departed from wife-initiated divorce cases in the Jerusalem court analyzed in this study. Judges required the wife to give up the deferred dower if she initiated divorce, but the wife did not have to compensate her husband for the advanced dower. The husband was exempt from paying any part of the advanced dower that he still owed the wife, however.[8] Hanafi law also called for a child to live with his or her mother until a certain stage of development, to which the courts adhered quite rigidly, as we will see in chapter 4.

Granqvist also offers some insight as to why many Palestinian men were reluctant to "release her with kindness," as the Qur'an instructs, even when their wives clearly no longer wished to remain married and were likely less than amicable spouses. First, she asserts that Palestinian men considered it "a shame and humiliation" for one's wife to wed another man, which was very probable in this period.[9] All the Artas divorcées whom Granqvist tracked from the late nineteenth to the early twentieth century remarried other men, except one who died and another who returned to her husband.[10] The other main incentive for men to retain their wives was the great expenses incurred to remarry, given the feasts involved and a new wife's dower. In Granqvist's study, a man was compensated for the dower he had paid when his wife initiated divorce, but a new wife's dower would have to be negotiated. Many factors could affect that amount, as we saw in chapter 1. Remaining single was typically not an option. Not only was it socially expected for a man to remarry in Palestinian society, but, as we saw in chapter 1, a man relied on his wife (or his daughters-in-law) to complete the manifold gendered tasks that his household required, particularly in rural areas. Indeed, Granqvist argues convincingly that the "economic loss is greater for a man who desires divorce than for a woman" because her family will need to repay the dower but they will regain their daughter, who can remarry for a new dower; but if a man initiates divorce, he receives nothing.[11]

A woman who was insulted or otherwise exasperated with her marriage usually did have the extralegal option of returning to her family's home, although this was often a short-term strategy. A woman in this situation was called "offended and angry" (*hardana*), and she typically returned to her father's house so she could demand fair treatment from her husband or in-laws.[12] Granqvist notes that whether or not the woman was able to succeed in her endeavor depended upon her family's support, if her community deemed her to be in the right, the extent of her usefulness to her husband, and her skill in handling the situation.[13] Being *hardana* could even be an indefinite state, thereby functioning essentially in the same way as wife-initiated divorce, but without the requirement of obtaining the husband's consent. Pregnancy, however, complicated matters for a woman who had returned to her family home, because then it was critical for her husband to acknowledge the child as his own. If he refused, the wife would be "disgraced in the village forever"; consequently, she usually returned to her husband after he made an announcement affirming his paternity.[14]

Compared to wife-initiated divorce or being *hardana*, it was far more advantageous for a woman to procure a judicial dissolution by petitioning the court (*tafriq*). In this type of divorce a woman is entitled to the financial divorce rights that she would receive in a divorce declared by her husband. In classical Hanafi law, the circumstances under which women could obtain an annulment were very limited, but Tucker shows that Ottoman courts were more flexible in practice. She demonstrates the standard conditions under which women could access judicial dissolutions in seventeenth- and eighteenth-century Palestine and Syria included the husband's impotence, insanity, desertion, or a contagious, dangerous disease.[15] Occasionally, women could also obtain this type of divorce for nonsupport by a present husband during this period.[16] The 1917 Ottoman family code attempted to expand women's access to judicial divorces by explicitly including grounds of desertion, as well as "discord and incompatibility." We will examine how the Jerusalem court applied the new code in Mandate Palestine, assessing the extent to which the court adhered to classical Hanafi law of the Ottoman period versus the 1917 Ottoman code of the Mandate period in court proceedings. As we saw in the maintenance cases, the Jerusalem court was quite resilient to change within the 1925–1939 period in the face of tremendous social and political transformations imposed on the Palestinian community from without. Palestinians were far more concerned with the threats posed by British imperialism and Zionist colonialism than with reforming family law and the *shari'a* court system. Indeed, it was these very forces and the ensuing upheaval that compelled Palestinians to preserve the one indigenous institution they still controlled.

In addition, we will examine examples of women's strategic negotiations in court, as well as the ways in which Palestinian women perceived Muslim family law and how this affected their lives. Unfortunately, the wife-initiated divorce records in this survey contained few details about the circumstances regarding the divorce, and none of them included information about the couple other than their names; the hometown of each family; and the city, village, or neighborhood of their current residence. While they contain less information than the maintenance and child custody proceedings, there are interesting variations in the divorce cases from which we can draw conclusions. Also, the interviews I conducted were valuable in that they helped validate findings, draw comparisons and distinctions between the Mandate period and the present, and shed light on the numerous questions that the wife-initiated divorce summaries raise. Finally, the interviews indicate some of the ways in which Palestinian women think and feel about Muslim family law today and how it affects their lives.

The Standard Wife-Initiated Divorce Case

The format for an ordinary wife-initiated divorce record proceeded in the following way. First, the court recorder (katib) stated the names of the couple, their respective cities or villages of birth, and, if they had moved, the place of their current residence. Then, usually accompanied by two witnesses, the wife told the court, "This man is my husband, we have consummated the marriage in accordance with shari'a, and we have a proper marriage contract." The husband confirmed her statements and told the court they had agreed to divorce. Then the wife declared, addressing her husband, "I give up all of my rights connected to the marriage, before and after the divorce, [including] maintenance during the waiting period. I will be free of you after you divorce me, and the marriage will be ended."[17] These financial rights implicitly included the deferred dower and any remainder of the advanced dower.[18] It is possible that the wife-initiated divorce proceedings did not explicitly stipulate the deferred dower because, as mentioned, only one-third of rural marriage contracts included one in Moors's research on the Nablus region; similarly, villagers used only one dower in Granqvist's study.[19] Returning to the standard case, then the husband replied to the wife, "Immediately, you are divorced, and you are free of me." Finally, the judge explained to the former spouses they had obtained a minor divorce and they would need a new marriage contract and a new dower if they wished to marry each other again. They could, however, remarry without negotiating a new contract if they did so within the wife's waiting period. In some instances, the court also announced that the couple had voluntarily chosen to divorce as adults, and the court had carried out this divorce in accordance with shari'a.

Wife-initiated divorce cases nearly always resulted in a minor, or revocable, divorce, which was consistent with classical Hanafi legal procedure.[20] This reflects common practice in the *shari'a* courts of Palestine today as well. In contrast, Palestinian women initiating divorce today may be more likely to insist on an irrevocable divorce. One of my interviewees, Hekmat, was able to initiate and obtain a major divorce in Gaza after a long ordeal and several court dates. Hekmat said that the judge tried repeatedly to convince her of the advantages to a minor divorce, but she was determined to leave her husband conclusively so she could move on with her life. Despite the court's pressure, Hekmat was resolute with the judge and the other court officials, and she succeeded in obtaining her major divorce; we will look at her experiences in more depth later in this chapter.[21]

One of the evident goals of the court was, and is, to keep families together, and it is logical from this position to encourage revocable divorces over irrevocable divorces because a couple may reconcile during the wife's waiting period.[22] Granqvist cites two examples of reconciliation in her discussion of the relatively few Artas divorces (11 out of 264 marriages). In these examples, a religious authority (the mufti of Jerusalem in one instance and a judge in the other) allowed a husband who had divorced his wife to take her back after paying a fee.[23] After an irrevocable divorce, however, all four Sunni schools of law require the wife to remarry another man and divorce him before she may marry her first husband again. The traditional origin of this doctrine was to prevent men from abusing their unilateral right to divorce during the time of the Prophet. With the finality of the third divorce, men could no longer repeatedly divorce their wives and take them back.

From Maintenance to Wife-Initiated Divorce

The most common way in which court records departed from standard wife-initiated divorce proceedings was they began as a maintenance claim and then abruptly shifted into a wife-initiated divorce. As we saw in the opening case of this chapter, a woman was likely to have started her lawsuit as a maintenance claim because it enabled her to broach divorce, the outcome she actually sought. If the woman had obtained her husband's agreement to divorce before the court date, then there would have been no reason for her to request support in court. There are, however, a few alternative situations to consider. Perhaps the woman was hoping her demand for maintenance would provoke her husband into divorcing her unilaterally so she could retain her divorce rights. Indeed, this happened in some proceedings. A man may have declared the divorce in hopes of saving face, but taking a financial loss, by making a public display of his authority in response to her summoning him to court. It is also possible that the wife was trying to retain her right to maintenance, in addition to initiating divorce, even though this was a most unlikely outcome. Or perhaps the woman could not convince her husband to agree to the divorce in private, so she resorted to summoning him to court for a maintenance claim. Now publicly embarrassed and confronted with his wife's request, the husband decided to take advantage of the considerably fewer costs in wife-initiated divorce, compared to a husband's unilateral divorce.

One rather unusual maintenance-to-wife-initiated divorce case demonstrates the latter of these circumstances, apart from the outcome, because the wife was unable to convince her husband to divorce her. In these 1931 proceedings in which the couple was from Jerusalem, Fatima stated that she had brought her marriage contract with her from seven years ago, and her husband had left her five months ago without maintenance or someone else to provide it. She requested maintenance, and her husband, Ibrahim, confirmed the marriage. Then Fatima told the court she did not want Ibrahim, support, or a house; she only wanted a divorce. Ibrahim refused to consent. The judge told Fatima he could not force Ibrahim to agree to the divorce, rejecting Fatima's request. Then the judge told Ibrahim he could ask him to order her to be obedient.[24]

This lawsuit illustrates the reality that if a husband refused to grant his wife a divorce, she had very little legal recourse. The only practical circumstances under which a woman could obtain a judicial dissolution in classical Hanafi law were the husband's impotence, insanity, or a dangerous disease. The husband's failure to support his wife was not a permissible reason in Hanafi law. Likewise, while the 1917 Ottoman family code expanded a few of women's divorce rights, it did not include a present husband's failure to provide maintenance. Not only was Fatima denied a divorce, but she probably also had to live in less than pleasant circumstances at home afterward.

Also, the judge added insult to injury by reminding Ibrahim that he could request an order for her to be obedient. As we have seen, jurists largely conceptualized obedience as meaning the wife was to reside in the marital home. In this case, it is apparent there was no agreement to divorce before the court date because the wife actually told the court she did not want her husband. If the couple had agreed in advance, Fatima would have allowed her husband to state they had agreed to divorce in accordance with the standard procedure. But as described previously, Fatima probably did have the extralegal option of returning to her family and living as a *hardana* ("offended and angry") woman, particularly because no children were mentioned in the court summary.

Another unique maintenance-to-wife-initiated divorce record demonstrates a very different possible outcome, in that the woman was able to retain the rights (*huquq*) that she would usually receive in a husband-initiated divorce. This 1929 case involving a Jerusalem couple began with 'A'isha requesting the court to assess an amount of maintenance. 'A'isha's husband, 'Abd Al-Salam, confirmed he had left her without maintenance and without a provider. Then he told the court they had agreed to wife-initiated divorce and asked for it to be recorded in court. 'Abd Al-Salam, however, also agreed not to oppose 'A'isha if she wished to request her rights, which rarely happened in a wife-initiated divorce. The proceedings end here, so apparently the court did not complete the divorce that day. They most likely continued the proceedings in another session, because the judge never announced that they were divorced, nor did he tell the couple they would need a new dower and contract in order to remarry.[25] There were likely extraordinary conditions that were withheld in the court summary, because it was very unusual for a husband to allow his wife to retain her financial divorce rights when he had no obligation to do so. Despite not knowing the circumstances, that is precisely the implication of this case: the wife received her rights entirely because her husband was willing to allow it.

We can try to deconstruct his potential motives by considering some possible situations. One was that the wife's family, or his own family, had insisted that he take such a course of action. Another possibility, which could have been present along with the first, was that 'Abd Al-Salam had behaved improperly and he felt a good deal of remorse. Neither of these circumstances would have affected the husband's absolute legal authority to dictate whether or not his wife would retain her financial rights because it was a wife-initiated divorce. The primary implication of the lawsuit is consistent with a number of maintenance claims in that many women secured their claims because their husbands were willing to cooperate with their requests or needs.

A more common variation from the standard wife-initiated divorce record was the sort that ended in a major, or irrevocable, divorce. This type of divorce is final, after which there can be no reconciliation without the wife first marrying and divorcing another man. Interestingly, two of the five wife-initiated irrevocable divorce lawsuits in my survey began as maintenance claims. An example of a maintenance-to-wife-initiated irrevocable divorce is the following 1936 case. Although the couple was living in Jerusalem, the wife was born in Manura, a town, and the husband was from the village of Tibih Tawakarim. The proceedings began with Fatima, the plaintiff, stating that "this man is my husband, there has been proper consummation of the marriage, we have a marriage contract in accordance with *shari'a*, and my husband has left me without maintenance and without a provider. I ask the court for a ruling to assess maintenance, for him to pay the costs of court, and for permission to borrow the monthly amount in his name." Her husband confirmed that Fatima was his wife and the marriage had been consummated. Then Faris stated that he and Fatima had decided to divorce by the wife's initiative. Fatima confirmed this and said, addressing her husband, "I give up my rights . . . and I am free of you"; and he replied, "[Effective] immediately, you are divorced" three times. Faris also told Fatima that he would return her possessions to her, including her clothing. Then Fatima asked the court for a commitment to compel him to fulfill this promise. The judge explained it was an irrevocable divorce and she could not marry him again unless she married and divorced another man. The judge also stated that Faris must give Fatima her belongings and dismissed her initial request for maintenance.[26] Because Fatima began her case requesting maintenance, it seems probable that they came to court without a prior agreement to divorce. Also, since the normal procedure for women-initiated divorces is a minor divorce, Faris likely decided to make it irrevocable on his own; he may well have done so because Fatima had dragged him into court requesting maintenance.

Overall, these court records indicate that women who initiated their divorces by requesting maintenance were strategically employing their right to support to do so. But occasionally, women came up with a different strategy altogether in an attempt to obtain a divorce; that is, a wife would appear in court and claim her husband had divorced her. The most likely circumstances in which a woman would have done so were if she was unable to persuade her husband to divorce her, or if she could only afford to divorce with her financial divorce rights intact. For example, Helwa, a woman from a village near Jerusalem, began her 1937 case by telling the court her husband, Nazal, had divorced her three times and that he needed to pay her deferred dower, which was 20 Egyptian pounds, as well as her maintenance during the waiting period. But Nazal claimed that he had not divorced her. Consequently, the judge asked Helwa to provide proof (*ithbat*) of the divorce, and he asked Nazal to swear there was no divorce. Helwa had no proof, and Nazal swore, "She is my wife and I did not divorce her," so the judge canceled Helwa's claims.[27] It is likely that Helwa was hoping to provoke her husband into divorcing her by compelling her husband to appear in court. She had nothing to lose by doing so, although she must have irritated her husband a good deal. It does not seem probable that Nazal had simply changed his mind about the divorce; Helwa would have insisted on swearing the divorce indeed had occurred if that had been true. In other proceedings as well, the wife claimed there had been a husband-initiated divorce but the husband denied it. It was of course to the wife's advantage if her husband initiated the divorce as opposed to a wife-initiated divorce in which she gave up her divorce rights and often had to negotiate her right to child support. It is not surprising, then, that women may have fabricated such a situation on occasion.

Other Variations

A somewhat common distinction from the typical wife-initiated divorce proceeding was a wife initiating divorce in the context of an unconsummated marriage. In this study, there are five wife-initiated divorce records with these circumstances: two from Jerusalem, one from Haifa, and two from villages.[28] These marriages were considered incomplete and failing to fulfill a major function for which marriage was intended, that is, satisfying the sexual needs of both partners.[29] There could be a variety of reasons for the consummation of a marriage not to occur, as we will see. In these cases, the judge did not require a waiting period because there was no chance of the woman being pregnant.

The following proceedings are from a standard wife-initiated divorce without consummation of the marriage. Mazihn and Muhammad, a couple from Haifa, were married (meaning they had signed the marriage contract) but had not consummated the marriage. They brought two witnesses to court to confirm these facts. The wife, Mazihn, said, addressing the husband, "I give up all of my rights before and after the divorce"; and Muhammad replied, "Immediately you are divorced." Then the judge explained that they had obtained a minor divorce and she could remarry another man right away without a waiting period.[30] This type of case may appear to indicate another way in which the court contravened the 1917 Ottoman family code and Hanafi law, both of which accept the husband's impotence or sexual inability as grounds for judicial dissolution. But it is not clear in these cases which partner was at fault, or if in fact anyone was at fault. Indeed, sometimes in Palestinian society today, a couple will sign the contract, but they never actually start their life together; so they end up dissolving the marriage as a wife-initiated divorce.[31] Often this happens because of financial reasons, such as the excessive costs of financing and equipping a new home, but there can be a variety of other factors as well.

Another variation of the standard wife-initiated divorce proceedings were proceedings in which the wife asserted there was aversion or incompatibility (munafara) between the couple. There were five wife-initiated divorce records with aversion stated as the wife's reason for divorce, all from 1925. The following proceedings between a couple residing in Jerusalem exemplify this sort of case. Shafiqa, whose family was from Nablus, told the judge she was the wife of Khamis, who was originally from al-Khalil (Hebron). She said they had a proper marriage contract and she had a three-year-old girl in her care. Then Shafiqa stated there was incompatibility between them and they could not live together. She maintained they had agreed she would compensate him with seven gold lira uthmani

(Ottoman) and she was giving up her rights before and after the divorce. Shafiqa vowed she would financially support her child through the mother's custody period and pay her husband the seven lira. Khamis agreed with these conditions and Shafiqa gave him the money in court. Then Khamis said, "I divorce you," and the court explained to them that they had obtained a minor divorce.[32]

The above case illustrates the great lengths some women had to go through to get divorced, and it shows why wife-initiated divorce would not have been an option for many women. In addition to giving up her divorce rights, Shafiqa had to pay her husband seven gold lira and waived child support for her daughter in order to obtain the divorce. And she only obtained a minor divorce, despite these additional expenses. Similarly, in another 1925 aversion record in which the couple was from Jerusalem, the wife also volunteered to pay for her son's upbringing expenses while he was in her temporary custody, but she also added a condition regarding her potential remarriage: If the wife remarried, and the son immediately went into his father's custody, then she would continue paying for her son only if he was in the care of someone other than his father.[33] The wife clearly had to give her husband additional incentives to agree to the divorce, but she was also very shrewd to add the stipulation in the event she remarried. It is unlikely that she would have had to continue paying support for the child, since he would probably live with his father. The court recorder in 1925 used the term "aversion or incompatibility" quite often during this year; in fact, almost every 1925 wife-initiated divorce case in my study included a reference to aversion between the couple. The term "aversion" did not emerge in any other year, so it is possible the recorder had a stylistic preference for the word. Another distinction in these 1925 records was the court recorder added to the usual format of the other years, adding the wife's promise not to come to court again regarding this divorce. Also, in 1939, the court recorder used the phrase "we lack integration" (*na'dm al-imtizam*) in a handful of proceedings, rather than the term "aversion."[34]

Cases Involving Child Custody

As the previous lawsuit alluded, wife-initiated divorce tended to become significantly more complicated when there were children involved because

there was more at stake. During the Ottoman period, Hanafi scholars instructed that a mother has the right to care for her daughter from
infancy until the beginning of physical maturity, approximately ages nine
to eleven, and a mother's caretaking rights for a son ends when he can
care for himself, about seven years old.[35] After reaching these development
stages, the child lives with the father, who is considered the child's permanent guardian and responsible for his or her upbringing expenses. In addition to conceding the deferred dower and maintenance during the waiting
period, it was not unusual for women to give up their right to receive child
support as well. Sometimes women also volunteered to pay other upbringing expenses, such as nursing or education costs, to obtain the divorce. For
example, in a Jerusalem couple's 1938 wife-initiated divorce record, Miriam
told her husband she would pay child support expenses, along with the
usual waiving of the dower and waiting-period maintenance, in exchange
for the divorce.[36]

There were, however, also cases where women were able to retain child
support and other payments for their children during the mother's temporary custody period. In the following 1936 case of a couple from Jerusalem,
Hekmat's lawyer began the proceedings by recounting the events of the
couple's previous court date. Hekmat had given up part of her deferred
dower (mahr mu'ajjal) and they had gotten a minor divorce, but she had
retained her right to ask for child support and other expenses for her daughter. Now her lawyer was asking the court to assess both of those costs. Then
their lawyers disagreed on the respected elders from the couple's community who were to determine the appropriate amount of maintenance, so
the court appointed them. The respected men estimated the child support
at one Palestinian pound per month, and the husband had to pay all the
court fees and his wife's lawyer's fees as well.[37] We can assume the divorce
was wife-initiated since Hekmat had given up part of her dower, especially
because she did so while employing a lawyer. As we saw in chapter 2 on
women's lawsuits requesting maintenance, female plaintiffs who employed
lawyers received more favorable rulings compared to their counterparts
without legal assistance.

But even if a woman had waived her right to receive child support so
she could obtain her husband's consent to divorce, she could sometimes

reverse her decision. In two wife-initiated divorce custody records, both women changed their minds about relinquishing their custody rights. In a 1936 case, Na'ma, the wife, told the court she and her former husband Sahi were divorced and she had one daughter in her care. Na'ma informed the court she had volunteered to pay for her child's support, but now she was asking her husband to pay support along with the court expenses. Sahi confirmed the divorce and the daughter in Na'ma's care, but he refused to volunteer an amount of child support. Then he disagreed with Na'ma regarding the respected elders who would determine the amount of support, so the court appointed the men. They assessed the daughter's support at thirty mils per day, which the judge ordered Sahi to pay, along with the court fees.[38] It is likely that Na'ma had volunteered to pay her daughter's child support to help convince her husband to consent to a wife-initiated divorce; then after obtaining the divorce, she had nothing to lose in seeking her forfeited rights. This tactic was one of the most effective means of women's manipulation of Muslim family law to their advantage that emerged in my research. It is also possible that Na'ma simply became impoverished and requested child support despite having relinquished it previously. She probably would have mentioned her desperate situation had that been true, however, because women did so in many other proceedings.

On the other hand, there were a few cases in which the wife had to give up her temporary child custody rights to secure the divorce. The following 1936 wife-initiated divorce record of a Bedouin couple from different villages shows this most unfortunate outcome for a woman seeking divorce. After the usual preliminary statements, 'A'isha told her husband that she was giving up her right to raise her daughter in exchange for a divorce.[39] This is an extreme example of what a woman may have had to concede to secure her husband's agreement. It is worth noting that even if a woman was able to retain her child custody rights with all of the corresponding payments for the children, life was often difficult for her, as Werda, one of my interviewees, indicated. Even though she was speaking of the post-1948 era, her insights on some of the difficulties that divorced women can experience must have been just as painful for women during the Mandate period, particularly the loss of a child. Werda said she knew a woman who initiated divorce and that she had a daughter. The woman and her daughter stayed with her parents for nine years, and the former husband paid child support throughout. Then he took the daughter. The woman's experience was very difficult, and she had to go to court more than once, where her interactions with the judge were also arduous for her.[40]

Grounds of Desertion

In classical Hanafi law, a woman must wait ninety-nine years from her husband's birth to obtain a judicial divorce on grounds of desertion. By comparison, it may appear that judges during the Mandate period were most reasonable. Tucker shows, however, that Ottoman courts regularly deferred desertion cases to non-Hanafi judges, who allowed women to gain judicial dissolutions in such situations.[41] Thus there was considerable continuity between Ottoman and Mandate court practices regarding women's access to judicial dissolution for desertion. For example, in the following 1929 case, Amira said her husband, Muhammad, had gone to America ten years before and that he had not provided her with maintenance or a provider since his departure. Amira maintained that she knew nothing of his whereabouts or even if he was alive. She also said she was very poor, and her husband had left no property, business, or any other way for her to procure living expenses. Then Amira told the court she could not borrow in his name because no one would lend her money, so she asked the judge to end the marriage. She added that she had tried very hard to contact him and to seek information about him, and the judge asked her for proof. Amira brought witnesses who confirmed her story by oath, and the judge granted her request. Also, he told Amira that she could remarry after the completion of her waiting period.[42] It is interesting that there was no mention of the deferred dower or maintenance in the desertion records, which women should have received in a judicial dissolution. Perhaps the judges were simply being practical, given that it would have been very difficult for women to claim their financial divorce rights unless the husband's family was held responsible.

Amira's case indicates a respect in which the Jerusalem court did apply the Ottoman family code of 1917. The Ottoman code stipulates that a deserted wife may obtain a judicial dissolution, but she must wait four years if the husband has provided support in his absence.[43] Accordingly, as we saw in Amira's lawsuit above, the Mandate-era Jerusalem court did not require women to wait the Hanafi-prescribed ninety-nine years to obtain a divorce on grounds of desertion and rather applied the Ottoman family code. In addition, the court granted immediate judicial dissolutions to all three women who sought divorce for desertion; the women's husbands had been absent for three, ten, and fourteen years.[44] Of course, as noted previously, Tucker has shown that Ottoman-period judges often deferred desertion cases to non-Hanafi judges who could grant a deserted wife a divorce. As for current court practices, the former Chief Islamic Justice told me that a woman must wait one year in order to obtain a divorce on grounds of desertion.[45]

Apparently some women were unconvinced that a judge would always follow the Ottoman code, however, and they were careful to secure the power to end their marriages in the event of desertion. There were a handful of proceedings in which the husband was going abroad for an indefinite period and the wife had her husband sign an agreement enabling her to divorce if he failed to return within a specified period. In one 1930 agreement between a couple from Beit Safafa, Fatima told the court her husband, Hasan, had left her without maintenance and without a provider, and now he planned to go to America. In addition to maintenance and a guarantor for it, Fatima asked Hasan to promise in court that if he did not return within three years she could divorce him without his consent. Hasan agreed but then he returned home to her, so the court withdrew her request for maintenance.[46]

An example of such an agreement coming to fruition is the following 1935 case of a Bedouin couple. Helwa came to court with an agreement she and her husband had signed three years before. The document stipulated if her husband failed to return from America within three years, Helwa could divorce him without his consent. Muhammad had not returned within the period, so Helwa asked the court to grant her a divorce. She also brought two witnesses, both of whom confirmed her account. Thus, the judge granted her the divorce and told Helwa she could remarry after the completion of her waiting period.[47] It does not appear that these women were able to retain their financial divorce rights; neither the balance of the dower nor maintenance during the waiting period were mentioned in the records. But as noted before, it would have been difficult for a deserted woman to claim her dower or maintenance unless her husband had appointed an individual to take on these responsibilities.

Interviewees' Insights

As is often true of oral sources, the interviewees' responses in this section tend to indicate more about their own experiences and views than perhaps anything else. This does not make interviewees' insights less valuable; indeed, giving voice to the voiceless, as cliché as it may sound, is still a meaningful goal for many who use oral sources. The senior women interviewees for this study can certainly be characterized as such given their people are still denied a state, their limited educational opportunities (see chapter 5 for statistics), and their gender. This method, however, does require researchers to either evaluate interviewees' contentions about the past carefully with more reliable sources or to use the information gained primarily to reveal interviewees' consciousness of the past and how it reflects their own experiences and perceptions of the present. I use a combination of these approaches here. Absolute historical accuracy cannot be the goal, especially when one is using a limited number of qualitative interviews, but we can certainly gain insights into how women think about Muslim family law and the shari'a court system today. We can also perhaps extrapolate how women from the previous generation may have felt about certain matters. Given the tremendous silences in the court records, interviews are arguably our only means of gleaning a sense of how women may have thought about Muslim family law in the past. This is particularly true when it comes to nonelite women as we have few to no memoirs, family histories, or other sources that we do have for Palestinian elites, though few elite sources address the topics of this study. Of course, there are many additional concerns and issues for researchers to consider when carrying out interviews, which I address in chapter 5.

Most often in the Mandate-era Jerusalem court, a female plaintiff appearing for wife-initiated divorce was accompanied by her father, who performed the role of witness. This indicates that women who sought wife-initiated divorce usually had the support of their families.[48] Interviewees suggested that most families in both the past and today would be sympathetic to a daughter in an unhappy marriage, and her family would facilitate a divorce if it was financially possible.[49] According to Werda, "Parents feel [sympathy] with their daughter, and if the marriage is bad they can help her divorce."[50] After gaining her family's support, a woman could then obtain a divorce as long as her husband agreed. If the family was elite, it likely had more means to entice a reluctant husband with additional financial incentives. A nonelite woman, on the other hand, had considerably less access to wife-initiated divorce because retaining the dower was far more important to her livelihood.[51] Also, the interviewees asserted that financial difficulties were the most important issue for women and their families during the Mandate period. This is likely accurate, given the tremendous economic difficulties that rural Palestinians experienced in the 1930s after the Great Depression and with the huge influx of Jewish immigrants.[52] Family support remains important for women seeking divorce in Palestine today, although not to the same extent, because far more women are employed outside the home and they are less dependent on their families financially. Another consequence that families of any class may have been unwilling to face was the possibility of social stigma that may have accompanied divorce, particularly in conservative villages or neighborhoods; therefore, some families may have been unwilling to support a daughter in such a decision.

Most interviewees, however, said Palestinians were generally less judgmental toward divorced women in the Mandate past compared to attitudes today. A word of caution is in order here. One should be mindful of an inclination among Palestinians, and their popular histories, to regard the past more optimistically in contrast to Palestinians' difficult lives today under Israeli occupation.[53] Nevertheless, Granqvist's discussion of the fourteen divorces that had occurred in Artas supports how the majority of interviewees claimed that divorced women experienced less of a stigma in the past. First, several of her examples indicate that it was the husband who feels "shame and humiliation that his wife goes to another man"; whereas no examples mentioned any shame experienced on the wife's part.[54] In addition, remarriage for divorced women appears to have been very common during the Mandate period because, as discussed in chapter 1, all of the divorced women in Artas were able to remarry (with the exception of one who died before she could remarry).[55] This suggests less shame associated with divorced women compared to the present.

Granqvist's data is very interesting given the interviewees' diverse responses to the question of whether it was easier for divorced women to remarry during the Mandate period compared with their situation today. Like many, if not most, of their responses, the women's views on this topic seem to have been very much linked to experiences and encounters in their own lives. Layla and Suad were the only women to say it was easy (*sihl*) for divorced women to remarry both in the past and now, although they proceeded to add conditions to their assertions.[56] Layla maintained that remarriage for divorced women was easy in the past, and today it is as well, but then she complicated this by adding, "if not then she can stay home."[57] She seemed to implicitly refer to the taboo still present in some parts of Palestinian society concerning single women living by themselves. But even for conservative families there are exceptions, such as if a woman is attending university. Suad also maintained it is easy for a divorced woman to remarry both now and in the past, but today women can choose their own spouses instead of parents choosing for them. Suad added that divorced women can remarry, but some women choose to stay with their children rather than remarrying.[58] Upon a divorced woman's remarriage to a new husband, her former husband can claim child custody immediately, regardless of the child's age or stage of development. Khader Salemeh, one of three male interviewees, said it was easier for divorced women to remarry during the Mandate period because of current societal expectations of expensive weddings, men's preference for a virgin (*bikr*) bride, and the near absence of polygyny.[59] Former Chief Islamic Justice Shaykh Tamimi alluded to the possibility of family pressure on a woman to stay in a marriage, and not only because it may be challenging for her to remarry. That is, if a woman divorces, it often makes it difficult for her sisters to find husbands.[60] I should mention that Salemeh and Shaykh Tamimi are probably less likely than the other interviewees to project their personal experiences onto their perceptions of the past because they are both very well educated and have extensive knowledge of Palestinian history.

Umm Khalid and Hamda both thought it was easy to remarry in the Mandate past, but neither of them directly commented about divorced women's capacity to do so today. Umm Khalid maintained it was easy to remarry in the past; she also said there are more divorces now than in the past.[61] Hamda contended it was easy for a divorced woman to remarry in the past (assuming there was an eligible man) because people did not talk badly about divorced women. But Hamda also asserted that it was not easy to find someone to marry because there were not many available men. She explained that each family only had one or two boys because of diseases and wars; Hamda proceeded to give some examples from families she knew. She also said, however, that divorced women could fairly easily remarry as an additional wife in the past. Hamda was assuming that men had the financial resources necessary for another dower and an additional household. She is from a fairly well-off Jerusalem family so it is perhaps not surprising she would make this assumption. Finally, Hamda seemed to imply that divorced women tend to encounter unkind talk today while discussing how this was not an issue in the past.[62]

Jehad and Haji Kowthar departed from the rest by contending that it is easier for a woman to remarry now than in the past. Haji Kowthar offered only one reason for this—that it was because of more shame connected to a divorced woman in the past.[63] As we have seen, Granqvist's research suggests strongly that the opposite was true, at least for rural Palestinians. Jehad asserted that, in the past, "it was not unheard of" for divorced women to remarry, and then she discussed examples of divorced women she knew who had remarried in recent decades. First she told me about a woman from Nazareth, a nurse who had gotten divorced and remarried in the 1970s. Jehad said that now it is easier for divorced women to remarry because friends and family try to help, and women can find someone via telephone or the internet.[64] She also mentioned two women in her family who had remarried in the United States. Perhaps Jehad's view is distinctive because she is Palestinian-Israeli and the others live in East Jerusalem or the West Bank. Jehad is from a well-off, rather liberal, mixed Muslim-Christian village near Haifa, whereas Palestinians in Jerusalem tend to be more conservative and there seems to be more of a tendency to stigmatize divorced women.

Interestingly, the issue of men's preference for virgins as a factor hindering divorced women from remarrying today emerged only in interviews with men. This perhaps reflects the interviewees' own concerns and values, those within their communities, or both. Since the focus of this study is on women's perceptions of and strategies in Muslim family law, I only interviewed three men. When I asked them about the prospects for divorced women to remarry in Palestine-Israel today, all three men mentioned that it is difficult in part because of men's preference for a virgin (*bikr*) bride today. Also, they situated this remark in opposition to the past, when men did not insist on virgin brides to the extent that they do now. Salemeh said it was much easier for divorced women to remarry in the past compared to today, because polygyny was still somewhat common and it was considerably less expensive to marry. He added that now it is "almost impossible" for a divorced woman to remarry because of the great expense of marriage and men's preference for virgins.[65] Nader, a jewelry maker and shop-owner in the Old City, also said it was easy for women to remarry in the past, but now it is the opposite because today men only want to marry virgins.[66] He suggested more critical attitudes toward divorced women, maintaining that people think the woman initiated the problem and thus they blame her. It is intriguing that they responded similarly, given these comments concerning virginity were completely unprompted; I did not broach the subject. Another interesting observation is that none of my female interviewees mentioned a greater male preference for virgins today, nor did any of them mention the issue of virginity at any point.

The court records did not allow me to determine how frequently wife-initiated divorce took place in the Jerusalem area during the Mandate period because the registers lacked a catalogue or indexed system, and some records may well have been stored elsewhere or were missing. It appears, however, that wife-initiated divorce occurred rarely in rural areas. Granqvist found that only 4.1 percent of 264 marriages in Artas ended by men divorcing their wives, and only one divorce was initiated by the wife.[67] In addition, only two of the sixty-five Artas women who married beyond the village were divorced, one by the husband and one via wife-initiated divorce (although it was "wholly" her brothers' doing).[68] When I asked interviewees about the frequency of wife-initiated divorce, most of them told me that it was "normal" (*'adi*) in both the Mandate period and today. The term *'adi* translates as "usual," "common," "ordinary," or "normal,"[69] but the women seemed to mean "normal" more in terms of "it happened" or "it was not unheard of." They apparently did not mean "common" or "usual" as I had initially assumed. Therefore, taking into consideration the context of their narratives, the interviewees tended to use "normal" in the sense that women-initiated divorce happened, but it was not an every-day occurrence during the Mandate period. This makes sense, considering the financial costs of wife-initiated divorce for women, particularly during a period in which most Palestinian women were nonelite villagers who did household and field work, as opposed to waged labor. In Kharbatha Beniharis, a West Bank village near Ramallah, Werda maintained that divorces of any kind only happened about once every five years in the past.

While more women said wife-initiated divorce was "normal" (or "known to happen") both in the past and in the present, three interviewees had divergent views. Also, Hamda, who lives in the Old City of Jerusalem, qualified her "it happened" assertion by saying divorce was not as common in the past because if a man was not content in his marriage, he would simply marry another wife.[70] This, again, reflects her urban, upper-class perspective. In contrast, Umm Khalid, Haji Kowthar, and Jehad all maintained that wife-initiated divorce is more common today than during the Mandate period. This is supported by Granqvist's research discussed above, showing far more husband-initiated divorces (approximately 92 percent of divorces) than wife-initiated divorces (about 8 percent of divorces) in Artas.[71] Welchman's study from the early 1990s showed the occurrence of husband-initiated versus wife-initiated divorces in the West Bank was 36 percent and 64 percent; for Gaza, the wife-initiated divorce rate was even higher at 82 percent.[72]

The interviewees gave different reasons for this trend. Umm Khalid, a Jerusalem resident, stated that wife-initiated divorce was "not possible" during the Mandate period, then conceded it happened "only if life was extremely difficult [for the woman];" she also said that today there are more divorces than in the past.[73] Haji Kowthar, also from Jerusalem, made the point that it was much more difficult for a woman to divorce in the past because of her lack of financial security, especially if she had children. She added that now it is easier for women to divorce because the government will provide maintenance if the ex-husband cannot pay it.[74] *Shari'a* courts in both Israel and Palestine provide limited maintenance if the husband is unable to provide it, but the amount is difficult to live on without other sources of income.[75] Jehad, from a well-off village near Haifa, asserted that wife-initiated divorce did happen in the past, but not too often because women were weak and they felt shy and inhibited. Jehad also said people would tend to think something was wrong with her if she had initiated divorce in the past, but today wife-initiated divorce is more accepted and more common.[76] The former Chief Islamic Justice's assertion that in the past women lacked awareness of their rights, placing them in an inferior position, suggests he would concur with Jehad's view of Palestinian women's past status. He stated that wife-initiated divorce is more common now than in the past, but he also said that it was not unusual in the past.[77]

While the research cited suggests that wife-initiated divorce is a far more common phenomenon today than it was during the Mandate period, it also seems to be more difficult for a divorced woman to get remarried now. This is largely because of the exorbitant costs of getting married, but societal attitudes toward divorced women also appear to have become less forgiving in Palestine-Israel. In addition, men seem to prefer virgin brides to a greater extent today and polygamy is far more limited, both of which decrease women's options for remarriage. The state of Israel has made polygamy illegal for all Israeli citizens, as well as for Palestinians who are "permanent residents" of Jerusalem. This law may appear to be a triumph for the improvement of women's rights, but many Palestinians consider it another manifestation of Israeli control over their lives. A few Palestinians explained they resent this total ban because polygamy offers an option when there is a fertility problem with the first wife, and they consider it cruel to divorce and abandon the first wife for a reason that is beyond her control.

Bushra and Hekmat

To get a better sense of how Palestinian women experience the process of going to court today, I interviewed two women in their thirties, Bushra and Hekmat, who had recently divorced their husbands in wife-initiated divorces. I also found these interviews useful for understanding the ways in which Palestinian women think and feel about family law and the court system today, such as their perceived protections and restrictions. I was particularly interested in whether or not the male-dominated and privileged system intimidates women, as well as how the men running the courts treat the women who use them. In doing so, I considered each woman's perceptions of the judge and his sympathy for them, or lack thereof, and to what extent he sought to protect her interests. Also, both women freely discussed the ways in which their communities treated them as well as their families' roles in their divorces. And each woman made it clear that maintaining custody of her children was her highest priority and greatest challenge in the process. While there is clearly much to be gained about women's present experiences and views of the court system from these interviews, they can also inform the Mandate period in a few ways, which I will discuss after telling their stories.

Bushra, a thirty-year-old from al-Khalil (Hebron) who has six children, said her divorce was very difficult for her. The family-associated, community-related, and financial stresses generated far more anxiety for Bushra than her experiences in the court. Bushra said her parents now live in Jerusalem, but they are from al-Khalil (Hebron), where the people have "special traditions." She described people from that city as being closed-minded and conservative, and she said they are unwilling to accept a divorce within one's family because they consider it shameful for the family. Bushra characterized her parents as being so fixated on shame that they seemed far less concerned about her suffering from her ex-husband's physical abuse or that he was imprisoned for such behavior. Bushra's mother told her not to tell anyone she was planning to divorce, and Bushra complied with her mother's wishes because their neighborhood would not accept a divorced woman. Although Bushra's parents ultimately enabled her divorce by renting her a living space next to them, she illustrated that they are still very opposed to it by pointing out the wall next to her house. Minutes from the wall that the Israelis have constructed, her parents have erected their own wall out of rusted roofing metal so they can avoid glimpsing Bushra and her children; their intolerance is evidently a major incentive for her to relocate her family outside of Jerusalem. "But now, thank God, everything is better," Bushra says, because she will marry a considerate man soon and they will live with her children in Acre.[78]

Bushra did not know her rights at all when she married at fifteen years old, and she said that she was "like a child" at that age. After Bushra's problems in her first marriage, she met many women with similar situations and now she understands her rights. Bushra emphasized that women have rights but they need to be aware of them or they will lose them. Her father had determined the conditions (*shurut*) in her first marriage contract (*'qad*). Now Bushra, however, will determine her own conditions in the contract for her second marriage. She said that it is far more common for Muslim women in Palestine-Israel to conduct their own second marriages, and to use stipulations in the contract, as opposed to doing so in first marriages. In first marriages, the father usually negotiates the marriage and determines the conditions, if he uses any, for his daughter; but in second marriages, women tend to be older, better informed, and more willing to insist on setting their own terms. Divorcées, and widows, are also unlikely to receive much of a dower, if anything at all. Thus families are often not overly concerned about whom divorced women decide to marry, particularly because it can be difficult to find a second husband.

Bushra will include the following conditions in her new marriage contract: her six children will live with her, her husband will respect her, she may go anywhere she pleases and work at her pleasure, and she will choose where they will live. Her fiancé, who is a schoolteacher in Acre, agreed with her stipulations because he respects her, he likes her children, and he wants the kids to continue their studies. Bushra explained that she is marrying someone outside of Jerusalem because they have a "different mind" in Acre: they respect women and do not use violence against women.

After her experiences with the courts under both Israeli and Jordanian authority, Bushra clearly favored the Israeli *shari'a* court system over the Jordanian one. She has two marriage contracts, one Israeli and one Jordanian, and she feels the Israeli *shari'a* courts (staffed by Palestinian-Israelis) were preferable because the judge was sympathetic to her situation. She claimed the judges in the courts under Jordanian authority dislike divorce and always try to fix the problems with family arbitrators before they will grant a divorce. The judge to whom she was assigned in an Israeli *shari'a* court fulfilled the ideal of being the protector of women's rights: he understood her, he gave her government-provided maintenance, he granted her the divorce, and he gave her all of her rights in Islam. That is, he gave her most of her rights. When I asked about her dower, Bushra said her ex-husband could not pay her deferred dower of 10,000 Jordanian dinars ($14,100). Bushra appeared in court with a lawyer from the government because it is the law in the Israeli *shari'a* courts, but she always spoke for herself. Overall, she considers the Israeli courts better because she feels they act in the interests of the woman, they are fair, and they pay maintenance. She did not mention that this amount is hardly sufficient on which to live, or that the *shari'a* courts in the Palestinian West Bank also pay support if the husband cannot provide it. It is less than the amount in Israel, but the cost of living is also less expensive in Palestine. In general terms, but obviously coming from her experience, Bushra said parents feel ashamed when there is a divorce and then they project this shame on the children. Therefore, every woman needs to be strong, she must know all of her legal rights, and she needs to maintain her respect. If a woman does not know her rights, she will be weak.[79]

Hekmat, a thirty-seven-year-old from Gaza who has five children and works for various nongovernmental organizations (NGOs), got married when she was eighteen years old. Hekmat recalled that she knew nothing about her rights in *shari'a* upon her wedding day. She maintained that most Palestinian women do not know much about their rights when they marry, and this is especially the case in Gaza, where women get married quite young. Hekmat said if one talks about women's rights in *shari'a* in Gaza, people will think you are liberal and western-oriented, and it will be difficult to be accepted by the more religious people.

Hekmat's experience in the Gaza *shari'a* court was very difficult. She described it as an intimidating environment in which the judge looked at her as though she were *nashiza* (disobedient), a disgraceful term. She went to court alone and chose to represent herself, which was possible because it was wife-initiated divorce. The judge tried very hard to convince Hekmat to agree to a minor divorce, but she was determined to have the marriage categorically over with an irrevocable divorce. Up until the very end, the judge was still trying to persuade Hekmat to reconsider. It is routine for courts in Palestine to pressure women, and to a lesser extent men, to reconsider a divorce in the interest of keeping families together, and it is not uncommon for women to change their minds at the last minute because of financial stresses, children, family pressures, or community concerns. But the judge was not the primary hurdle in Hekmat's story. In order to obtain her divorce and keep her five children, Hekmat first had to get her husband to agree to her conditions. It took her six months to persuade him to go to court the first time, and even longer to convince him to give her child custody. Hekmat did so via several persuasive means, stressing the fact that his new wife would want her own children. After her ex-husband remarried very quickly, Hekmat promptly recruited his new wife to help her cause, since she certainly had no interest in raising Hekmat's five teenage children.

Hekmat emphasized that it was very unusual for her to be able to keep her children, to have the support of most of her family, and then to find a wonderful new husband whom she loves very much—and at the age of thirty-seven with five kids! She generally tried to keep her family out of the whole divorce process, but she also felt that it was important to get their approval. Hekmat really only needed the support of her uncle, who is the head of her extended family, and he quickly silenced those who were opposed to her decision. The most important factors that enabled Hekmat to obtain a divorce on favorable terms were that she is from a well-off, understanding family, she is well-educated, and she has a good job. Being able to keep her children was a major accomplishment, particularly because she initiated the divorce. She also gave up her right to child support, which was possible with her income and probably with some family help. For any divorced woman, however, the rate of maintenance for children in Gaza is a pittance at only 100 NIS (Israeli shekels, about US$20) a month per child.[80]

Hekmat's new husband was from Ramallah, he had never been married, and his family was supportive of his engagement to Hekmat.[81] His family's attitude very much surprised her. She had expected them to oppose the match because of her background as a divorcée, particularly since her community in Gaza had talked rather badly about her after the divorce. Hekmat even lost many friends because of the divorce; girlfriends were suspicious of her trying to steal their husbands and male friends had to stop meeting her because of "talk." She felt like she had to be meticulous about her public appearance in every respect, from the shade of her lipstick to the volume of her laugh. Hekmat never expected to marry again, nor did her neighbors think she would remarry. People gossiped that if she ever got remarried, it would be as a fourth wife. But women Hekmat knew generally did not pity her, because she said many of them wished they could get a divorce too. Hekmat concluded that most Palestinian men generally dislike strong women and prefer submissive types. She said this is especially true of religious men, and we can infer that she was including the men whom she encountered in the Gaza court.[82]

I learned a great deal from Bushra and Hekmat about Palestinian women's experiences in court and divorce today. In addition, a few of the insights gained from them can inform the Mandate period to some extent. Throughout their narratives, both Bushra and Hekmat emphasized the crucial importance of knowing one's rights in Muslim family law when negotiating marriage and divorce. Neither had known much about their rights when they were married at fairly young ages, but both later gained knowledge about women's rights in *shari'a* and Bushra was careful to include conditions in her second marriage contract. (Hekmat has a professional occupation and can support herself, so protecting her financial rights was not necessary.) Knowing one's rights surely would have been very important for women during the Mandate period as well, even though women would have been less likely to be informed about them given the younger ages of marriage and the very limited access to education compared to recent decades.

This points to another valuable contribution to this study, which is how the experiences of the younger women illustrated some of the same concerns and points that the older interviewees had mentioned. As discussed above, only by educating themselves were the younger women able to take advantage of the very rights the older women emphasized as being so important in Islam. Both divorcées also emphasized that it is far more difficult for a woman to obtain a second marriage compared to a first marriage and that they were stigmatized by their communities, and even by family in Bushra's situation, after their divorces. This confirms the majority of older interviewees' contentions, as well as the research cited, that it is more difficult for Palestinian women to remarry today and that women experience more of a stigma today versus the past.

Finally, several challenges faced by the younger women were those that women in the Mandate period also experienced, such as not receiving one's deferred dower, facing financial stresses, being unaware of one's rights (initially), and the importance of family support for wives to initiate divorce, however reluctantly it was given in Bushra's story. Thus, the younger women's perceptions of and feelings about those various challenges can perhaps give us an idea of how Mandate-era women may have perceived and thought about them as well.

Conclusion

Palestinian Muslim women had greater access to divorce in the Mandate period than in most, if not all, contemporaneous societies in the west. Wife-initiated divorce in Muslim family law was, and is, not the ideal divorce situation for a woman, however. This is primarily because women nearly always had to give up their financial divorce rights when they initiated divorce, especially the deferred dower and maintenance during the waiting period, and they often gave up child support as well. It could be challenging for women to convince their husbands to divorce even when waiving these rights, as suggested by the number of divorces initiated by women as maintenance claims. Demanding maintenance gave a woman an excuse to bring her husband to court if he was unwilling to agree to divorce beforehand, and many times she was then able to secure his consent. Perhaps the most notable example of women's creative negotiating tactics in this chapter was the wife's strategy of relinquishing child support as leverage to obtain her husband's consent to divorce, and then later requesting it in another court session. Another example of this trend was the wife claiming in court that her husband had divorced her, while he maintained that he had not done so. By bringing their husbands to court, wives were sometimes able to prod their husbands into actually divorcing them.

We have also seen that women were able to divorce unilaterally on grounds of desertion during Mandate Palestine. This was the only way in which the Ottoman family code of 1917 expanded the terms for women to request judicial dissolution, as compared to classical Hanafi law. Whereas classical Hanafi jurists expected a woman to wait ninety-nine years from her husband's birth before she could obtain a judicial dissolution on these grounds, Mandate-period judges granted divorces immediately when a woman demonstrated desertion. But in practice, Ottoman courts had already been granting women judicial dissolutions for desertion because they were willing to defer such cases to non-Hanafi judges, as Tucker has shown.[83] In other respects, the Ottoman code reinforced conventional Hanafi ways in which women could unilaterally request a judicial dissolution, such as for the husband's impotence, dangerous illness, or insanity. In addition, women typically waived the same financial rights—the deferred dower and maintenance—during the waiting period, in both Ottoman- and Mandate-era wife-initiated divorce records. The one divorce-related innovation of the Ottoman code, compared to classical Hanafi law, was to include "discord and incompatibility" as grounds for judicial dissolution, but it does not seem to have been used during the Mandate period. Thus it appears that there was considerable continuity between Ottoman- and Mandate era court practices in terms of wife-initiated divorce and judicial dissolution.

Judicial dissolutions were rare, however, and the vast majority of women who were able to obtain divorces did so via wife-initiated divorce. But this was not really an option for many women. In addition to concerns about finances and the rigid ages for child custody rulings, there were serious consequences for a woman to take into account if her husband denied her the divorce; this must have prevented many women from broaching the topic. Umm Khalid told a story that reflected one of the realistic motivations for a woman to remain in an unhappy marriage: she related the likely possibility that a husband will refuse his wife a divorce and proceed to make life very difficult for her. She knew a woman who asked her husband to divorce but he refused, and instead he found himself an additional wife. Umm Khalid's first lesson of the story was that a woman must understand her husband and communicate with him well. But her most important lesson was that a woman needs to know everything regarding her husband before the marriage.[84]

Overall, women's access to wife-initiated divorce during the Mandate period was probably not an option for most nonelite women because of the financial consequences for the wife and her family. But as Palestinian women have worked outside the home to a far greater extent since that period, their recourse to wife-initiated divorce has expanded a great deal as well. Somewhat paradoxically, however, many of my interviewees suggested the stigma that comes with divorce is far more significant today than it was during the Mandate period. Accordingly, divorced Palestinian women probably had an easier time finding a husband during the 1920s–1930s than they do today. Other factors that contribute to this trend include today's decreased rates of polygyny, the greater cost of marriage, and perhaps men's stronger preference for virgins than in the past.

Muslim women in Palestine and Israel today, however, have greater access to protection in their marriages and divorces. There is a major contingency that, if executed well, has the potential to dictate the terms of a woman's marriage and to solve the predicament of a woman losing her rights in a divorce. As we have seen with Bushra, a woman has the important opportunity of including stipulations in her marriage contract, which can range from preventing her husband from taking another wife to guaranteeing she may continue working. While women appear to have used conditions in the marriage contract infrequently during the Mandate period, the practice is more common among educated Palestinians today.[85] The most usual stipulations today involve a wife's wish to continue her education, to work, or to live in a certain area, which is usually near her family or separately from his family. Sometimes the conditions are less significant, however, and can involve the type and location of the wedding (*zafaf*), the wedding dresses, the trousseau, or items in the household. Jehad told me about the importance of including stipulations in the marriage contract regarding major life decisions:

Women must always put conditions in the marriage contract. Yes, I knew about this right before my marriage. But it makes me sad to think about this because when my daughter Layla got married, her husband agreed to the condition that Layla could continue her studies to become a nurse, but we did not write it in the contract. Then later Layla's husband refused to let her continue her education, and it makes me so sad that I cry about it sometimes. Islam gives women a big opportunity to take their rights and to connect them to their lives, and I know so many women who must divorce because they did not include conditions in the contract.[86]

In order for a woman to be able to protect her interests, she must, of course, be informed of her right to include stipulations in the marriage contract; but there is another important nuance to take into account. It is the woman's father who tends to negotiate the terms of a first marriage, thus it is his attention to his daughter's future that is most critical in a first marriage. She may ask her father to include stipulations, but in many situations it is up to the father to think of including protections for his daughter. Stipulations can only go so far to protect women, however. When there is the issue of child custody to negotiate, Hekmat's story illustrates that a woman must often convince her husband to give up his right to custody. This of course complicates the situation a great deal, as we also saw in lawsuits where women negotiated the terms of their divorces with children to consider. We will examine this topic, along with several more factors, more closely in the next chapter on the mother's temporary caretaking period.

4

He Took My Child

The Mother's Temporary Caretaking Period

SA'DA, A WOMAN FROM THE VILLAGE OF AL-WALJIH, near Jerusalem, was separated from her husband when she appeared in the Jerusalem *Shari'a* Court in 1926. First, she stated that her husband, Shahada, had taken their daughters from her without a valid reason in *shari'a*. Sa'da requested the return of her six- and four-year-old girls, and she asked for maintenance for herself and her children. Shahada confirmed their daughters' ages and that they were in his home, but claimed that Sa'da had left his house without his permission and was living with her father against his wishes. He requested for Sa'da to return to his house. The judge ordered Shahada to return the girls to their mother and to pay maintenance for his wife and the children.[1] This case is significant because it, and others like it, indicate that the Jerusalem court in this period valued a mother's right to care for her child more than a husband's right to his wife's obedience. Even if a woman was actively disobeying her husband, Sa'da's lawsuit demonstrates that the court upheld the woman's prerogative to raise her child.

As in Sa'da's case, "He took my child without legitimate reason in *shari'a*" was an appeal that many Palestinian women made to *shari'a* court judges, claiming their right to raise their young children. As we saw in a number of maintenance and divorce proceedings, certain child custody disputes demonstrate that Palestinian women were able to use creative strategies to gain benefits and exploit this male-privileged system during the British Mandate period. This chapter analyzes gendered strategies that women used to secure their interests in child custody disputes, as well as circumstances under which women tended to be successful in their lawsuits. Another theme we will revisit is how the Jerusalem court's application of Hanafi law in Mandate Palestine demonstrates both transformation from and continuity with the Ottoman period, with a focus on child custody. As I argue in the preceding chapters, the Palestinian community had little incentive to overhaul the one indigenous institution that it still controlled in the face of significant external threats, British imperialism and Zionist colonialism.

We have seen how it can be difficult to assess the actual motivations driving female plaintiffs in maintenance and wife-initiated divorce cases. In each maintenance claim, the wife began by requesting support payments from her husband. But whether or not compensation was the plaintiff's actual objective or a pretext for appearing in court for another reason was often ambiguous; sometimes the lawsuits ended in husband-initiated or wife-initiated divorce, either of which the plaintiff may well have sought. In short, there were a number of motivations and factors that could have influenced a woman's decision to appear in court to demand maintenance. In wife-initiated divorce proceedings, women's motivations for seeking divorce were generally not recorded, with two exceptions. In a small number of cases, either aversion or failure to consummate the marriage was stated as the reason for divorce. As long as the husband gave his consent, the court allowed the couple to end the marriage. Although imposed arbitration is conspicuously absent from these court records, my interviews suggest that arbitration likely took place prior to the actual divorce. Also, the interviews indicate that women's reasons for initiating divorce both in the Mandate past and in present-day Palestine-Israel were diverse and complex.

In contrast to the wide range of incentives in and reasons for maintenance and wife-initiated divorce proceedings, it is far more straightforward to discern women's, and men's, motivations in child custody disputes. The child custody cases examined here demonstrate that a Palestinian woman's main objective was usually to prolong the time she was able to live with her children. That is, she wished to extend her caretaking period (*hadana*) during which she had the right to raise her children and maintain temporary custody. In addition, my interviews indicate that a Palestinian woman's children tended to be the most important part of her life in both the

Mandate past and present-day Palestine, and only in the most desperate of circumstances would she be willing to relinquish them. But compared to the other types of cases, the long-term outcome for women who succeeded in their custody disputes was also more ephemeral because the right to child custody would revert to the father when children reached the age of seven or nine during the Mandate era.

This emphasis on the child's age was a departure from Hanafi practices during the Ottoman period. Tucker demonstrates that Ottoman legal experts (muftis) and judges alike usually discussed child custody and decided lawsuits in terms of childhood stages, rather than ages. Upon the divorce or separation of a couple, or the father's death, they interpreted Hanafi law as giving a mother the right to raise her son from birth until he could perform basic functions by himself, such as feeding, dressing, and using the toilet.[2] For girls, the muftis and judges tied the end of the stage to the initiation of physical development, but legal discourse was silent as to why.[3] Perhaps the later end of a girl's stage with her mother was to prepare her for future marriage duties. Thus developmental ability and the beginning of adolescence were what marked the end of a mother's caretaking period for boys and girls, as opposed to age: "Indeed, numerical age was rarely mentioned at all in legal discussion or court session, with occasional reference to the Hanafi [age] rule."[4] Nevertheless, the body of Hanafi jurisprudence established the corresponding ages for these stages, and the end of a mother's custody, as seven years for boys and nine for girls. Hanafis did, however, allow an extension to nine years for boys and eleven for girls.[5] In contrast, Mandate-era judges interpreted Hanafi law less flexibly, considering the end of the mother's custody to be age seven for boys and nine for girls. Also, while Ottoman legal scholars were little concerned with children's ages, judges were very mindful of them in general, and court recorders nearly always stated the age of the child in years. Most significantly, Mandate judges based their decisions entirely on the child's age when there was any question concerning the child's proper custodian.

In other respects, Mandate-era judges tended to conform to classical Hanafi law, which highly privileged the father's custody rights over those of the mother. Hanafi law was often the least considerate of women among the four Sunni bodies of law, including the terms under which women could initiate divorce unilaterally, the inability of women to sue for back payments of maintenance, and the restricted duration of the mother's caretaking period. In contrast to Hanafi law, the Hanbali and Shafi'i schools allowed the child to choose with which parent she wished to live. Malikis permitted girls to live with their mothers until marriage, while boys stayed with the mother until puberty.[6] There is, however, a dearth of scholarship analyzing the extent to which these terms were applied prior to modern codifications of Muslim family law. It is important to note that while modern codes and reforms have made some important improvements concerning women's status, they have also tended to preserve male privileges, and in certain respects these male advantages can be exploited to a greater degree than was typical under the classical laws. In this chapter, we will examine to what extent child custody cases actually did correspond with Hanafi law in the context of Mandate Palestine.

The advantages for men in classical Hanafi law were particularly acute in child custody, and these advantages were amplified in the Mandate era. Because Mandate-era judges meticulously applied the end of mother's custody at ages seven and nine, narrowly interpreting what historically were more flexible stages in Hanafi law, there was little leeway for a mother to negotiate her position within the court system. This was the reality that women faced regardless of which party had initiated the divorce, without accounting for fault in the dissolution of the marriage, and with almost no consideration for the well-being of the child. One lawsuit suggests that even child abuse was not grounds for stripping the father of his right to child custody. In a 1936 Jerusalem case, a father demanded the return of his daughter, who was twelve years old. The mother said she was ready to bring the girl to the father, but she also asked the judge to listen to the girl. The daughter said her father had beaten her and harmed her emotionally, so she had gone to live with her mother. The judge, apparently unmoved by her statement, ordered the wife to give the girl to her father, presumably because she was older than nine years.[7]

Not only was the child's father privileged over the mother, but Hanafis also favored the paternal family over the mother of the child. In the event the father was unwilling or unable to maintain or care for his child, guardianship reverted to a member of his family. Also, if the mother remarried during her caretaking period, she immediately lost her short-term custody rights unless the marriage was to a paternal relative of the child. While the paternal extended family was clearly privileged over the maternal, the mother's family did have precedence in custody during the mother's period of caretaking; this was also true in the event the mother was deceased or otherwise unable to care for her child. In these circumstances, the court gave the child to her maternal grandmother for the duration of the mother's caretaking period. In general, classical Hanafi law gave priority to female relatives on the mother's side over women on the father's side during the mother's caretaking period.[8] Despite the gender inequalities entrenched in Hanafi child custody doctrine, the 1917 Ottoman family code failed to improve women's custody rights. Clearly, the architects of the new family code were reluctant to challenge the patriarchal basis for the father's ultimate guardianship of his children.

But one should not conclude that mothers had no rights concerning the raising of their children. Also, we will also see how women came up with strategic approaches to make the best of an uneven playing field. As mentioned, classical Hanafi law expected a girl to live with her mother until she reached her physical development, at approximately age nine. Tucker shows, however, that once a girl reached her legal majority, evidenced by being physically and mentally mature, she could choose any "trustworthy relative" with whom to live; of course a boy of the same legal status could choose with whom he lived as well.[9] Also, Tucker demonstrates that a widowed mother could obtain guardianship of her children if her husband had designated her as guardian before his death or if a judge appointed her as one.[10] But it must have been a rather uncommon occurrence because the Chief Islamic Justice was required to approve a local judge's appointment of a mother as guardian.[11]

The rationale for the father's preferential status in child custody comes down to his role as the provider and protector of the family. Thus, the father, and the paternal family, is further constructed as the natural guardian of his children. As we saw in the chapter on maintenance, a husband's privileged status in marriage came with compulsory responsibilities to provide for his wife and his family. Likewise, the husband's privileged status in husband-initiated divorce (*talaq*) was accompanied by the requirements to give his former wife the remainder of the dower and to provide main-tenance during her waiting period. In much the same way, the father had financial obligations that came with his preferential position in child cus-tody law. As the ultimate guardian of the child, the father was responsible for monthly child support payments while the child was in her mother's custody (also termed *nafaqa*), as well as nursing (*rada'a*) payments if the child was under two years old or until she was weaned.[12]

What Is the Typical Format of a Child Custody Case?

The child custody cases surveyed here are considerably more diverse than the maintenance and wife-initiated divorce lawsuits that we have seen in previous chapters. Beyond the process by which the two parties came to an agreement if there was a child support payment to determine, the court recorders adhered to far less formulaic structures in the majority of child custody disputes compared to other types of cases, especially divorce.[13] This was probably because of the great amount of variation among the proceedings, with the exception that female plaintiffs usually had a com-mon goal of extending the caretaking period so they could continue liv-ing with their children. For male defendants, the objective was typically to keep the children living with them, as we will see in the next section on contesting ages. Beyond these general aims, many disputes involved a mother asking for child support payments during her caretaking period. Also, all the mothers in these lawsuits sought the return of their children, with the exception of a few cases involving divorce. Their requests were in response to the husband having taken his child while she was in the mother's rightful care.

Why was it so common for the father to take his children during the mother's caretaking period, and why did the mother's family allow this to happen? Granqvist's ethnographic work on family life in a Palestinian vil-lage in the late 1920s suggests that, in practice, society expected divorced women to return their children to their fathers after weaning, thus disre-garding both classical Hanafi- and Mandate-era court interpretations of the mother's caretaking period.[14] This considerable disjuncture between social practice and family law could well explain why fathers found themselves summoned to court for this reason. Of course, as we saw in chapter 1, there were other respects in which social practice and the law were inconsistent, such as a woman's right to live apart from her in-laws per the Ottoman code of 1917. I found no records in which women demanded this right in court, whereas many women demanded their children during their caretaking periods. This suggests that Palestinian women were quite willing to breach social expectations in order to be with their children, even if doing so only extended their caretaking period for another year or two.

Some disputes also involved a female plaintiff's request for maintenance for herself during the waiting period in the event of a husband-initiated divorce, and occasionally a divorcée demanded her deferred dower. Other lawsuits involved the wife's request for maintenance for herself in the event of a separation but without a divorce. The fact that a good deal of these child custody cases occurred within the context of marriage was an unexpected finding. The women who came to court in circumstances of a separation from their husbands while they were still married, however, still sought the same objectives as divorced women: they claimed their children and maintenance for themselves and their children. The outcomes in such disputes tended to be very similar to proceedings in which the couple was actually divorced. That is, judges tended to rule according to their interpretation of classical Hanafi ages for the mother's caretaking period: from birth to age seven for boys and birth to age nine for girls.

While there was little format to which court recorders conformed in summarizing child custody cases, the following 1934 proceeding was more straightforward than most. This lawsuit involved a divorced couple from at-Tirah, a village near Ramallah. The mother and plaintiff, Khadijah, told the court that her former husband, Hassan, had divorced her once, and he had taken their three-year-old daughter, Latifa, from her. Khadijah told the judge that she had the right to care for her daughter and that Latifa was within the age of the mother's custody period. Thus, Khadijah asked the judge to make Hassan return her daughter. Hassan confirmed all of her statements but he claimed Latifa was five years old instead of three years. The judge ordered Hassan to return their daughter to Khadijah and explained that she had the right to ask for maintenance for Latifa after she received her daughter. The judge also ordered Hassan to pay all the court costs.[15] Since Khadijah and Hassan's daughter was well within the age of the mother's caretaking period, despite their disagreement on her age, there was very little that Hassan could challenge.

Contesting the Child's Age

Khadijah and Hassan's case points to a reoccurring theme in many of the child custody proceedings, that is, a dispute over the age of the child. The spouses disagreed on the child's age in fourteen out of forty-three proceedings, a third of the child custody and child support lawsuits examined. It happened in a variety of types of custody cases ranging from 1928 until 1939, and thus it was a common feature of child custody disputes during this period. Disagreements on the child's age also occurred in a number of child support proceedings in which there was no legal argument over custody. Interestingly, not a single parent produced a birth certificate as evidence in any lawsuit with a disagreement over the child's age, suggesting that the Mandate government's efforts to enforce birth registrations were rather ineffective. Also, the uncertainty about people's ages in general, discussed in chapter 1, must have amplified the tendency for parents to disagree on their child's age when the right to child custody hinged upon it.

We can most likely assume that the discrepancy in ages reflected each parent's desire to retain his or her custody for a longer period. Even in cases that were exclusively about child support, parents would have been mindful that their statements, including the child's age, would be on record and could thus be consulted in the event of a later custody dispute. In lawsuits involving a disagreement concerning the child's age, the mother consistently said the child was one to four years younger than the father claimed. It is quite reasonable that the mother would favor a younger age than the child's father since Mandate-era judges interpreted the end of the mother's custody as nine years for a daughter and seven for a son. There was one exception to this trend in a 1928 custody dispute from Bab Hata, a Jerusalem neighborhood, in which the child's paternal uncle claimed the boy of his deceased brother was eleven, and the mother told the court her son was fourteen.[16] But the mother's motivation for her son to be older was very likely the same as the mothers in the other cases. That is, the mother's objective was to extend the period during which her son could live with her, but after he was a legal adult. Because the son was well beyond the mother's caretaking period, she must have wanted her son to reach his legal majority more quickly. Upon the end of the paternal family's legal guardianship of the son, the mother was probably hoping that her son would choose to live with her. Once a father's guardianship, or that of the paternal family, had ended, his son was a legal adult; he could contract his own marriage and transact property as an adult, and he could decide with whom he wished to live.[17]

The same argument can be made for the father and the father's family, in that the father also wished to increase the time during which the child lived with him. It is possible that some portion, if not all, of these age-dispute cases were those in which the father was disingenuous about the age of his child. It seems more probable, however, that it was either the mother who made the most use of this device because of her disadvantaged position, or that both parents were stretching the truth a bit in hope of gaining an advantage in the custody struggle. There is a financial incentive on the part of both parents as well: for the father, to stop or avoid paying child support; and for the mother, to begin or continue receiving those payments. This motivation seems to be more of an incentive for the father, since the collection of child support payments could have been problematic for the mother. Nevertheless, in an era where much of the population resisted the British demand for registering births, it would have been difficult to prove who was right. And because judges determined a child's age only when it was necessary, we cannot establish whether the judge tended to believe the mother or the father more frequently. Even in lawsuits that did hinge on the child's age, and there was a dispute over it, it is not usually clear why the judge made his ruling. But in a few proceedings we can discern some factors that emerged; this possibly alludes to how the court tended to tilt in custody disputes. For example, in the record below, it was necessary for the judge to determine the child's age in order to decide the case, and he ruled in accordance with the mother's statement. One should note that the mother also swore on the Qur'an while the father provided no such validation for his testimony.[18] A person's willingness to swear on the Qur'an was taken very seriously, and it was particularly effective when the other party was unwilling to do so.

One of the most common types of child custody cases were those in which the father had taken the children from the mother while they were within her caretaking period. The mother then came to court to request the return of her children as well as maintenance payments for them. Another frequent characteristic of the custody disputes was that some aspect of the mother's caretaking period was negotiated in the context of divorce, which was often wife-initiated.

The following 1932 case of a couple from Malha is similar in both of these respects, but it is unique in that it ended in an irrevocable husband-initiated divorce. Sabiha, the plaintiff, began the proceedings by stating to the court: "This man is my husband, Muhammad, we have a proper marriage contract, and we have consummated the marriage. We have three children: Na'ma is ten, Fatima is seven, and Hussein is five years old. My husband left us without maintenance and without someone to provide it, and then he took my children from me."[19] Sabiha asked for the return of her kids, child support, and maintenance for herself. Then her husband, Muhammad, announced to the court "I divorce her" three times. Muhammad also claimed the children were fourteen, eleven, and seven, and accordingly he asked the court to cancel Sabiha's request for their custody. Sabiha said Muhammad needed to pay maintenance during her waiting period, maintenance for the kids, and to return Fatima and Hussein because they were within her caretaking period. The judge asked Muhammad to prove their ages, but he could not. Sabiha swore on the Qur'an in order to validate the ages she stated for Fatima and Hussein. The judge ruled in accordance with Sabiha's statement, presumably because she was willing to swear that she was correct, and Muhammad was not willing to do so. The respected elders from their community assessed the amount of maintenance at 30 mils per day for Sabiha, 15 mils per day for Fatima, and the same amount for Hussein. The judge also gave Sabiha permission to borrow the monthly payment in her husband's name if he failed to pay, and he ordered Muhammad to provide a house for them and to pay the court costs.[20] Sabiha therefore received custody of two of her children, full maintenance for herself during her waiting period, and child support for her kids. The judge was forced to determine the ages of both Fatima and Hussein because the question of child custody hinged on this point; the children's ages determined whether they were to live under the mother's provisional custody or the father's permanent custody. The ruling indicates the judge's decision was based upon the fact that Sabiha swore her statement was true, as well as Muhammad's lack of validation for his claim, but there may have been unrecorded factors involved as well.

As in the lawsuit above, many other custody cases involving the mother requesting the return of her child also took place in the context of marriage, or at least they began with a marriage. The outcome of these custody disputes was the same: the mother gained temporary child custody for the duration of her caretaking period. This is not to suggest that women always won custody disputes; rather, it indicates that judges adhered to classical Hanafi custody ages. Most of the proceedings in which the father had taken the kids from the mother were far more straightforward than the first one between Sabiha and Muhammad discussed above, regardless of whether the couple was still married or if they had divorced. We will see that in cases in which the divorce was wife-initiated, there were considerably more complications because the mother often needed to negotiate some of her rights to obtain the divorce.

Negotiating Mothers' Caretaking Rights

The child custody disputes we have examined up to this point are those in which the mother's primary goal was clearly to gain custody of her children, and her secondary motivations were based on securing child support. The mothers in the next set of disputes had the same aims, but they faced a more complicated situation because they also sought a wife-initiated divorce. As soon as a woman also tried to obtain a divorce, many of her rights connected to child custody tended to become bargaining chips. That is, she had to relinquish many of her rights to persuade her husband to consent to the divorce. These rights that were now up for negotiation could include child support, nursing costs, educational expenses, and sometimes even the right to care for her child. But sometimes women were proficient negotiators and were able to retain many, and occasionally all, of their rights.

An example of a skilled negotiator emerges in the following 1932 wife-initiated divorce case involving a couple from Jerusalem. The plaintiff,

Amna, was able to acquire an irrevocable divorce and retain her child care-taking rights while relinquishing only her divorce rights, which she would have had to give up anyway. As was standard in wife-initiated divorce, Amna stated to the court that she was giving up her rights before and after the divorce, which included maintenance during her waiting period and the deferred dower. Also, she told her husband, 'Arif, that she promised to educate his four-year-old son, Hussein, with her own finances until the end of her caretaking period (at age seven). But Amna did ask for child support for her son. Then 'Arif said, three times, "Immediately, you are divorced," and he offered her maintenance for their son at 15 mils per day, to which Amna agreed. The judge consulted respected elders from their neighbor-hood to see if this amount was sufficient, and they confirmed that it was. The judge explained to them that they had an irrevocable divorce and ordered 'Arif to pay maintenance for his son.[21]

The judge seemed to have been looking out for Amna, because he ordered the community elders to check the maintenance sum for the son even though she had agreed to her husband's proposed sum. Also, it is significant that Amna was able to obtain an irrevocable divorce without losing custody of her child or child support. Unless the husband agrees to make it irrevocable, wife-initiated divorces are revocable divorces in which the couple may reconcile during the wife's waiting period. It is not clear if Amna convinced her husband to make the divorce an irrevocable one or if he did so on his own accord. Nevertheless, considering that women were not always able to initiate divorce while maintaining child support for their kids, or even caretaking rights in some circumstances, Amna did very well. Furthermore, the only concession she made to obtain this divorce was offering to finance her son's education for a few years; he was already age four and her custody would end at age seven. Amna was likely to edu-cate her son if her husband was unwilling to do so anyway. Unfortunately, the court summaries are silent as to the reasons why men agreed to allow their former wives to retain their rights in custody disputes like this one. A probable reason was that the husband was concerned about the well-being of his children. Or perhaps he was thinking about the potential social and economic consequences if the wife was from a prominent family. Of course, there would have been a number of overlapping reasons and motivations that varied by each case.

Women used a range of other strategies as well, as the following divorce-custody lawsuit illustrates. The plaintiff in the proceedings asserted her husband had divorced her while the husband initially denied it. In addition, the wife evidently decided it was worth sacrificing the possibility of one more year with her son in exchange for a husband-initiated, irrevocable divorce. The 1934 case, involving a couple from the village of Bira, began with the plaintiff, Halima, telling the judge that her six-year-old child, Hassan, was in her husband's house. She also claimed that her husband, Salman, had divorced her three times. Halima asked the court to assess maintenance during her waiting period and for the return of her son. Salman said that he had their son, but Hassan was eight years old and there had been no divorce. The judge asked Halima to prove the divorce but she had no witnesses. Then the two sides agreed that he had divorced her three times, and Salman offered Halima three Palestinian pounds for the entire waiting period. Halima accepted the amount of maintenance, asked the court for a commitment (*ilzam*) for it, and said she would give up short-term custody of her son in return for the divorce. The judge explained to the couple that they had concluded an irrevocable divorce, and he dismissed her request for child custody.[22] Had Halima decided to demand custody of her son without negotiating a divorce, she would have had a year with her son at best, and only if the court had ruled according to Halima's account of her son's age. Given this situation, it is quite reasonable that she bargained her right to caretaking as leverage to gain a major divorce. More importantly, she got her husband to admit that he had initiated the divorce, so she was able to retain her financial divorce rights. Finally, securing an official record of the divorce would later enable Halima to claim her deferred dower if Salman refused to pay it.

Women were able to use some of their rights as bargaining chips to convince their husbands to divorce in other cases as well. As we saw in Halima's custody dispute above and in the wife-initiated divorce chapter, sometimes it would be in the form of the actual custody of the child. But in other situations, women were able to maintain custody while relinquishing child support, usually in conjunction with another child-related payment, such as nursing. For example, in the following 1934 case involving a divorced couple from Jerusalem, the husband agreed to his wife's proposal of her giving up maintenance payments and child support, in return for (provisional) custody of her son and an irrevocable divorce. It is interesting that the wife, Bahia, actually tried to obtain a great deal more than custody and the divorce when she first appeared in court, despite a prior agreement with her husband, Ibrahim. Bahia also asked for maintenance for herself and her child, as well as her deferred dower, but Ibrahim told the court her waiting period had finished and that Bahia had offered to give up child support in exchange for custody and a major divorce. Bahia admitted as much and the court cancelled her request for maintenance and the deferred dower.[23] Despite the unusual aspect of Bahia attempting to contravene her agreement, the case represents a somewhat common phenomenon. In a handful of other wife-initiated divorce records the mother also gave up child support payments as a means of retaining custody. But as we saw in Amna's lawsuit, some women were able to initiate divorce while retaining child support for their children.

Rather than negotiating rights, other women took a different approach in attempting to stay with their children. In a handful of proceedings, the female plaintiff requested the return of her children and maintenance and denied that her husband had divorced her. In all of these cases the child was beyond the age range of the mother's temporary custody, and we can probably deduce the woman resorted to such ends precisely for that reason. In a 1934 lawsuit concerning a couple from 'Anata, Hamda, the claimant and child's mother, said her husband, Abd al-Ghani, had left her without maintenance and had taken their daughter, Fatima, from her. Hamda said Fatima was within the age of the mother's caretaking period, and she asked the court for her daughter and maintenance. Abd al-Ghani confirmed that their daughter was living with him, but said Fatima was ten years old and he had divorced Hamda three times. Hamda denied that Abd al-Ghani had divorced her, but she confirmed that Fatima was over the age of the mother's custody and accepted his proposed amount of maintenance during her waiting period. The judge explained it was an irrevocable divorce and refused her request for child custody. He did order Abd al-Ghani to pay the court fees, however.[24] Hamda's denial of the divorce very likely indicates that her first priority was to be with her child. Because Fatima was over the age of the mother's caretaking period, remaining in the marriage was the only way Hamda could have stayed with Fatima. This case points to the cruelest reality of divorce and child custody in Hanafi law; even when the woman did not wish to divorce, or was willing to stay in the marriage for her child, she was still denied permanent child custody if her husband decided to divorce.

Most of the child custody disputes examined above demonstrate the range of ways in which women could use their custody rights to negotiate the terms of their divorces or as leverage in convincing their husbands to agree to a divorce. Amna's case shows that sometimes a woman was able to secure relatively good terms for her divorce because she only had to give up her financial divorce rights, which nearly always happened in a wife-initiated divorce anyway. For Halima, it made sense to give up custody in order to secure her divorce because her son was nearly beyond the mother's caretaking period. Bahia's case represents a more common trend of women giving up child support rights as bargaining chips to maintain temporary custody and to obtain their divorces. And Hamda's situation particularly shows the harsh implications of the rigid age categories in Mandate-era judges' application of Hanafi law; because her child was over the mother's caretaking age, she tried to deny the divorce so she could stay with her child.

Privileging the Paternal Family

The child custody cases we have examined demonstrate how the shari'a court was intimately involved in maintaining the privileged child custody and guardianship rights of the men who found themselves involved in custody disputes. As Tucker explains, there is a critical distinction between child custody and guardianship, which is very much a gendered difference.[25] The custody of a child could be held by the mother or the father, but it was only a short-term period for the mother. We have seen how the Jerusalem court decided to grant custody in this period primarily depended upon the age of the child. Guardianship, however, was a right almost exclusively reserved for the father and, in his absence, the paternal side of the family. A woman could only hold the position if her husband designated her as his child's guardian; Tucker shows this occasionally happened on a man's deathbed during the Ottoman period.[26] The court system was most concerned about protecting the custody and guardianship rights of the paternal side of the family as a whole, rather than merely the father's rights.

The systemic interest in upholding paternal privilege is apparent in the way that judges were particularly meticulous in upholding Hanafi child custody law when the mother had remarried during her caretaking period. For example, in the following 1930 case involving a mother and the paternal grandmother from Jerusalem, the judge comes across as unduly inflexible. This was in spite of the paternal family's willingness to compromise, presumably out of concern for the interest of the child. Rashida, the child's paternal grandmother, came to court because her son, the child's father, had died six months before. Rashida told the court her family had been paying maintenance for the small child, who was in the custody of her mother, Safia.[27] Rashida asked the court to end her family's child support payments and to give her the girl because Safia had recently remarried. Safia explained that she had married a man from Lifta and she requested that the court allow her to keep her little daughter for two more years without any child support. Rashida agreed to extend Safia's custody for an additional two years as long as her family did not have to pay maintenance. The judge ruled the girl must go to her grandmother; Safia's custody was not an option because she had remarried.[28] This indifference to the best interests of the child is rather surprising, and it seems we can attribute this harsh attitude to the court's ardent desire to safeguard the father's family's privileged status in child custody. The court was determined to preserve the paternal family's position as providing the only legitimate space for children to ultimately belong. This was despite the willingness of the father's family to compromise, which likely was in consideration for the welfare of the child.

This concept of family guardianship of the minor, far from being the exclusive responsibility of the parents, also extended to the maternal family during the mother's caretaking period. In the following 1935 case involving a maternal grandmother and a child's father from Jerusalem, we begin with almost the reverse setting as in the proceedings above. The maternal grandmother, Latifa, came to court seeking the custody of her grandchildren, who were ages four, six, and one. She also sought financial support so she could take care of them. Latifa's daughter, Ne'mty, had had custody of her three children, but after she died the children's father, Judat, took them from her, and he had since remarried. The judge ordered the father to bring the children to their grandmother, and he explained to Latifa that she could ask for maintenance for the children after they were returned to her.[29] Even though the father of the children had found a new wife who could presumably raise his children, the judge ruled in favor of the children's maternal grandmother. The apparent reason for his decision was because of the children's ages, which were all within range of the mother's caretaking period.

Female Plaintiffs with Lawyers

Just as we saw in the maintenance claims, women who had the means to hire a lawyer were often at a distinct advantage in child custody cases in comparison with women who could not afford a legal representative. For uncomplicated custody disputes in which the father had taken the child while she was in her mother's care, women had little or no need for a lawyer. For more complex lawsuits, however, especially those involving divorce or marriage rights, an attorney was a great benefit for a woman appearing in court; this was true for both female claimants and defendants. The next set of cases illustrates the profoundly different experiences of women who appeared in court with legal representation. The outcomes of their proceedings are particularly distinctive in contrast to otherwise similar lawsuits that we have seen in which women were not accompanied by lawyers.

In a 1932 case involving a divorced couple from Jerusalem, Yusuf, the father, stated to the court that he had been paying maintenance of 40 mils for his wife and 30 mils in total for his two daughters. Yusuf had come to court in order to end the maintenance payments for his former wife, Wafia, because her waiting period was over. Wafia's lawyer told the judge the amount of support for the girls was not sufficient because of expensive living costs and nursing costs. He added that Yusuf still owed Wafia 10 pounds for her deferred dower but she had received all of her maintenance. Yusuf replied that he was ready to pay the dower in payments, but he did not agree with increasing the amount of support for the girls. The judge asked respected men from their community to assess maintenance. They decided on 75 mils total, which included both of the girls' expenses, and they said Yusuf could afford this amount. The judge ordered Yusuf to pay this amount and the 10 pounds he owed Wafia for her dower. The judge also ordered Yusuf to pay the court costs and Wafia's lawyer's fees.[30] It was clearly an advantage for Wafia to employ a lawyer, because she was able to get more than double the maintenance for her children, from 30 mils to 75, and the remainder of her deferred dower. Yusuf also had to pay for both parties' court fees and Wafia's lawyer's expenses. While Wafia may have been able to gain some of these benefits without a lawyer representing her, this case is unusual in regard to the tremendous increase in maintenance for the children. The fact Wafia had a lawyer likely contributed to her success, which was a trend we saw with maintenance claims in chapter 2 as well.

The next case demonstrates the advantages to employing a lawyer to an even greater extent. It is a 1932 lawsuit involving a married but separated couple from 'Arab al-Mas'udi, a village near Nablus. The mother and claimant, Hamida, told the court that her husband, Hawash, had taken her three-year-old son and forced her to leave, leaving her without maintenance, clothing, and a house. Hamida asked the court for her son and maintenance. Her husband said he would give her the boy if she returned to him, and he claimed he had a proper house.[31] The judge asked the court in Nablus to check the house, and in the next session Hamida sent a lawyer to represent her. Her lawyer said the defendant did not have a proper house and he asked for the boy and maintenance and for Hawash to pay all of Hamida's court and lawyer's fees. The court ordered Hawash to return the child and to pay 25 mils per day for him.[32] This is very significant because it is the only court record in this entire study in which the judge had the house checked and it was found to be noncompliant with *shari'a*. It could be a coincidence that it also was one of the few lawsuits with a lawyer representing the winning side. Lawyers won nearly all the cases with which they were involved in my study, however, suggesting that it was a considerable advantage for any woman appearing in court to hire legal representation.

The Significance of Social Practice

While we should not dismiss the importance of judges' application of child custody law, we also should avoid overestimating the extent to which Palestinian Muslim society adhered to the dictates of the law. Perhaps the most significant way in which rural Palestinians disregarded Hanafi law was, as previously explained, how they expected children to return to the father upon weaning, rather than according to either classical stages or ages.[33] Also, the following 1934 custody dispute between a widow and her stepson well illustrates how Muslim family law could only be enforced to the degree that the community actually conformed to it. It also echoes the theme that once a divorced or widowed woman had remarried outside the child's paternal family, her child went to the custody of her former husband's family. This dispute over the custody of a ten-year-old girl was between Halima, the girl's mother and a widow, and Khalil, who was her stepson and the plaintiff. Khalil demanded the custody of the girl for his family after Halima remarried because she had married a "stranger."[34] The judge ruled in favor of the girl's half-brother and ordered Halima to bring her daughter to Khalil.[35] This case shows that even a half-brother had more claim to the permanent custody of a child than a girl's own mother who had remarried. In addition to the great extent of the paternal family's rights, this custody dispute also illustrates the circumstances under which some Palestinians were most likely to adhere to Hanafi custody law. It is very interesting that the paternal family allowed Halima to maintain custody of her ten-year-old daughter for at least a year past the mother's caretaking period, even though they had the right to demand the girl since her ninth birthday. It was only when Halima remarried that her deceased husband's family decided to claim custody of the girl, suggesting that the paternal family was more likely to adhere to custody law when the child's mother had remarried. For this family, it was unacceptable for a so-called stranger to raise a child who belonged to them.

Conclusion

The child custody cases examined here well demonstrate the patriarchal nature of the law, yet the court consistently upheld a mother's right to child custody during the mother's caretaking period. In every child custody dispute examined, women were granted provisional child custody so long as the child was within the classical Hanafi age range of the mother's caretaking period. This may seem trivial in and of itself in comparison to men's greater privileges in child custody, but the court also supported women's caretaking rights regardless if she was performing her wifely obligations. In addition, we have seen that the court enforced both the father's preferential status in custody law and his burden of providing for his children while they were in the mother's care. Thus the *shari'a* court structure attempted to protect divorced or widowed women and their children from impoverishment to some extent. Unless the mother had relinquished this right to obtain a divorce from her husband, the child's father was responsible for paying child support during the mother's caretaking period. It is also worth noting that judges appeared to treat girls and boys with few distinctions, apart from the age differences determining the end of the mother's custody.

The proceedings we have examined in this chapter also illustrate that Mandate-era judges consistently adhered to their narrow interpretation of classical Hanafi law, using the child's age to determine the end of the mother's custody period. But the deciding role of the child's age in custody disputes quite frequently led to disagreements between the child's parents regarding her age. Thus this strategy was used by both women and men. We can likely assume that the main reason for such disagreements, as well as the objective of the parents in such custody disputes, was to prolong each parent's period of time with her or his child. There often must have been other incentives as well. A father would likely wish to end child support payments and a mother sometimes sought a divorce, which frequently involved negotiating child support or even child custody rights to get her husband's consent. Beyond the principal aim of extending one's time with one's child, the cases examined in this chapter were overall quite diverse and contained many variables.

The child custody disputes analyzed also demonstrate aspects of transformation from the Ottoman period to the Mandate period. In particular, Mandate judges' strict adherence to the child's age in deciding custody cases was a remarkable departure from the Ottoman period. During the Ottoman era it was unusual for judges to reference the child's age in custody rulings; rather, they favored childhood stages based on developmental abilities and appearance. Jerusalem judges were, however, sometimes lenient about the age constraints in custody disputes that took place within the context of marriage and strictly dealt with child support. There were a handful of lawsuits in this study in which the judge allowed children who were older than the mother's caretaking age to remain with their mother as long as the father did not request their return. It is possible that these judges did not always rely on the classical Hanafi age as their standard for the onset of puberty for girls, or that some judges took a case-by-case approach. But the most likely explanation is that, in the event the father did not request the children, judges did not feel compelled to order their return to him while the marriage was still technically intact. It is also possible that judges may have taken special circumstances into consideration when they deemed it necessary, even if those considerations rarely appeared in the court summaries. But what of women's perspectives on how judges and the court systems deal with matters of maintenance, wife-initiated divorce, and child custody today? We will examine these topics, as well as considerations for using oral sources, information about the interviewees, and the issues they brought up, in the following chapter.

5

A Muslim Woman Is Free

Further Insights from Interviewees

Considerations for Using Oral Sources

Before discussing the views of and insights from my senior interviewees, we will address methodological issues in using oral sources. Any document-based research will have its silences, and *shari'a* court records especially contain numerous gaps for historians; many times the court proceedings will raise more questions than they answer. In addition, the court documents that I analyzed contain the court recorder's summary of each case or sometimes a series of cases. The maintenance and wife-initiated divorce lawsuits in particular largely adhere to a fill-in-the-blank type of format, and they do not appear to include many of the participants' exact statements. There is, however, a good deal more variation and detail in the child custody and maintenance lawsuits than in the wife-initiated divorce proceedings.

Consequently, it was useful to conduct interviews with Palestinian women who had memories of the late Mandate period, and I used my findings from these interviews to inform my research of the court registers. I also interviewed two much younger divorcées to get a sense of how women experience the court system today. All of these interviews were valuable for discerning how Palestinian women think and feel about Muslim family law, *shari'a* court judges, and their legal status today and in the past. Of course, perceptions and feelings change over time; but given the silences in the historical sources, interviews are often the only means of gleaning insights into how nonelite Palestinian women may have felt about certain issues. Rosemary Sayigh points to another advantage of using interviews: Palestinians can be less reticent when discussing sensitive topics compared to authors writing their own memories or histories.[1] For example, Rochelle Davis discusses a number of conspicuous omissions, or in some instances glossed-over facts, on matters such as poverty, disease, and class in the written Palestinian histories of pre-1948 villages she examined.[2] I would imagine that such silences are also found regarding certain family law topics as well, particularly divorce. Finally, whenever possible, I have substantiated my tentative findings gained in the interviews with other sources, as seen in chapter 3.

When employing oral history, it is necessary to keep in mind a number of potential variables that could influence the interviewee's responses, as well as any personal and external factors that could influence the interviewer's interpretation of their accounts. Stephan Miescher and his colleagues in *African Words, African Voices* discuss a number of these issues concerning oral history methodology, many of which informed my research. Among the most important are the power relationship between the interviewer and interviewee and the issue of subjectivity for both roles.[3] Regarding power relationships, I think being a woman and much younger than most of my interviewees helped offset any perceived power imbalance in my favor. In Palestinian society, older women are more esteemed and tend to hold more powerful positions in their families compared to younger women. The fact I am not Israeli was also an asset. Many of my interviewees probably conceptualize "Israeli" as synonymous with colonizer, which would have been a major hurdle to overcome. But because I am American, some of my interviewees may well have placed me in a similar category, that is, as a colonizer-enabler. I will discuss that possibility and its potential effect on the interviewees' responses shortly. As for subjectivity, I took a somewhat nontraditional approach, but one that is becoming more common in terms of measuring the subjectivity of the interviewee. Rather than trying to tease out which parts of each interview may be considered ostensibly "objective," I considered all the interviews to be inherently subjective.[4] Indeed, the interviewees said a great deal more about how they generally perceive, experience, and feel about Muslim family law and the *shari'a* court system than anything else; their responses also provided insight about the ways in which the court system and family law affect their lives and relationships.

Regarding the interviewer's own subjectivity, she must be self-aware of her own biases in an attempt to avoid the pitfalls of over-interpretation or misrepresentation. It is worth noting that subjectivity is an issue that must be considered in written histories as well. Indeed, Davis finds that authors of pre-Nakba Palestinian village histories tend to approach certain issues, such as folk religious practices and women's work, "through the lens of modern sensibilities and impose on history today's modern conventions."[5] In my case with interviews, I had to consciously try not to impose my anticolonial positions, my antioccupation politics, and my feminist agenda on my interpretations and my questions. Because all my interviewees share similar anticolonial views and oppose the occupation, overinterpretation in those respects was a nonissue. But feminism is an entirely different matter. Perhaps my most challenging undertaking in this project has been trying to balance my feminist worldviews with respect for other cultures, both of which include a healthy dose of pragmatism—after all, women must deal with the realities they face on the ground or in the courts. When one studies Muslim family law, it can be difficult not to feel outraged at the inherent gender inequality and systemic injustices in the male-privileged structure. Of course Muslim women, regardless of whether they self-identify as feminist, are also upset when they are subject to discrimination in family law. Indignation because of gender injustice, however, is not the equivalent of feminism. The main reason I avoided using the term "feminism" (*nisa'iya*) in my interviews is because of the hostility to men and to family life that it can unintentionally imply and the western imperialist constructs that it often carries in the Middle East. It is worth mentioning that all three outlooks—anticolonial, antioccupation, and feminist—did emerge, unprompted, in the interviewees' responses.

Also in regard to subjectivity, there were a number of considerations of which I had to be mindful. Many of these factors involved the interviewees' confidence and trust in my motives and abilities. First of all, I considered the interviewee's perception of me and how it may have affected her responses. Was she concerned that I may misunderstand or even misrepresent my sensitive topic of inquiry? This issue of the interviewees' trust in me was probably the greatest hurdle that I encountered, and I found the most effective way to resolve it was to use a trusted contact to initiate or help with the interviews.[6] Another possibility to consider was regarding the interviewee's confidence in my moral character, or lack thereof, which could add to or detract from her trust in my motivations and abilities. Did she assume I was a spoiled American who could not possibly understand the Palestinian-Muslim way of life? Even if she had been aware that I received a fellowship to complete my work, living abroad to conduct research may well have seemed an extravagant way to make a living. Margaret Strobel points to a number of obstacles that cultural misunderstandings can produce, but she also mentions that an "insider" actually may be more likely to confide in an "outsider" who is not subject to the same cultural taboos.[7] In a similar way, a Palestinian woman may have been more inclined to excuse an undesirable behavior on my part, such as doing research abroad alone for a year, as opposed to criticizing a local Palestinian woman for the same action.

But even if an interviewee saw me more as a genderless academic, and dismissed the yearlong abandonment of my husband as a western failing, she probably still viewed me as an American, with the distinct possibility of being a Jewish American. None of my interviewees asked me if I was Israeli or Jewish, as it would have been considered impolite for them to inquire, although I did resort to volunteering my Christian identity to an East Jerusalem community center so I could conduct interviews with the members of its senior ladies' club. The director clearly suspected that I was Israeli, Jewish, or both. I realized that she was not going to allow me to conduct interviews if the answer to either was yes, so I explained to her that I was an American Christian. Once this was cleared up, I was welcome to conduct interviews, and the employees at the center were very accommodating.

Another issue concerning the interviewees' trust is they may have been apprehensive about the possibility of my rehashing old stereotypes of Arab or Muslim women. Also, whatever perception a woman might have of me and my potential objectives, did she have a motivation, unconscious or conscious, to present a certain image of her national history as a Palestinian, a Muslim, or both? Did she have an inclination to depict the past in a more sanguine light to me than she would to a Palestinian? Did she want to emphasize how her community is worse off now, because it is under

Israeli occupation, and particularly because of to whom she was speaking? This is particularly relevant to me since I am American, given the unbalanced role of the United States in the conflict and peace efforts. It did not take me long to discover that politics are everywhere in Palestine, and I am sure my interviewees were very conscious of my nationality. This was especially true for interviewees whom I met at the East Jerusalem community center, because I did not have a trusted intermediary help me arrange the interviews. I did, however, have a female Palestinian friend accompany me during many of those interviews and I conducted them in Arabic; both aspects likely helped the question of my credibility.[8]

Then there was the question of an interviewee's religious identity and the possibility of her desire to impart a certain depiction of Muslim women in general and Palestinian Muslim women in particular. Did she hesitate to tell me about any injustices that Palestinian women may encounter in the *shari'a* court system because of a desire to challenge the rampant biases against Islam in the west? The question concerning the politics of American involvement in the conflict was probably an important factor for many women, but only a few of them brought it up. The concern regarding women's rights in Islam emerged far more frequently in the interviews. Two women in particular had a strong desire to defend Islam, as we will see.

In addition to these factors that may have influenced interviewees' responses, I quickly acquired an awareness of and sensitivity to women's reticence to speak about certain issues. Employing oral history as a non-Muslim American in Palestine is complicated enough when one is pursuing an innocuous topic; but when one is asking questions about a subject that is borderline taboo, the task becomes much more complex. Divorce is apparently one of those very nearly taboo topics in this context, or at least it often is when a Palestinian Muslim woman is speaking with someone outside her community. Not only did it make arranging the interviews more difficult once I mentioned the word "divorce," but most of the older women with whom I talked were not very outspoken about divorce. Many even seemed reticent to speak of women who had simply appeared in court; only some of the women said they even knew a woman who had gone to court. While it is possible that some of these women did not in fact know a woman who had gone to court, it seems rather unlikely. Tellingly, the

women who did state they knew someone who had been to court participated in contexts in which I had been able to have a trusted intermediary
arrange the interview. All of the women, however, were quite comfortable
talking about Muslim family law without reference to divorce or appearing
in court, and they were happy to answer questions about women's rights
and family law. Indeed, some of my interviewees very much enjoyed demonstrating their knowledge.

Another issue I kept in mind was the potential tendency of an interviewee to project her current understandings onto what she had actually
known as a young bride. I wanted to make this distinction because I asked
the women what they had known about their rights in Muslim family law
before marriage. I was trying to discern to what extent Palestinian Muslim
women were familiar with their rights before they would have an opportunity to take advantage of them at the critical juncture when the marriage
contract ('qad al-zawaj) is negotiated. I was especially interested in learning
whether or not any of the women's fathers had included conditions (shurut)
in their marriage contracts, or if they had known it was possible to do so.
I also sought to understand how their experiences in marriage and divorce
processes informed their perception of Muslim family law, shaped their
dealings within the court system, and influenced their family relationships.

I should also mention that there was to some extent a culture divide
regarding certain meanings and perceptions, because a few terms in my
questions proved to be somewhat problematic. For example, my interviewees seemed to interpret the word 'adi, which the standard Arabic-English
dictionary, defines as "usual, common, or ordinary," more along the lines
of "it happens" or "is not unheard of."[9] Context, while always important
in determining meaning, became very important to discern more precisely
what my interviewees meant to convey. Another difference in perception
that I encountered was when I asked interviewees whether they knew
about women's rights (huquq al-mar'a) in Muslim family law at the time of
their marriage. I had meant the whole range of women's rights, including
maintenance, dower, inheritance, the mother's caretaking rights in child
custody, and so on. But when I asked Layla about the rights of women,
her perception of these rights was quite reasonably limited to her personal
experience. What she considers her rights is what she received: the actual

gold, dresses, and household items that her parents had bought her with her dower money.[10] The rest of women's rights were irrelevant to her experience, because she never needed to go to court and demand maintenance, child custody, and so forth.

One last point I should note in terms of meanings and perceptions is in regard to periodization and my interviewees' likely lack of concern for it. Even though I explained to my interviewees that my research was on the British Mandate (*intidab britani*) period, their answers were contextualized more generally, as "in the past" (*min zaman*). Whereas I was initially concerned about examining processes in that period specifically, I rather doubt any of them distinguished the British era from the post-1948 period in their memories concerning family law or the courts because the Israelis largely preserved the existing family law systems intact. Muslim family law is also often perceived as being removed from the influence of secular governments. Likewise, it is difficult to overstate the influence of the national cause and the Israeli Occupation on peoples' memories of the past. As Ted Swedenburg notes, "What I found particularly remarkable about the memories of the old people I interviewed was the degree to which their sense of history was overdetermined by the current situation."[11]

The Ladies or the Interviewees

The women I interviewed came from a variety of backgrounds, in terms of class, occupation, place of birth, and where they reside today. The majority were in their mid-seventies when I interviewed them, which made most of them around the age of eighteen at the end of the British Mandate in 1948. Some were only in their sixties, however, and the only two divorced women with whom I was able to procure interviews were thirty and thirty-eight years old. Although I did not specifically ask the older women their age when they were married, some of them volunteered it. Sixteen was the average marriage age of the older ladies, but their ages varied to a considerable extent. For example, Hamda from al-Khalil (Hebron) was only fourteen, while Jehad, from a village near Haifa, was twenty-four years old. The average age of the older women when they were married was 17.6 years, and this reduces to 15.5 if we take out Jehad's exceptional age of 24 years. The younger women were fifteen and eighteen years old when they

Table 1. **Senior Women Interviewees' Personal Data**

Name	Year of Birth	Age in 2006	Place of Birth	Current Residence	Age Wed	Means of Contact
Haji Kowthar	1931	75	Wadi Joz (East Jerusalem)	Wadi Joz (East Jerusalem)	[?]	Aunt of my student
Ruwaida	1933	73	Homs (Syria)	East Jerusalem	[?]	Community center
Raghda	1931	75	East Jerusalem	East Jerusalem	[?]	Community center
Umm Khalid	1944	62	East Jerusalem	East Jerusalem	16	Community center
Layla	1946	60	Kharbatha Beniharis	Kharbatha Beniharis	[?]	Lutheran church network
Werda	1955	51	Kharbatha Beniharis	Kharbatha Beniharis	16 1/2	Lutheran church network
Hamda	ca. 1935	mid-70s	Al-Khalil (Hebron)	Old City (East Jerusalem)	14	Friend's relative
Suad	1932	74	Old City [?]	Old City	[?]	Friend's relative
Jehad	1942	64	'Abalin (village near Haifa)	'Abalin (village near Haifa)	24	Friend's relative
Bushra	1976	30	Al-Khalil (Hebron)	Beit Haninia	15	Friend's contact
Hekmat	1969	37	Gaza City	Ramallah	18	Auspicious meeting

married. These data are of a very limited scope, but they do demonstrate the wide range of experiences of Palestinian Muslim women.

As for place of birth, half of my older interviewees were born and raised in some part of Jerusalem, including Haji Kowthar, Raghda, Umm Khalid, and Suad. Ruwaida was born in Homs, Syria, and her family moved to Jerusalem when she was quite young. Hamda was born in al-Khalil, and she moved with her husband to Jerusalem. Layla and Werda were both born and still reside in Kharbatha Beniharis, a village near Ramallah in the Palestinian West Bank. Jehad is from I'billin, a well-off Muslim-Christian village near Haifa that Israel seized during the 1948 war. Hekmat and Bushra, the younger women who were profiled in chapter 3, were both born outside of Jerusalem. Hekmat was born and raised in a well-off family in Gaza City, but she now lives in Ramallah with her new husband. Bushra was born in al-Khalil; she had moved with her family to Jerusalem, but she was planning to move at the time of our interview. After she remarries, she and her children will move to Acre, where her fiancée resides.

Women's Rights, Respect, and Choice in Islam

I asked each interviewee a list of questions, some of which were open-ended and others more specific. Many interviewees spoke well beyond the topics raised by my questions. I welcomed extraneous stories, and made a point of asking each interviewee to add anything she wished to the interview. About half of the interviewees were quite determined to teach me about Islam's benevolent treatment of women and women's rights in Islam and *shari'a*, and they took advantage of the opportunity to educate me. When my interviewees mentioned a woman's rights in *shari'a*, they were mostly referring to women's rights in Muslim family law, such as the right to the dower, to receive maintenance, and so on.

It soon became clear, however, that the interviewees also conceptualized women's rights in more abstract terms. Several women emphasized that a major part of woman's rights in *shari'a* consists of the right to be respected and treated well by her husband. No one may use violence against her.[12] Jehad added that a woman can disagree with and fight with her husband.[13] During her interview, Ruwaida provided an interesting facet to the issue of domestic violence.[14] Before I asked her any questions, she asked me if she could tell me her story, and I was happy to hear it. At the end, Ruwaida said her father was a very good man and never used violence, and that he respected women.[15] While I am sure she was sincere, Ruwaida may have also wished to counter negative stereotypes about Muslims and Palestinians, or her statement may suggest that it was not unheard of for men to use violence against women. Or perhaps both speculations have some degree of truth.

Many interviewees very much wanted to convey to me that a woman's rights in *shari'a* give her independence, agency in her life choices, and everything a woman needs in her life. As soon as I mentioned women's rights in *shari'a*, Raghda was quick to tell me that "a [Muslim] woman is free," and she makes her own decisions. Accordingly, she has the choice to live with her parents or alone, a woman still gets her inheritance if she does not marry, a woman can get a divorce if she is not happy, and the "man is not better than the woman" in Islam.[16] Ruwaida also told me the Qur'an allows a woman to divorce and return to her family if she is not happy; if her family gives her a bad life (that is, if they find her a bad husband and will not help her get a divorce), she can go to court.[17] Other interviewees also made sure I was aware that women had the right to divorce in Islam. In addition, a few women mentioned the husband's responsibility to provide maintenance for his wife or face imprisonment.

Werda, who is obviously a devout Muslim, emphasized that everything women need is in the Qur'an, God cares for women, and Islam gives women all the rights she needs.[18] She went on to say no one can use violence against women, and that women have more rights in Islam than in other religions. Muslim women can even ask for help with the housework if the house is too big for her to handle on her own.[19] It was fascinating how some of the interviewees tended to personalize women's rights in *shari'a* in a way that addressed their own situations. Werda also explained that other people think Islam is a difficult religion, but in fact it is easy. For example, if a woman wants to go out, she must ask her husband for permission, and she must wear Islamic dress if he tells her to do so. Werda added that a woman cannot talk badly about her husband, but she does have a lot of rights.[20]

Some women discussed a woman's rights in *shari'a* in the context of a major condition: if she's right. Being "right" implies a woman is not "disobedient" (*nashiza*); that is, she obeys her husband and has done nothing wrong, so she will receive her rights. Interestingly, the interviewees' definition of being obedient was broader than jurists' historical conception of obedience. As discussed previously, jurists usually defined obedience as a woman living in the marital home, and this obligation was enforced only by linking it to her right to maintenance. Jehad gave the example that when a woman requests maintenance or her dower in court, she can take it if she is justified; if not, she feels shame and takes nothing.[21] Suad echoed this claim and told me a woman will take her rights in *shari'a* if she is right.[22] Likewise, Werda and Layla both stressed that if a woman is justified, the judge will give her what she requests.[23] In addition to educating me about advantages for women in Islam, Raghda pointed out men's privileged status in marriage: if the woman initiates the divorce, she cannot take anything and "the man can take her hair!"[24] Along similar lines, Ruwaida provided an anecdote to illustrate the lack of say that daughters and sons had in their marriages in the past. Ruwaida was betrothed when her father and uncle agreed to marry their two boys to their two girls, and the fathers only told the children when they gave them the rings.[25] She said they agreed because they could not do anything about it anyway, and they continued their simple life with her extended family. To end her story, Ruwaida said they broke the bed on their wedding night![26]

Contextualizing Women's Understandings of Muslim Family Law

The interviewees' knowledge about women's rights in Muslim family law, and their wishes to demonstrate it, likely reflect significant trends that have taken place during their lives, including the great expansion of girls' and women's access to education, the rise of Islamist movements in Palestine, and the activism of women's rights nongovernmental organizations. First we will consider girls' increased educational opportunities. During the Mandate period, Palestinian girls' access to education was very limited, especially in rural areas in which only 4 percent of girls attended school as of 1940.[27] Education has expanded a great deal, from 44.5 percent of Palestinian children attending primary school at the end of the Mandate period to nearly universal education in the early 1990s.[28] In 1993, Palestinians aged fifteen through nineteen had completed a mean of nine years of school.[29] Another indicator is the literacy rate, which was 97.1 percent for Palestinians aged fifteen through nineteen in 1995.[30]

Since 1948, most Palestinian refugees have attended schools funded and operated by the United Nations Relief and Works Agency for

Palestinian Refugees (UNRWA). Palestinians who are not refugees attend private or government schools, the latter of which represents the largest sector.[31] Jordanian authorities ran government schools in the West Bank and East Jerusalem from 1948 until 1967, while Egypt did so in Gaza. After 1967, all government schools came under Israel control. The Palestinian Authority took over this function for the West Bank and Gaza in 1994. As of 2000, UNRWA provided 31 percent of education for Palestinian children in the West Bank and Gaza overall, and over 50 percent of education in Gaza alone; only 8 percent of Palestinian students attended private schools.[32] Unfortunately, I did not ask about the level of education attained by my interviewees, with the exception of Jehad, but it is likely that few of the seniors received more than a primary education with the probable exception of Werda. In 1993, the mean number of completed school years for Palestinian females sixty and older was one year, which would apply to my interviewees who were in their seventies in 2006 (Haji Kowthar, Ruwaida, Raghda, Hamda, and Suad).[33] For those in their sixties in 2006 (Umm Khalid and Layla), the mean number of completed years was a little over two years in 1993; the mean was eight years for Werda, who was in her early fifties during the 2006 interview.[34] These statistics do not apply to Jehad, as she is a Palestinian citizen of Israel. Jehad attended her village primary school for six years. Also, it is probable that Suad and Hamda completed more school years than the one-year mean because their affluent homes indicate they are from elite families.

Second, the rise of Islamist groups, and particularly the activism of Islamist women, may have influenced my interviewees' knowledge of family law. Beginning in the mid-1970s, the West Bank and Gaza saw a revitalization of the Muslim Brotherhood, partly reflecting a wider expansion of Islamist movements in the region.[35] This was coupled with a rise in religiosity among Palestinians, which "increasingly manifest[ed] itself in the politicisation of Islam and the support for the Brotherhood and other Islamic organisations."[36] These changes have amplified since Hamas's emergence and popularity during the first intifada and has also affected gender constructs. In the 1990s, Palestinian women who had participated in the secular nationalist movement as university students were now veiling and becoming attracted to Hamas.[37] Many factors have contributed to Hamas's soaring popularity during and since the 1990s, including the failure of Oslo, corruption within the Palestinian Authority, and Hamas's ability to "reinvent [itself] as a nationalist movement."[38]

The most interesting aspect of Hamas's rise for our purposes is how its women members' activism has played a critical role in changing the group's positions on gender ideology, starting in the late 1990s. Previously, although women were active in Hamas's student blocs, the group's 1988 charter constructed the ideal Islamist woman as "dependent on men, confined to their homes, and segregated from public space."[39] Islah Jad analyzes Islamist women activists' conference papers from the late 1990s to show how they have changed Hamas's gender ideology to more progressive interpretations of Islam, including supporting women's public lives and activism "side by side with men," as one workshop booklet put it.[40] Similarly, Islamist women's views on women's rights in Muslim family law were progressive at these conferences, with numerous calls for new interpretations of the Qur'an and other religious texts. Their views were not uniform, however. At one workshop, many Hamas leaders, male and female, were skeptical about universal women's rights, while other attendees advocated banning polygamy outright (and others wished to restrict it).[41] Jad demonstrates that a major conclusion of these conferences was "women have to claim their rights," which my interviewee Jehad likewise articulated when discussing marriage contract stipulations (see discussion at the end of chapter 3). Jad also highlights a paper presented in which an Islamist woman argued that Islam "gives the woman all of her rights: education, free choice of a husband . . . and social or professional work."[42] These views were reflected in many of my interviews as well. Beyond family law, Hamas women demanded equal pay and even pressured their leaders to allow women's participation in armed resistance, which led to the establishment of the women's brigade (*Mojahidat al Qassamyat*) in 2005.[43]

The last relevant trend that may have affected my interviewees' views and knowledge is the proliferation of women's rights nongovernmental organizations in the Occupied Territories, such as the Women's Centre for Legal Aid and Counselling (WCLAC). Established in 1991, WCLAC has offices in Jerusalem, Ramallah, Hebron, and Bethlehem, and it receives financial support from many international organizations, including the

European Union, United Nations Development Project, and OXFAM.[44] The group's key roles are offering legal advice, representation in court, and counseling for Palestinian women in need.[45] WCLAC also works with community groups to organize workshops and information sessions promoting women's rights, including those in Muslim family law, for both men and women. In addition, the group provides pamphlets and other literature on a range of issues.[46] Finally, as mentioned, WCLAC is participating in efforts to create a unified Muslim family law code. WCLAC is only one of many women's and human rights groups that reach out to Palestinians and try to effect change in the Muslim family law system. It is very feasible that one or more of these organizations have influenced the women in my study or the women in their communities.

The Past: Better Women, Better Society, Better Occupation

Another common theme in my interviews, which came up completely unprompted, was the idea that Palestinian society was inherently better in the past than it is today for a variety of reasons. Of course, this sentiment comes up in many if not most ethnographic works on Palestinians, particularly those on refugees, as well as in Palestinians' own village histories.[47] Some women expressed that people were more genteel, religion was more important, and "people behaved better than they do today."[48] Haji Kowthar, who is from the East Jerusalem neighborhood of Wadi Joz, said women better cared for their families, wore the hijab more often, and knew more about *shari'a* than they do now. She summed it up well: "In the past, women were more Muslim."[49] Similarly, Ruwaida mentioned life was simple in the past and she lived with forty of her relatives in one house, which was a "beautiful life."[50] Finally, Umm Khalid also maintained that "the past was more beautiful than now," and she went on to mourn the state of society today. Now, she said, everyone prefers people who are rich, while in the past there were fewer class distinctions and most men were poor or middle class. Even judges were better in the past, she asserted.[51] But more than emphasizing the morally superior past, Umm Khalid stressed the ills of Palestinian society today.

First she attacked women: "Now too many girls marry and then divorce after three months because life is hard. And women go on trips, visits, and forget about their homes. People have changed, and God does not like people now because of usury and *zina* [sexual relations outside of marriage], both of which are *haram*!" (*Haram* means "forbidden"; she said this a lot, actually.)[52] Later on, her commentary became very political: "Life was very difficult under the British Mandate, there was no food, no help, and it was Occupation . . . now it is the Americans! God take them away! Life is very bad now and God watches it."[53] It is difficult to say if or to what extent Umm Khalid's remarks were directed at me. For example, the "women going on trips and forgetting about their homes" comment could well have been a reprimand, and the "God take away the Americans" plea could have been intended for me as well. Or perhaps she was just ranting and I was willing to listen. It is interesting that Haji Kowthar and Umm Khalid both expressed their comments concerning the better society of the past in a highly gendered context. Not only were they were more concerned about women's roles and behavior than men's, but they also seemed to consider these factors as the main indicators of their society's moral condition.

A Masculine Sphere

Many of the older women seemed to view Muslim family law as more of a male domain in that men were more likely than women to be knowledgeable about and familiar with it. In fact, at the community center where I interviewed several women who are part of an elderly ladies club, some of my interviewees suggested visiting a men's club because men know more about *shari'a*. But that is certainly not to say that women are ignorant about family law. Most of the interviewees knew a good deal about their legal rights and obligations; they seemed to know at least as much if not more than the average woman knows about family law issues in the west.

Many of my interviewees also did not think men have privileged status over women in Islam, and they insisted that "Islam gives women all their rights." And very interestingly, the men I interviewed echoed this sentiment of gender fairness in Islam, because they did not seem to consider the courts or family law to be biased in their favor. A few men argued that women actually have it much better, because a woman has the right to be supported throughout her life, and men are responsible for maintenance.[54] And despite men having legal advantages over women in many respects, in some cases the prestige of the woman's family in the community can favor the wife. That is, the status of a woman's family could empower her position in the relationship with her husband despite his privileged legal status, which would lessen the likelihood of her husband exploiting his legal advantages. Of course, if the husband's family is the more prominent one, this could work against the wife as well.

In regard to another common perception, all the women and men with whom I spoke had a very high regard for judges (*quda'*) and the *shariʿa* court system in general. When I asked about *shariʿa* court judges, all the elderly women and men had the utmost respect for them and offered only positive remarks. The interviewees often made the association of *shariʿa* as God's law, and every nonacademic (most of my interviewees) stated that judges were always fair to women. This is consistent with Shehada's finding that judges in Palestine today perceive themselves as "protecting weak members of society" and will interpret the law flexibly in order to do so.[55] The only exceptions to this sentiment came from the younger women divorcees, who were rather critical of judges. Hekmat felt that the judge in her case looked at her as if she were disobedient and kept trying to convince her to accept a revocable marriage. On the other hand, Bushra had much respect and appreciation for her (Muslim) judge in the Israeli system. She did not think that Jordanian judges represent women's interests, however, because she felt they were more concerned about preserving marriage and trying to impose arbitration.

Conclusion

In this chapter, we have examined some of the key challenges and considerations involved in using oral sources, as well as several specific challenges that I encountered during my interviews. The most relevant topics to my work that Miescher et al. mention on oral methodology include issues of power relationships and subjectivity. I have tried to be sensitive to these matters throughout my research; however, in terms of subjectivity I found it impossible to distinguish between what is objective or subjective in each interview. In addition, how the interviewees feel and think about Muslim family law today is more interesting to me than trying to determine what can be considered objective.

Regarding issues that complicated my own research, I found my status as an outsider, a non-Muslim, and an American influenced my interviewees' responses to many of my questions about Muslim family law. This was particularly the case for interviewees who had overt political and religious motivations driving their narratives. In addition to considering such factors in my interpretations of the interviewees' responses, I also had to be mindful of my own biases regarding my feminist and political views. That is, I had to be careful not to impose my preconceived notions, including feminist perspectives and antioccupation politics, on my interviewees' responses when such ideas where not present.

Many of my interviewees had their own agendas to push, one of which was the desire to educate me about women's status in Muslim family law. A number of my interviewees tried to convince me that Islam treats women kindly, apparently assuming that I held the opposite view, and some argued it is gender-equal. They were likely seeking to counter western stereotypes about Islam, Muslim women, and Muslim men. Some women also made an effort to convey their political views concerning Israel's occupation of Palestine, although this was less common than the attempts to enlighten me about Islam's treatment of women. Finally, while I was not surprised to find women insisting that Islam promotes gender fairness, I did not expect the handful of men I interviewed to adhere to this view even more strongly. My interviewees were also candid in discussing the injustices that women encounter in the current system, however, which suggests they would most likely be open to family law reform that is rooted in *shari'a* principles.

Conclusion

PALESTINIAN MUSLIM WOMEN did not have much choice but to use the *shari'a* court system under the British Mandate, particularly in the face of the challenges their community was facing. But they exploited the system to their own ends whenever possible, in effect pushing back against its patriarchal framework. Using innovative, and often gendered, strategies to negotiate their lawsuits, women tacitly accepted the male-dominated structure of the court while obtaining benefits from it, at least in successful claims.[1] One of the most common tactics that emerged in this study was women requesting maintenance as a way of broaching divorce. Perhaps the most innovative maneuver was women giving up child support as leverage to obtain their husband's consent to divorce, then requesting the support after the divorce. We have also seen how men had financial obligations that went along with their systemic privileges and how other factors, such as family prestige and influence, could shape the extent to which Palestinians adhered to Muslim family law.

The maintenance, wife-initiated divorce, and child custody court records from 1925 to 1939 that are analyzed here also demonstrate how the actions of the Mandate-period Jerusalem *Shari'a* Court reflected both transformation and continuity from the Ottoman era. In doing so, the court records confirm the reluctance of the British to institute Muslim family law reform, as well as Palestinians' resistance to change family law in the face of tremendous political upheaval beyond the realm of the court. Indeed, the different cases illustrate how the Jerusalem court tended to follow classical Hanafi law more than it observed the Ottoman family code of 1917. Another finding of this study was the circumstances under which women were most likely to succeed in court, which included employing a lawyer, having a cooperative husband, having children in her care, and the presence of a second wife. While the latter two situations affected maintenance claims uniquely, the former two applied to wife-initiated divorce and child custody proceedings as well. But the three types of court records diverged from one another regarding women's motivations for suing, the strategies they used to maneuver within the system, and to what degree a successful lawsuit could change a woman's life. Finally, in conjunction with interviews, the cases suggest in what respects women were informed of their rights in *shari'a*, and the ways in which women took advantage of them. Possessing this knowledge, along with the tenacity to use it, could have had profound implications for a woman's life. The interviews also give us an idea of how Palestinian women feel about Muslim family law and the *shari'a* court system today.

We have seen the theme of transformations from the Ottoman era to the Mandate-period Jerusalem court emerge in these cases in diverse ways. In chapter 2, we saw how judges adhered to a major shift regarding expectations about a wife's living conditions vis-à-vis her in-laws and a wife's right to receive maintenance. In Ottoman Palestine, a husband could compel his wife to live with her in-laws, but in the Mandate period, judges required husbands to provide separate living quarters for their wives per the Ottoman Law of Family Rights of 1917. If a husband failed to do so, the wife was entitled to collect maintenance payments. Regarding wife-initiated divorce, explored in chapter 3, a seeming break from the past was in the conceptualization of desertion. Compared to classical Hanafi law, which required a woman to wait ninety-nine years from her husband's birth before obtaining a unilateral divorce on these grounds, judges during the Mandate period were very reasonable. In every record where a woman sued for divorce on grounds of desertion, the judge granted her the divorce immediately, again per the 1917 Ottoman family code. But as Tucker shows, Ottoman-era judges did not follow classical law either, because they regularly assigned desertion cases to non-Hanafi judges who could grant dissolutions for desertion.[2] As for the mother's temporary caretaking period, chapter 4 showed that judges tended to rule with a narrower interpretation of classical law compared to Ottoman-period muftis' opinions and judges' rulings, but even in these lawsuits, there was room for women to maneuver somewhat.[3] In situations where a woman had not remarried and her former husband had not demanded his child, one who was older than the mother's custody age, judges often did not require the child to return to the father.

Despite these changes between the Ottoman and Mandate periods and the major upheaval that affected Palestinians' lives, there was overall more continuity in the Jerusalem court over the 1925–1939 period. We must consider two parties, both of whom could have instigated change, in deconstructing the reasons for continuity in the system: the British administrators of Palestine and the leaders of the Palestinian-Muslim community. It may be surprising that the British did so little to effect change when they interfered in Palestinians' lives in numerous other respects. But when it came to family law, British administrators were reluctant to involve themselves and instead allowed the various religious groups in Palestine to run their own affairs. The British were simply not interested in improving the legal status of colonized women, nor did they wish to cause more resentment among Palestinians.

As for Palestinian Muslims, the *shari'a* court system was the only institution that they were permitted to control under British rule. This had the effect of amplifying the importance of Muslim family law as a component of Palestinian-Muslim identity, and it came to represent a major part of Palestinians' cultural heritage as it remained untainted by colonial rule. Thus Palestinians had little motivation to reform family law under these conditions, and resisting change and interference in the *shari'a* system actually became a form of resistance. Beyond this, Palestinians were also far more concerned with challenging both British imperialism and Zionist settler colonialism than with reforming Muslim family law. Even the Palestinian women's movement that emerged in this period did not call for family law reform at this point because they too were most preoccupied with the national cause. Also, as I show elsewhere, new employment, education, and other prospects for socioeconomic mobility were not emerging for most Palestinian women, which compounded their natural inclination to support their indigenous but unequal legal system in a time of crisis.

But both the British and the Palestinians did have an important precedent that could have guided them. Had the courts of Palestine followed the Ottoman family code of 1917, this would have improved women's legal position in some respects, and it would have been a good starting point for further reform. My research, however, shows the Jerusalem court adhered to classical Hanafi law more closely than it applied the Ottoman code. Most notably, the code granted women the right to sue for delinquent payments as a cumulative debt, while the court only allowed women to start collecting maintenance from that day in court. Judges did grant women judicial divorces on grounds of desertion per the Ottoman code, an improvement in women's rights on paper, but it was happening previously in practice.

Although its impact was not too extensive in the Mandate period, the Ottoman family code did provide a basis for expanding women's rights in the post-1948 period. Israel retained the millet system and upheld the Ottoman code in its entirety, whereas Jordan and Egypt used the Ottoman code as the basis for the family laws applied in the West Bank and Gaza. This has caused a gradual but limited application of certain reforms that the courts had ignored during the Mandate period. One important example of this phenomenon concerns the Ottoman code's sanction of stipulations in the marriage contract that would empower a wife to divorce her husband if he took a second wife. While the architects of the Ottoman code included this reform to curb polygyny, we have seen how educated women in Palestine-Israel today sometimes use this right to include stipulations to determine the terms under which they enter their marriages. Most conditions address a wife's right to work, the right to continue her education, and where the couple will live. This trend among some well-educated, urban Palestinians has the potential to make an important impact on other sectors of Palestinian-Muslim society as well, if it has not already done so, given women's greater access to higher education in the last few decades, as chapter 1 discussed.

Despite that the code's encouragement of stipulations had little impact during the Mandate period, there were other ways in which family law could affect women's lives, such as the conditions under which women were likely to be successful in court. Beyond proceedings with straightforward claims, certain factors were very important to a woman's success. Perhaps the most important asset a woman could have was a lawyer, and the increased presence of professional lawyers in the courts was another way in which the court system had shifted since the early nineteenth century. In case after case, female plaintiffs and defendants who had legal representation fared considerably better than their counterparts without lawyers. The women may have won their lawsuits even without legal representation, but their lawyers were often able to procure significantly more money for them than was the norm. The additional benefits gained by women who could afford to lawyer up raises an obvious point that manifests itself perhaps universally, in that elites tend to be privileged over nonelites in legal systems.

Another reason for the increased success of elite women is they could more often afford to negotiate their financial rights or to give them up entirely if necessary. In wife-initiated divorce, they could more easily close the deal by offering further incentives to a reluctant husband. In addition, when a plaintiff initiated her claim in circumstances in which there was a second wife, she won every case. It is worth mentioning again that polygyny was mostly limited to elites. Then what of the elite husbands in these records? The court summaries are silent on this issue, as they often are, but family support was more important for women who initiated lawsuits than for the male defendants. Thus the woman's family was most likely already supporting their wronged daughter when she appeared in court and may have contributed by pressuring her husband. In contrast, it is less certain that the husband was fully supported by his family, because as the defendant he was being summoned to court.

Women who were seeking child support in addition to maintenance for themselves also tended to do better in their maintenance claims than women without children in their care. But this may have had more to do with the former or separated husband's compassion for his children than with the judge's sympathies. Most likely, both were factors in women's improved chances for success in such cases. In child custody disputes, women who were separated but still married to their husbands could sometimes extend the mother's caretaking period as long as the father did not request his child. This could happen after divorce as well, but if a woman remarried, all bets were off. This was because of the court's increased compliance with the law, and that of the paternal family's, in such circumstances. Overall, situations in which women won cases involving children often seemed to hinge on the cooperation of the husband and his compassion for his children more than anything else.

Examining the conditions under which women most often won lawsuits leads to the question of the extent to which women were informed of their rights in *shari'a*. Were they winning claims because the judges explained their rights to them, or did women tend to know their rights independently? The reality that women initiated their claims in court, and often alone, suggests they were quite aware of their basic rights at the very least. In addition, the innovative strategies that many women used in court suggest that they had more than a rudimentary understanding of Muslim family law. For example, the most common tactic women used in child custody disputes was lying about the child's age. When a woman claimed that her child was several years younger than her husband stated, she was clearly aware of her right to caretaking and the court's interpretation of classical Hanafi law in this respect. And when a woman had trouble obtaining her husband's consent to a divorce, a common strategy was to drag him into court for a maintenance claim. It seems that such an affront often persuaded the husband to grant her the divorce rather than to lose additional face.

My interviews confirmed that Palestinian-Muslim women had a general understanding of their *shari'a* rights in this period, and many of them knew considerably more than the basics. In fact, about half my interviewees from my initial set of interviews took it upon themselves to ensure that I was fully informed about women's rights in *shari'a*. The interviewees were especially helpful in conveying how women perceive and feel about Muslim family law and the *shari'a* court system. They were all quick to point out women's rights in Islam, but they did not hesitate to discuss the difficulties that women often encounter in court and under the law. Many also openly spoke of the problems that divorcées face—from the stigma her community and neighborhood often ascribe to her to the common inability of a divorcée to remarry so she may keep her children. Interestingly, even this seeming black-and-white line in Muslim family law is not actually fixed in practice. The two divorcées demonstrated that women can in fact keep their children after remarrying, but only after convincing their former husbands to relinquish their right to custody.

My older interviewees were extremely respectful toward the *shari'a* court in general and held judges in especially high esteem. The younger divorcées were considerably more critical of the court and its male privileges, but they had both recently gone through the system and encountered its gender injustices personally. While many of the older women mentioned that it is a woman's duty to obey her husband, neither of the younger women said anything along those lines. Rather, they focused on the need for a woman to know her rights so she can protect herself and determine the terms of her marriage by using stipulations. Similarly, we heard Jehad's personal story at the end of chapter 3, which illustrates the importance of including stipulations in the marriage contract in order to protect a woman's life choices. When her daughter, Layla, was married, Jehad's son-in-law agreed to the stipulation of allowing his wife to attend nursing school, but they did not write it in the contract. Later, he refused to let Layla continue her studies.

Jehad's story about her daughter well demonstrates the need for women to protect their interests as they negotiate the terms of their marriages. While it would not solve all the forms of gender discrimination that are entrenched in Muslim family law, more extensive use of stipulations in the marriage contract would at least enable Muslim women to enter marriages on their own terms. It is an encouraging sign that well-educated Palestinian young women whom I interviewed in 2014 discussed the importance of including stipulations in marriage contracts. Also, the recent efforts of women's groups, other nongovernmental organizations (NGOs), the Palestinian Authority, and the *shari'a* judiciary to draft a unified Muslim family code for the West Bank and Gaza suggests that Palestinian society may be on its way to a comprehensive reform of Muslim family law in the years to come. This is not as likely to happen, however, in the current political context in which Palestine remains under Israeli military occupation. It may take a solution to this crisis to enable Palestinian society to fully take on the challenge of Muslim family law reform.

Glossary

Notes

Bibliography

Index

Glossary

'aqd al-zawaj: the marriage contract.

ahl khubra: see *mukhbirin.*

baynuna kubra: irrevocable, or major, divorce after which a divorced couple cannot remarry unless the wife marries another man and divorces him.

baynuna sughra: revocable, or minor, divorce after which a divorced couple may reconcile without negotiating a new marriage contract during the woman's three-month waiting period.

dukhul: sexual intercourse or the consummation of a marriage.

fatwa: a respected but nonbinding legal opinion issued by a mufti.

fiqh: jurisprudence.

ghiyabi: in absentia.

hadana: the mother's caretaking period for her child that lasts from infancy until approximately age seven for boys and age nine for girls in Hanafi law.

hardana: offended and angry (describing a woman).

hukm: court order.

'idda: a woman's three-month waiting period after divorce or her husband's death during which she cannot remarry another man.

irth: inheritance.

istidana: borrowing money in another person's name.

isti'naf: appeal

kafa'a: suitability or compatibility of spouses in marriage.

kafil: enforcer or guarantor.

kashaf: to check; in this study, checking a house to ensure it meets *shari'a* standards.

khul': colloquial Arabic for *mukhal'a.*

kuswa: clothing.

mahkama shari'a: an Islamic court.

mahr: the dower, or marriage gift, that the husband provides the wife.

mahr mu'ajjal:[1] the advanced dower that the husband is supposed to give the wife when the wedding contract is signed.

mahr mu'ajjal: the deferred dower that the wife receives upon her husband's death or if he divorces her.

meskin shar'i: housing that meets *shari'a* standards and includes all the elements that encompass maintenance; see *nafaqa*.

mudd'a: female plaintiff (male: *mudd'*).

mudd' alehi: male defendant (female: *mudd'a alehi*).

mufti: a legal expert in Islamic jurisprudence.

muhami: lawyer.

mukhal'a: divorce that the wife initiates, relinquishing her divorce rights, and to which the husband must consent; formal Arabic term for *khul'*.

mukhbirin: respected community members.

munfiq: someone a maintenance provider has designated to distribute maintenance.

nafaqa: the food, shelter, clothing, and any additional household items that a *nafaqa* provider must provide his dependent to support her or him, or the cash equivalent. Often translated as maintenance or support.

nashiza: disobedient (describing a woman).

qadi (pl. quda): judge.

Qadi al-Quda: Chief Islamic Justice, the head of the *shari'a* court system in Palestine.

sijill (pl. sijillat): *shari'a* court register.

ta'a: obedience.

tafriq: judicial dissolution of a marriage.

waqf (pl. awqaf): religious endowment.

꽃

Notes

Introduction

1. Jerusalem *Shariʻa* Court, box 104/*sijillat* 473–479, case 62, page 137, 1936.

2. For other studies that analyze constructs of gender and women's strategies in *shariʻa* court registers, see Leslie Peirce, *Morality Tales: Law and Gender in the Ottoman Court of Aintab*; and Iris Agmon, *Family and Court: Legal Culture and Modernity in Late Ottoman Palestine*.

3. "Bargaining with Patriarchy," 286, n. 1. A decade later, Kandiyoti critiqued her analysis in "Gender, Power and Contestation: Rethinking Bargaining with Patriarchy." As she explained in a 2006 interview, Kandiyoti had become "increasingly sceptical about using frameworks that were primarily geared to explaining class relations (such as the work of Gramsci . . .) to understand the forms of negotiations that crystallize around gender." See Rema Hammami, "Reflections: Deniz Kandiyoti," 1349. However, as mentioned, I am using her concept quite broadly.

4. In addition to Peirce, *Morality Tales*, and Agmon, *Family and Court*, another example is Annelies Moors, *Women, Property and Islam: Palestinian Experiences, 1920–1990*.

5. See, for example, Brinkley Messick, *The Calligraphic State: Textual Domination and History in a Muslim Society*; Iza Hussin, *The Politics of Islamic Law: Local Elites, Colonial Authority, and the Making of the Muslim State*; and Agmon, *Family and Court*.

6. "Disobedient Wives and Neglectful Husbands: Marital Relations and the First Phase of Family Law Reform in Egypt." Flavia Agnes makes a similar argument for colonial India in "Patriarchy, Sexuality, and Property: The Impact of Colonial State Policies on Gender Relations in India."

7. For collections of articles based on gendered analysis of court registers, see *Women, the Family, and Divorce Laws in Islamic History*, edited by Amira Sonbol; *Women in the Ottoman Empire*, edited by Madeline C. Zilfi; and *Family History in the Middle East: Household, Property, and Gender*, edited by Beshara Doumani.

8. See, for example, Moors, *Women, Property and Islam*; Martha Mundy and Richard Saumarez Smith, "'Al-Mahr Zaituna': Property and Family in the Hills Facing Palestine,

1880–1940"; and Margaret Meriwether, "Women and *Waqf* Revisited: The Case of Aleppo 1770–1840."

9. See, for example, Mounira Charrad, *States and Women's Rights: The Making of Postcolonial Tunisia, Algeria and Morocco*; Marina Lazreg, *The Eloquence of Silence: Algerian Women in Question*; and Lynn Welchman, *Beyond the Code: Muslim Family Law and the Shari'a Judiciary in the Palestinian West Bank*.

10. For example, see the articles in *Family History*, edited by Doumani; and Agmon, *Family and Court*. Also, Cuno examines the construction of a family ideology and its impact on marriage practices and Egypt's first family law code in *Modernizing Marriage: Family, Ideology, and Law in Nineteenth- and Early Twentieth-Century Egypt*. Judith Tucker's *In the House of the Law: Gender and Islamic Law in Ottoman Syria and Palestine* focuses on muftis' constructions of gender within the family by examining their *fatwas* (legal opinions).

11. Doumani, *Family Life in the Ottoman Mediterranean: A Social History*, 44–45.

12. Ibid.

13. See Tucker, *In the House*; and Agmon, *Family and Court*. Doumani's *Rediscovering Palestine: Merchants and Peasants in Jabal Nablus, 1700–1900*, is a tremendous contribution to Palestinian social history that draws on *shari'a* court records and family papers, but gender and women's roles and status are not prominent themes.

14. Welchman, *Beyond the Code*.

15. I borrow much of this definition from Stephen Humphreys, Professor Emeritus of History at the University of California, Santa Barbara.

16. The Ottoman Empire had long issued legal codes as *qanun* (canon), and before the *Tanzimat* (Reorganization) reforms of the mid- to late nineteenth century, judges had applied both *shari'a* and *qanun* law in *shari'a* courts. The *Tanzimat* introduced a civil court system and secularized law codes, modeled after French laws, and stripped *shari'a* courts of their comprehensive jurisdiction except in family law and religious endowments. See Welchman, *Beyond the Code*, 32–36.

17. In certain Muslim countries *shari'a* still dictates other aspects of the law as well, such as in Saudi Arabia, Iran, and Sudan.

18. For this trend in Egypt, see Cuno, "Disobedient Wives." For India, see Agnes, "Patriarchy, Sexuality, and Property."

19. Ellen Fleischmann, *The Nation and Its 'New' Women: The Palestinian Women's Movement, 1920–1948*, 32–33.

20. Leila Ahmed, *Women and Gender in Islam: Historical Roots of a Modern Debate*, 137, 153. Ahmed also notes that Cromer fared little better when it came to his treatment of English women, as he helped found the Men's League for Opposing Women's Suffrage.

21. Ibid.

22. See *Women of Jordan: Islam, Labor and the Law*, 10.

23. Abadan-Unat, "Legal and Educational Reforms on Turkish Women," 179–80.

24. For a similar phenomenon in Algeria, see Marina Lazreg, *The Eloquence of Silence*, 80–88; or Allen Christelow, *Muslim Family Courts and the French Colonial State in Algeria*, 133; for Egypt, see Margot Badran, *Feminists, Islam, and Nation*, 124–25; for Syria, see Elizabeth Thompson, *Colonial Citizens: Republican Rights, Paternal Privilege and Gender in French Syria and Lebanon*, 127–40, 148–54.

25. Partha Chatterjee makes the same argument to explain Indians' resistance to British legislation and reforms concerning women in *The Nation and Its Fragments: Colonial and Postcolonial Histories*, chap. 6. For Central Asia, see Adrienne Edgar, "Bolshevism, Patriarchy, and the Nation: The Soviet 'Emancipation' of Muslim Women in Pan-Islamic Perspective."

26. Sherene Seikaly, *Men of Capital: Scarcity and Economy in Mandate Palestine*, 5.

27. Rashid Khalidi, *The Iron Cage: The Story of the Palestinian Struggle for Statehood*, 37.

28. Seikaly, *Men of Capital*, 4–5.

29. Khalidi, *The Iron Cage*, 42.

30. See Elizabeth Brownson, "Colonialism, Nationalism, and the Politics of Teaching History in Mandate Palestine"; and Brownson, "Enacting Imperial Control: Midwifery Regulation in Mandate Palestine."

31. Khalidi, *The Iron Cage*, 14–15. For Palestinians' extremely restricted access to secondary education, see Brownson, "Colonialism, Nationalism," 13, 22.

32. Khalidi, *The Iron Cage*, 45.

33. Charles D. Smith, *Palestine and the Arab-Israeli Conflict*, 134.

34. For legislation that disadvantaged Palestinian midwives, see Brownson, "Enacting Imperial Control," 28. For patriarchal employment and other laws, see Brownson, "Legislating Gender in Mandate Palestine: Colonial Laws on Midwifery, Employment, and Marriage"; or Assaf Likhovski, *Law and Identity in Mandate Palestine*, 92–99.

35. For Tunisia and Morocco, see Mounira Charrad, "Family Law Reforms in the Arab World: Tunisia and Morocco." For Egypt, see Hoda Elsadda, "Women's Rights Activism in post–Jan 25 Egypt: Combatting the Shadow of the First Lady Syndrome in the Arab World," 92.

36. Sonbol, *Women of Jordan*, 20.

37. See ibid., 48–51 for the incorporation of customary law into Jordan's civil code and how it continues to be perpetuated. For the continued and perhaps increasing influence of customary law in parts of Palestine today, see Lynn Welchman, "The Bedouin Judge, The Mufti, and the Chief Islamic Justice: Competing Legal Regimes in the Occupied Palestinian Territories."

38. Ziba Mir-Hosseini points outs that Muslims generally perceive *shariʿa* and jurisprudence with few distinctions, and I found this to be true anecdotally during my research as well. See *Marriage on Trial: A Study of Islamic Family Law in Iran and Morocco*, 5.

39. This is perhaps best explained in Wael Hallaq, *A History of Islamic Legal Theories: An Introduction to Sunni usul al-fiqh*.

40. For an overview of the Ottoman's nineteenth-century partial secularizing legal reforms and the 1917 Ottoman family code, see Robert Eisenman, *Islamic Law in Palestine and Israel*, 19–51. For how Jordanian judges negotiate and "accommodate the diversity of local custom" when dealing with rural populations, see Richard Antoun, "The Islamic Court, the Islamic Judge, and the Accommodation of Traditions."

41. For Jordan, see Sonbol, *Women of Jordan*, 34–53.

42. Although the term "Muslim family law" may seem to imply uniformity and a homogenous code, it is extremely diverse and varies a great deal by milieu. For an overview of family law in the contemporary Muslim world, see Abdullahi an-Na'im's website, https://scholarblogs.emory.edu/islamic-family-law/; or his edited book, *Islamic Family Law in a Changing World: A Global Resource Book*.

43. Wael Hallaq, "Was the Gate of Ijtihad Closed?" 22–26.

44. See chapter 2 for the necessary conditions for a house to meet *shari'a* standards.

45. Cuno, "Disobedient Wives," 6.

46. See Haim Gerber, "Social and Economic Position of Women in an Ottoman City, Bursa, 1600–1700," 233; and Ronald C. Jennings, "Women in Early 17th Century Ottoman Judicial Records—The Shari'a Court of Anatolian Kayseri," 61.

47. See Jennings, "Women in Early 17th Century," 61–62; and for modern Palestine, see Nahda Shehada, *Justice without Drama: Enacting Family Law in Gaza City Shari'a Court*, 70.

48. I only use the first names of my interviewees who are private citizens (rather, noncitizens because Palestinians in East Jerusalem and the West Bank live under military occupation). However, I will use the full names of those in the public eye, such as judges. Author's interview with Layla, Kharbatha Beniharis, Palestine, July 12, 2006.

49. Antoun, "The Islamic Court"; and Mir-Hosseini, *Marriage on Trial*.

50. The original documents of the court registers (*sijillat*) are located in the neighborhood of Abu Dis. The apartheid wall/security barrier separates Abu Dis from East Jerusalem, where I was based. Because the trip to, and particularly from, Abu Dis can be quite time-consuming, the director at the Al-Aqsa Library, Khader Salemeh, was kind enough to let me examine copies of the Jerusalem *Shari'a* Court registers on microfilm.

51. Erika Cohn, *The Judge*.

52. There have been women judges working in the offices of Sudan's *shari'a* judiciary since the 1970s. As Carolyn Fluehr-Lobban notes, however, they "do not work openly in court." When her book was published in 2013, there were four women *shari'a* judges in Sudan. *Islamic Law and Society in the Sudan*, 63.

1. The Historical, Legal, and Social Setting

1. This is perhaps best demonstrated in Khalidi's *The Iron Cage*.

2. See Brownson, "Colonialism, Nationalism"; and Brownson, "Enacting Imperial Control."

3. Samuel, *Memoirs*, 164.

4. Smith, *Palestine*, 109.

5. Ibid., 25.

6. Likhovski, *Law and Identity in Mandate Palestine*, 24.

7. Ibid., 25.

8. See Bentwich, *My Seventy-Seven Years: An Account of My Life and Times, 1883–1960*, 67.

9. Likhovski, *Law and Identity*, 57.

10. Sarah Graham-Brown, *Palestinians and their Society 1880–1946*, 24.

11. See Bernard Wasserstein, *The British in Palestine: The Mandatory Government and the Arab-Jewish Conflict, 1917–1929*, 92; and Smith, *Palestine*, 104.

12. Agmon, *Family and Court*, chaps. 4 and 5.

13. Ibid., 148–51.

14. Eisenman, *Islamic Law*, 26, 6.

15. Naomi Shepherd, *Ploughing Sand: British Rule in Palestine: 1917–1948*, 76.

16. Eisenman, *Islamic Law*, 45; and Tom Segev, *One Palestine Complete: Jews and Arabs under the British Mandate*, 170.

17. Likhovski, *Law and Identity*, 55, 57.

18. Shepherd, *Ploughing Sand*, 74; and Bentwich, *My Seventy-Seven Years*, 274–75.

19. Likhovski, *Law and Identity*, 55–56; and Shepherd, *Ploughing Sand*, 76.

20. Likhovski, *Law and Identity*, 56–57.

21. Ibid., 27.

22. Ibid., 29.

23. Ibid.

24. Segev, *One Palestine*, 170.

25. Likhovski, *Law and Identity*, 29.

26. Qadri Basha developed an Egyptian code for judges to reference in the late nineteenth century; however, it was not officially promulgated.

27. Eisenman, *Islamic Law*, 35.

28. Ibid.

29. Ibid., 34; and Welchman, *Beyond the Code*, 38, 43.

30. Welchman, *Beyond the Code*, 44.

31. Telegram from unidentified Palestinian leaders in Cairo to the Colonial Secretary in London, 1941 PRO CO 733/474/1/98.

32. Criminal Code Ordinance, Articles 182–83; Ruth Woodsmall, *Muslim Women Enter a New World*, 100.

33. Welchman, *Beyond the Code*, 44. Also, see Eisenman, *Islamic Law*, 34–45.

34. Tucker, "Revisiting Reform: Women and the Ottoman Law of Family Rights, 1917," 12–13.

35. See, for example, J. N. D. Anderson, *Law Reform in the Muslim World*, 118–120; Noel Coulson, *History of Islamic Law*, 186; or Aharon Layish, *Women and Islamic Law*, 16–17.

36. See Tucker, "Revisiting Reform," 16.

37. Samih K. Farsoun, *Culture and Customs of the Palestinians*, 27.

38. Tucker, *Women, Family, and Gender in Islamic Law*, 53–54.

39. See Jerusalem *Shari'a* Court, box 99/*sijillat* 440–447, case 254, page 464, 1928 C.E.; and Jerusalem *Shari'a* Court, box 104/*sijillat* 473–479, case 58, page 3, 1936.

40. Granqvist, *Marriage Conditions in a Palestinian Village II*, 202.

41. Granqvist, *Marriage Conditions in a Palestinian Village*, 78, 67.

42. Moors, *Women, Property, and Islam*, 97–98; Granqvist, *Marriage Conditions*, 119.

43. Granqvist, *Marriage Conditions*, 69, 85, 121–23; and P. J. Baldensperger, "Birth, Marriage and Death among the Fellahin of Palestine," 133–34.

44. Granqvist, *Marriage Conditions*, 121–22.

45. Moors, *Women, Property, and Islam*, 96.

46. Ibid., 96; and Granqvist, *Marriage Conditions*, 132–33, 135.

47. Granqvist, *Marriage Conditions*, 71–72.

48. Ibid., 53.

49. Ibid., 94.

50. Granqvist, *Marriage Conditions II*, 144.

51. Ibid., 85, 69.

52. Granqvist, *Marriage Conditions*, 86–87.

53. Ibid., 85.

54. Granqvist, *Marriage Conditions II*, 208, 304.

55. Granqvist, *Marriage Conditions*, 86.

56. Ibid., 38.

57. Granqvist, *Marriage Conditions II*, 149.

58. Ibid., 293; Graham-Brown, *Palestinians*, 49; and C. T. Wilson, *Peasant Life in the Holy Land*, 117–28, 132–36.

59. Graham-Brown, *Palestinians*, 50.

60. Granqvist, *Marriage Conditions II*, 293.

61. See Fleischmann, "*The Nation*," 28. Also see lengthy quote from Baldensperger on p. 51 on rural women's authority in the household and great influence on their husbands.

62. See Fleischmann, "*The Nation*," 30.

63. Ibid.

64. See Ottoman Law of Family Rights, Articles 92–101. Also, see Eisenman, *Islamic Law*, 41.

65. Esposito, *Women*, 26.

66. Welchman, *Islamic Family Law: Text and Practice in Palestine*, 25–26.

67. Ibid., 25.

68. Tucker, *Women, Family and, Gender*, 61.

69. Tucker, *In the House*, 44; and Eisenman, *Islamic Law*, 38–39.

70. Ottoman Law of Family Rights of 1917, Article 5. Also, see Layish, *Women and Islamic Law*, 16–17.

71. Granqvist, *Marriage Conditions*, 38.

72. Ibid., 38–39, n. 1.

73. Moors, *Women, Property, and Islam*, 96.

74. Report on polygamy, from Dr. Hamzeh, Medical Officer of Health, Ramallah, to Director of Health, Jerusalem, May 23, 1923, ISA RG10.

75. Graham-Brown, *Palestinians*, 69.

76. Wilson, *Peasant Life*, 95.

77. Tuqan, *A Mountainous Journey: An Autobiography*, 13–14.

78. Ibid.

79. Moors, *Women, Property, and Islam*, 96.

80. Ibid.

81. Woodsmall, *Muslim Women*, 100.

82. Ibid., 101.

83. Criminal Code Ordinance, 1010.

84. Greenberg, *Preparing the Mothers of Tomorrow: Education and Islam in Mandate Palestine*, 152.

85. Qtd. in ibid., 153.

86. Ibid., 115.

87. Nancy Stockdale, *Colonial Encounters among English and Palestinian Women, 1800–1948*, 137–38.

88. Dr. Hamzeh, *Report on Polygamy*.

89. Granqvist, *Marriage Conditions*, 41.

90. Tucker, "Revisiting Reform," 9.

91. Ibid., 11.

92. Tucker, *In the House*, 61–62.

93. Granqvist, *Marriage Conditions II*, 141.

94. Ibid.

95. Ibid.

96. Ibid., 238.

97. Ottoman Law of Family Rights of 1917, Article 38.

98. Welchman, *Islamic Family Law*, 67.

99. Tucker, *Women, Family, and Gender*, 49.

100. Ibid.

101. Rapoport, *Marriage, Money and Divorce in Medieval Islamic Society*, 56–57.

102. Ibid., 56.

103. Ibid., 58.

104. Hanna, "Marriage among Merchant Families in Seventeenth-Century Cairo," 147–48.

105. Ibid., 148; Tucker, "Revisiting Reform," 12; Kenneth Cuno, "Disobedient Wives," 7.

106. Abdal-Rehim, "The Family and Gender Laws in Egypt during the Ottoman Period," 110, 103.

107. Tucker, *Women*, 63.

108. Granqvist, *Marriage Conditions II*, 208.

109. Granqvist, *Marriage Conditions*, 3.

110. Granqvist, *Marriage Conditions II*, 211.

111. Tucker, *In the House*, 62.

112. Baldensperger, "Birth, Marriage," 131.

113. Granqvist, *Marriage Conditions*, 141.

114. Granqvist, *Marriage Conditions II*, 214.

115. Ibid., 191.

116. Ibid., 205.

117. Wilson, *Peasant Life*, 104.

118. See Brownson, "Colonialism, Nationalism," 15.

119. See Moors, *Women, Property, and Islam*, 102.

120. Ibid.

121. Ibid., 246.

122. Ottoman Law of Family Rights, Article 90.

123. Granqvist, *Marriage Conditions*, 132.

124. Moors, *Women, Property, and Islam*, 96–97.

125. Ibid.

126. Granqvist, *Marriage Conditions II*, 256.

127. Granqvist, *Marriage Conditions*, 139.

128. Tucker, *In the House*, 92.

129. Ibid.

130. Granqvist, *Marriage Conditions II*, 269–70; and Granqvist, *Marriage Conditions*, 12. In both books, Granqvist tracks four to five generations of marriages in Artas up to 1927, going back about a century.

131. Granqvist, *Marriage Conditions II*, 169.

132. Ibid.

133. Ibid., 269.

134. Ibid., 285.

135. Esposito, *Women*, 34.

136. Tucker, "Revisiting Reform," 13, 15–16.

137. Granqvist, *Marriage Conditions II*, 218.

138. Ibid., 248.

139. Ibid.

140. Ibid.

141. Ibid., 225.

142. Ibid., 285, n. 1.

143. Ibid., 222–24, 233.

144. Granqvist, *Birth and Childhood among the Arabs*, 110.

145. Ottoman Law of Family Rights, Articles 104, 105.

146. Ottoman Law of Family Rights, Article 110. Also see Layish, *Women and Islamic Law*, 133; and Eisenman, *Islamic Law*, 43.

147. Tucker, "Revisiting Reform," 16.

148. Ibid., 13.

149. Ottoman Law of Family Rights, Articles 122–123.

150. Ottoman Law of Family Rights, Article 130.

151. Tucker, "Revisiting Reform," 16.

152. Layish indicates this as well in *Women and Islamic Law*, 206.

153. See Anderson, *Law Reform*, 118–19 for a discussion on how these grounds have been applied in various Muslim countries.

154. See Rouhana, "Practices in the Shari'a Court of Appeal in Israel; Gendered Reading of Arbitration Decisions."

155. Welchman notes that Hanafis allowed a "limited extension" to nine for boys and eleven for girls. *Islamic Family Law*, 215. In the cases examined in this study, judges consistently adhered to the age of nine for girls.

156. Tucker, *In the House*, 116.

157. Ibid., 118.

158. E. N. Haddad, "The Guest-House in Palestine," 280.

159. Granqvist, *Marriage Conditions II*, 286.

160. Granqvist, *Marriage Conditions*, 49–50.

161. Baldensperger, "Birth," 133.

162. Granqvist, *Marriage Conditions II*, 324.

163. Moors, *Women, Property and Islam*, 60–62.

164. Granqvist, *Marriage Conditions II*, 156. The Palestinian pound was tied to the British pound, one of which was worth approximately $4.00 during World War II. See Robert Nathan, Oscar Gass, and Daniel Creamer, *Palestine: Problem and Promise*, 3.

165. Granqvist, *Birth and Childhood*, 110.

166. The IDF may not have directly expelled all Palestinians, but those who fled did so because they feared for their lives. See Benny Morris, *The Birth of the Palestinian Refugee Problem Revisited*, chaps. 3–4; or Smith, *Palestine*, 200. Although Israel eventually allowed Palestinians within its borders to become citizens, many of them had to wait decades before the state granted them citizenship. From 1948 until 1966 most Palestinians in Israel lived under martial law and were forced to live in separate communities from the majority Jewish population. For the status of Palestinian women in Israel see Rhoda Kanaaneh, *Birthing the Nation: Strategies of Palestinian Women in Israel.*

167. Welchman, *Islamic Family Law*, 19.

168. "NGO Report: The Status of Palestinian Women Citizens of Israel," 60.

169. Ibid., 62.

170. Ibid., 61.

171. Ibid., 57.

172. Ibid.

173. Jonathan Lis, Yair Ettinger, and Jack Khoury, "Israeli Ministerial Committee Okays Bill Raising Marriage Age to 18."

174. Ibid., 58.

175. Rouhana, "Muslim Family Laws in Israel: The Role of the State and Citizenship of Palestinian Women."

176. Ibid. For the numerous ways in which Israel discriminates against its Palestinian citizens, see Ilan Peleg and Dov Waxman, *Israel's Palestinians: The Conflict Within;* or the Equality Index and other reports on the unequal status of Palestinian citizens by Sikkuy, a joint Palestinian-Israeli and Jewish NGO that seeks full equality for Palestinian citizens, at http://www.sikkuy.org.il/en/.

177. Rouhana, "Muslim Family Laws."

178. Rouhana, "Practices in the Shari'a Court."

179. Ibid.

180. Ibid.

181. Ibid.

182. Welchman, *Beyond the Code*, 216; and Moors, *Women, Property, and Islam*, 86.

183. Moors, *Women, Property, and Islam*, 86.

184. Welchman, "The Development of Islamic Family Law," 875.

185. Ibid.

186. Shehada, *House of Obedience: Social Norms, Individual Agency, and Historical Contingency*, 40, 48n16.

187. Welchman, *Islamic Family Law*, 103.

188. Ibid., 102–3.

189. Ibid., 104.

190. Moors, *Women, Property, and Islam*, 142; Welchman, *Islamic Family Law*, 171.

191. Welchman, *Islamic Family Law*, 172.

192. Welchman, *Beyond the Code*, 13.

193. Welchman, *Islamic Family Law*, 180.

194. Ibid., 172.

195. Ibid.

196. Ibid., 161.

197. Ibid.

198. Ibid., 137.

199. Ibid., 215.

200. Ibid.

201. Ibid., 217.

202. Author's interviews with Wafa Al-Arj, legal advisor for the PA's Ministry of Women's Affairs, and an anonymous lawyer at the Women's Centre for Legal Aid and Counselling, Ramallah, Palestine, 2014.

203. Welchman, *Islamic Family Law*, 215.

204. See Article 5, Welchman, *Islamic Family Law*, 28–29; or An-Na'im, *Islamic Family Law*, 120.

205. Welchman, *Islamic Family Law*, 26–27.

206. Ibid., 29.

207. Ibid.

208. Ibid.

209. Reem Al-Botmeh, "A Review of Palestinian Legislation from a Women's Rights Perspective," 27.

210. Ibid., 30.

211. Welchman, "The Bedouin Judge, The Mufti, and the Chief Islamic Justice," 6.

212. Ibid., 16.

213. Ibid., 6, 20.

214. Ibid., 18, 20.

215. An-Na'im, *Islamic Family Law*, 133.

216. In surveys conducted in 2000 and 2013, 90 percent of women and 86 percent of men favor increasing the marriage age to eighteen. Hammami and Penny Johnson, "Change and Conservation: Family Law Reform in Court Practice and Public Perceptions in the Occupied Palestinian Territory," 10, 35.

217. Author's interviews with Judge Kholoud Al-Faqih and Wafa Al-Arj, Birzeit and Ramallah, January 2014. Judge Somoud Damiri was more circumspect, and followed the Chief Justice's line that judges should be able to make exceptions to a minimum marriage law of eighteen years. Author's interview, Ramallah, 2014. Judge Kholoud and Al-Arj were adamantly opposed to this, advocating eighteen years with no exceptions.

218. *Palestinian Children—Issues and Statistics Annual Report* (Ramallah: Palestinian Central Bureau of Statistics, April 2013), 24.

219. Author's interview with former *Qadi al-Quda* Shaykh Tamimi, Abu Dis, Palestine, June 2006.

220. Author's interview with Judge Al-Faqih.

221. Author's interview with a WCLAC lawyer, Ramallah, Palestine, 2014.

222. Author's interview with Al-Arj.

223. Hammami and Johnson, "Change and Conservation," 46.

224. Author's interview with Judge Al-Faqih.

225. Ibid.

226. Erika Cohn, *The Judge*.

227. As noted in the introduction, Sudan has appointed women judges since the 1970s, but they work in the *shari'a* judiciary's offices, not in court. See Fluehr-Lobban, *Islamic Law*, 63.

228. Al-Faqih's inspiring story is the subject of an award-winning documentary called *The Judge*. Unfortunately, Al-Faqih's international popularity from the film and willingness to speak truth to power has also led to her being reassigned to a court four hours from her home. She is, however, determined to continue her important work as a *shari'a* court judge.

229. Diaa Hadid, "Palestinians Chip Away at Male Divorce Monopoly."

230. Hammami and Johnson, "Change and Conservation," 18.

231. See n. 223.

232. Welchman, *Beyond the Code*, 222–30.

233. Ibid., 223.

234. Ibid., 228.

235. Ibid., 229.

236. Shehada, "Flexibility versus Rigidity in the Practice of Islamic Family Law," 35.

237. Ibid., 36.

238. Ibid.

239. Welchman, "The Development of Islamic Family Law in the Legal System of Jordan," 873.

240. Ibid.

241. Welchman, *Islamic Family Law*, 67.

242. Ibid., 68.

243. Ibid.

244. Ibid., 72.

245. Ibid.

246. Moors, *Women, Property and Islam*, 246–47.

247. Percentage Distribution of Persons (15 Years and Over) by Educational Attainment, Region and Sex, 1995, 1997, 2000–2016, Palestine Central Bureau of Statistics.

248. Ibid.

249. Welchman, *Islamic Family Law*, 69.

250. Author's interviews with female university students, Ramallah and Birzeit University, January 2014.

251. Ibid.

252. See Moors, "Debating Islamic Family Law: Legal Texts and Social Practices."

2. He Left Me without Maintenance

1. Jerusalem *Shari'a* Court, box 98/*sijillat* 434–439, case 220, page 369, 1926. In this case, the judge had to appoint the community representatives to determine the amount because the couple could not agree on them.

2. Tucker references Khalil ibn Ishaq's fourteenth-century work in *Women, Family, and Gender*, 51.

3. Rapoport, *Marriage, Money, and Divorce*, 59.

4. Tucker cites the medieval Shi'i jurist, al-Hilli, in *Women, Family, and Gender*, 51.

5. Tucker, *Women, Family, and Gender*, 53; Cuno, "Disobedient Wives," 3, 6; and Welchman, "A Husband's Authority: Emerging Formulations in Muslim Family Laws," 8–9.

6. Tucker, *In the House*, 63–65.

7. Tucker, *Women, Family, and Gender*, 44; and Mai Yamani, "Introduction," 5.

8. Ehud Toledano, *Slavery and Abolition in the Ottoman Middle East*, 3.

9. Welchman, *Beyond the Code*, 217.

10. Mir-Hosseini, *Marriage on Trial*, 46–47.

11. Ibid., 48–49.

12. The female plaintiff did not always include lack of clothing in her initial statement.

13. For example, see Jerusalem *Shari'a* Court, box 103/*sijillat* 466–472, case 278, page 470, 1935.

14. Tucker, *In the House*, 61–62.

15. Ibid., 62.

16. Ibid.

17. Granqvist, *Marriage Conditions II*, 141.

18. Ibid., 141.

19. Ibid., 238.

20. The appeal process is quite similar today in Palestine. Author's interview with Shaykh Tamimi, former Chief Islamic Justice.

21. Tucker, *Women, Gender, and Islam*, 52.

22. Tucker, "Revisiting Reform," 13.

23. Ibid., 16.

24. The British linked the Palestinian pound to the British pound in the mid-1920s.

25. Jerusalem *Shari'a* Court, box 104/*sijillat* 472–479, case 65, page 109, 1936. See chapter 3, this volume, for the procedure involved in wife-initiated divorce and women's strategies in securing them.

26. Jerusalem *Shari'a* Court, box 98/*sijillat* 434–439, case 79, page 151, 1928.

27. Jerusalem *Shari'a* Court, box 104/*sijillat* 472–479, case 26, page 39/61, 1939.

28. Granqvist, *Marriage Conditions II*, 261.

29. Ibid., 144.

30. Ibid.

31. Judith Tucker clarified this for me when we spoke at the June 2006 World Congress for Middle Eastern Studies conference in Amman, Jordan.

32. Esposito, *Women*, 25.

33. Jerusalem *Shari'a* Court, box 98/*sijillat* 434–439, case 51, page 28/73, 1928.

34. Tucker, *In the House*, 62.

35. Another common reason for this type of case was that the period of the mother's custody of the child had ended. For women's strategies in negotiating child custody cases, see chapter 4.

36. Jerusalem *Shari'a* Court, box 98/*sijillat* 434–439, case 213, page 325, 1926.

37. Jerusalem *Shari'a* Court, box 104/*sijillat* 473–479, case 72, page 175, 1936. The couple was from Hizma, which is about five miles north of Jerusalem.

38. *Wakil* can mean representative, guardian, or attorney. Only the first two definitions apply in these cases, because the court recorder used a more specific word for lawyer (*muhami*).

39. Jerusalem *Shari'a* Court, box 102/*sijillat* 460–465, case 10, page 88, 1933. They were from Selwan, a neighborhood just south of the Old City of Jerusalem.

40. See n. 5.

41. Moors, *Women, Property, and Islam*, 76.

42. Jerusalem *Shari'a* Court, box 104/*sijillat* 473–479, case 49, page 140, 1936.

43. Israeli forces destroyed most of Lifta, along with approximately four hundred other Palestinian villages, during the 1948 war.

44. Jerusalem *Shari'a* Court, box 98/*sijillat* 434–439, case 52, page 28/93, 1928. They were from the Old City of Jerusalem.

45. Jerusalem *Shari'a* Court, box 103/*sijillat* 466–472, case 273, page 454, 1936.

46. See Tucker, *In the House*, 62.

47. Al-Walaja no longer exists. Israeli forces razed it during the 1948 war.

48. Note that the plaintiff did not request a house.

49. Jerusalem *Shari'a* Court, box 103/*sijillat* 466–472, case 274, page 473, 1935.

50. Jerusalem *Shari'a* Court, box 104/*sijillat* 473–479, case 49, page 140, 1936.

3. I Gave Up All of My Rights before and after the Divorce

1. This phrase signifies a divorce initiated by the wife, as we will see. In the late 1920s and 1930s court cases examined here, this type of divorce was referred to as *mukhal'a*. It is a wife-initiated divorce in which the wife gives up her financial divorce rights in exchange for the divorce and to which the husband must consent. In colloquial Arabic, Palestinians and other Arabs refer to wife-initiated divorce as *khul'*.

2. After a minor divorce, a couple may reunite and resume the marriage during the three-month waiting period without a new contract.

3. Jerusalem *Shari'a* Court, box 104/*sijillat* 473–479, case 26, page 71, 1936. The couple in this case was from the village of Al-Waljhi.

4. Granqvist, *Marriage Conditions II*, 283.

5. Moors, *Women, Property and Islam*, 128.

6. Granqvist, *Marriage Conditions II*, 282, 287.

7. Moors, *Women, Property and Islam*, 128.

8. The Jerusalem court's practices in these respects reflect those typical of Ottoman courts. See Tucker, *In the House*, 98.

9. Granqvist, *Marriage Conditions II*, 285.

10. Ibid., 269–70.

11. Ibid., 283.

12. Ibid., 218.

13. Ibid., 234, 248.

14. Ibid., 227–29.

15. Tucker, *In the House*, 81–87.

16. Tucker, "Revisiting Reform," 13, 15–16.

17. A closer translation is "I am free of your obligations [for me] and all of the rights connected to the marriage, [including those] before and after the divorce," but this reads a bit awkwardly.

18. Tucker, *In the House*, 95.

19. See notes 4 and 5.

20. Esposito, *Women*, 32.

21. Author's interview with Hekmat, Beit Sahour, Palestine, July 2006.

22. For more recent examples of the court encouraging reconciliation, see Antoun, "The Islamic Court in Jordan," 261–62.

23. Granqvist, *Marriage Conditions II*, 261, 266.

24. Jerusalem *Shari'a* Court, box 100/*sijillat* 448–453, case 94, page 147, 1931.

25. The court recorder also stated there were no witnesses, which are usually present in a wife-initiated divorce case. Jerusalem *Shari'a* Court, box 100/*sijillat* 448–453, case 80, page 24/76, 1929.

26. Jerusalem *Shari'a* Court, box 104/*sijillat* 473–479, case 41, page 90, 1936.

27. Jerusalem *Shari'a* Court, box 104/*sijillat* 473–479, case 9, page 37/24, 1937.

28. Additionally, there were five major, irrevocable divorce cases that were wife-initiated, two of which began as maintenance.

29. When men recorded unilateral divorces, they would occasionally say there had been no consummation of the marriage in their statement as well. This is despite that they were not required to provide a reason for the court. See Jerusalem *Shari'a* Court, box 104/*sijillat* 473–479, case 160, page not written, 1938, and Jerusalem Shari'a Court, box 101/*sijillat* 454–459, case 79, page not written, 1932.

30. Jerusalem *Shari'a* Court, box 103/*sijillat* 466–472, case 109 (page not written), 1935.

31. Moors also saw this phenomenon in the 1980s. See *Women, Property, and Islam*, 145.

32. Jerusalem *Shari'a* Court, box 98/*sijillat* 434–439, case 27, page not written, 1925.

33. Jerusalem *Shari'a* Court, box 98/*sijillat* 434–439, case 34, page not written, 1925.

34. For example, see Jerusalem *Shari'a* Court, box 104/*sijillat* 473–479, case 108, page not written, 1939.

35. Tucker, *In the House*, 117–19.

36. Jerusalem *Shariʻa* Court, box 104/*sijillat* 473–479, case 157, page not written, 1938.

37. Jerusalem *Shariʻa* Court, box 104/*sijillat* 473–479, case 71, page 102, 1936.

38. Jerusalem *Shariʻa* Court, box 104/*sijillat* 473–479, case 62, page 137, 1936.

39. Jerusalem *Shariʻa* Court, box 104/*sijillat* 473–479, case 45, page obscured, 1936.

40. Author's interview with Werda, Kharbatha Beny Haris (a village near Ramallah), Palestine, July 12, 2006.

41. Tucker, "Revisiting Reform," 15–16.

42. Jerusalem *Shariʻa* Court, box 100/*sijillat* 448–453, case 86, page 398, 1929.

43. Tucker, "Revisiting Reform," 15.

44. The women did still have waiting periods. See Jerusalem *Shariʻa* Court, box 98/ *sijillat* 434–439, case 71, page 395, 1928.

45. Interview with Shaykh Tamimi.

46. Jerusalem *Shariʻa* Court, box 100/*sijillat* 448–453, case 94, page 197, 1930.

47. Jerusalem *Shariʻa* Court, box 103/*sijillat* 466–472, case 308, page 433, 1935.

48. Moors finds this in her study of women's access to property in the Nablus region as well. See *Women, Property, and Islam*, 143–44.

49. I mostly interviewed Palestinian women from East Jerusalem, but I also interviewed two Palestinians from the West Bank, one Palestinian-Israeli, and one Palestinian from Gaza who now lives in Ramallah. See chapter 5 for more information on my interviewees.

50. Author's interview with Werda.

51. Moors, *Women, Property, and Islam*, 140.

52. Brownson, "Colonialism, Nationalism, and the Politics of Teaching History," 9.

53. See, for example, Rochelle Davis, *Palestinian Village Histories: Geographies of the Displaced*, 23–26.

54. Granqvist, *Marriage Conditions II*, 259–84.

55. Ibid., 270.

56. Interestingly both Layla and Suad responded quite differently from their relatives whom I also interviewed. Layla is Werda's mother-in-law, and Suad and Hamda are sisters.

57. Author's interview with Layla.

58. Author's interview with Suad, Old City, Jerusalem, May 29, 2006.

59. Author's interview with Salemeh, Jerusalem, May 31, 2006. Salemeh is a former shaykh and was the director of the Al-Aqsa Library in 2006.

60. Author's interview with Shaykh Tamimi.

61. Author's interview with Umm Khalid, Wadi Joz, Jerusalem, June 22, 2006.

62. Author's interview with Hamda, Old City, Jerusalem, May 29, 2006.

63. Author's interview with Haji Kowthar, Wadi Joz, Jerusalem, June 6, 2006.

64. Author's interview with Jehad, Jerusalem, June 29, 2006.

65. Author's interview with Salemeh.

66. Author's interview with Nader, Old City, Jerusalem, June 3, 2006.

67. Granqvist, *Marriage Conditions II*, 268.

68. Ibid., 271.

69. *The Hans Wehr Dictionary of Modern Written Arabic*, 767.

70. Author's interview with Hamda.

71. Granqvist, *Marriage Conditions II*, 268.

72. Welchman, *Islamic Family Law*, 140–41.

73. Author's interview with Umm Khalid.

74. Author's interview with Haji Kowthar.

75. In the West Bank, the Palestinian Authority established the Nafaqa Fund in 2007, which provides 200 Jordanian dinars (US$282) per month for women, and 130 Jordanian dinars (US$211) per child as of 2013. Rema Hammami and Penny Johnson, "Change and Conservation: Family Law Reform in Court Practice and Public Perceptions in the Occupied Palestinian Territory," 60.

76. Author's interview with Jehad.

77. Author's interview with Shaykh Tamimi.

78. Although she is from al-Khalil, Bushra probably was able to obtain a residency card in her first marriage because she was married before 2003. In July of that year, the Knesset passed a law banning Palestinians from the West Bank who marry Palestinian residents of Jerusalem or Palestinian-Israelis from obtaining residency permits.

79. Author's interview with Bushra, Beit Hanina, Jerusalem, June 27, 2006.

80. This rate was in 2006.

81. Both Hekmat and her new husband work for NGOs, and their occupations give them more freedom of movement than is the case for most Palestinians under the Occupation.

82. Author's interview with Hekmat, Beit Sahour, Palestine, July 24, 2006.

83. Tucker, "Revisiting Reform," 15–16.

84. Author's interview with Umm Khalid.

85. See Moors, *Women, Property, and Islam*, 102.

86. Author's interview with Jehad.

4. He Took My Child

1. Jerusalem *Shari'a* Court, box 98/*sijillat* 434–439, case 141, page 222, 1926.

2. Tucker, *In the House*, 117–19.

3. Ibid.

4. Ibid., 116.

5. Welchman, *Islamic Family Law*, 215.

6. Jamal Nasir, *The Status of Women under Islamic Law*, 134–35.

7. Jerusalem *Shari'a* Court, box 103/*sijillat* 466–472, case 21, page 83, 1936.

8. After the maternal grandmother, the paternal grandmother was next in line for custody during the mother's caretaking period. If both grandmothers were not capable of

caring for the child, custody would revert to the child's full sister, followed by a half-sister who shared the same mother, and then a half-sister who shared the same father. Maternal aunts were next, followed by paternal aunts. For the full list of grantees of custody during the mother's custody period, see Nasir, *The Status*, 122.

9. Tucker, *In the House*, 119, 121.

10. Ibid., 143.

11. Ibid.

12. Tucker, *In the House*, 124; and Esposito, *Women*, 35.

13. Compared to maintenance cases, it was less common in child custody cases for the mother to contest the amount offered by the father.

14. Granqvist, *Birth and Childhood*, 100.

15. Jerusalem *Shari'a* Court, box 102/*sijillat* 460–465, case 162, page 268, 1934.

16. Jerusalem *Shari'a* Court, box 98/*sijillat* 434–439, case 68, page 146, 1928.

17. Tucker, *In the House*, 139–40.

18. Jerusalem *Shari'a* Court, box 101/*sijillat* 454–459, case 47, page 58, 1932.

19. Ibid.

20. Ibid.

21. Jerusalem *Shari'a* Court, box 101/*sijillat* 454–459, case 125, page obscured, 1932.

22. Jerusalem *Shari'a* Court, box 102/*sijillat* 460–465, case 51, page 101, 1934.

23. Jerusalem *Shari'a* Court, box 102/*sijillat* 460–465, case 23, page 23, 1934.

24. Jerusalem *Shari'a* Court, box 103/*sijillat* 466–472, case 182, page 344, 1934.

25. See Tucker, *In the House*, chap. 4.

26. Ibid., 144.

27. Quite atypically, neither parent specified the girl's age, and Rashida merely described her daughter as "little."

28. Jerusalem *Shari'a* Court, box 100/*sijillat* 448–453, case 153, page 261, 1930.

29. Jerusalem *Shari'a* Court, box 103/*sijillat* 466–472, case 270, page 480, 1935.

30. Jerusalem *Shari'a* Court, box 103/*sijillat* 466–472, case 25, page 40, 1932.

31. See chapter 2 on maintenance for the definition of a proper house.

32. Jerusalem *Shari'a* Court, box 101/*sijillat* 454–459, case 188, page 273, 1932.

33. Granqvist, *Birth and Childhood*, 100.

34. This is of course the reason classical Hanafi law provides for stripping remarried women of their caretaking rights.

35. Halima was from Qatnih, and Khalil was from Beit Mahseer. Jerusalem *Shari'a* Court, box 103/*sijillat* 466–472, case 317, page 545, 1934.

5. A Muslim Woman Is Free

1. Sayigh, "Review of Palestinian Village Histories: Geographies of the Displaced by Rochelle Davis," 120.

2. Davis, *Palestinian Village Histories: Geographies of the Displaced*, 101–13.

3. Cohen, Miescher, and White, *African Words, African Voices: Critical Practices in Oral History*, 4, 19.

4. This approach seems to becoming more common among younger scholars of African history. See ibid., 18–19.

5. Davis, *Palestinian Village Histories*, 102.

6. As Sherna Gluck shows, a personal contact is the best way to establish credibility with one's interviewee, but introducing one's research to the interviewee can also be effective. I arranged interviews via a personal contact whenever possible, and I told my interviewees briefly about my research before the interview. See "What's So Special about Women?" 10.

7. Strobel, "Doing Oral History as an Outsider," 46.

8. I should add that since my Arabic is still considerably influenced by Modern Standard Arabic, my friend sometimes had to translate my rather stuffy Arabic into local dialect.

9. *The Hans Wehr Dictionary of Modern Written Arabic*, 767.

10. Author's interview with Layla.

11. Swedenburg, *Memories of Revolt: The 1936–1939 Rebellion and the Palestinian National Past*, xxvi.

12. Ruwaida, Raghda, Werda, and Jehad all mentioned this specifically, and incidentally, it was also mentioned by Nader, my jewelry shopkeeper friend in the Old City.

13. Author's interview with Jehad.

14. Author's interview with Ruwaida, Wadi Joz, Jerusalem, June 6, 2006.

15. Ibid.

16. Author's interview with Raghda, Wadi Joz, Jerusalem, June 6, 2006.

17. Author's interview with Ruwaida.

18. Author's interview with Werda.

19. Ibid.

20. Ibid.

21. Author's interview with Jehad.

22. Author's interview with Suad.

23. Author's interviews with Werda and Layla.

24. Author's interview with Raghda.

25. Author's interview with Ruwaida.

26. Ibid.

27. C. W. M. Cox, "Arab Education in Palestine," Advisory Committee on Education in the Colonies, Palestine Subcommittee, 27 January 1942, Bowman Collection 2/2/99/3, Middle East Centre Archive.

28. Khalidi, *The Iron Cage*, 14–15.

29. Marianne Heiberg, "Palestinian Society in Gaza, West Bank and Arab Jerusalem: A Survey of Living Conditions," 133.

30. "Literacy Rate of Persons (15 Years and Over) in Palestine by Age Groups and Sex, 1995, 1997, 2000–2016," Palestine Central Bureau of Statistics.

31. Graham-Brown, "Education," 105.

32. Ibid.

33. Heiberg, "Palestinian Society," 136.

34. Ibid.

35. Mohammad Shadid, "The Muslim Brotherhood Movement in the West Bank and Gaza," 662.

36. Ibid.

37. Islah Jad, "Between Religion and Secularism: Islamist Women of Hamas," 264.

38. Ibid., 259, 261.

39. Ibid., 267.

40. Ibid., 272.

41. Ibid., 273–74.

42. Ibid., 273.

43. Ibid., 276.

44. Women's Centre for Legal Aid and Counselling, "Our Work: Service Unit" and "Documentation and Advocacy Unit."

45. Ibid.

46. Ibid.

47. See Davis, *Palestinian Village Histories*, 23–26.

48. This precise wording came from Nader, but many women echoed his sentiment.

49. Author's interview with Haji Kowthar.

50. Author's interview with Ruwaida.

51. Author's interview with Umm Khalid.

52. Ibid.

53. Ibid.

54. Author's interviews with Nader and Khalid, a freelance journalist.

55. See her piece, "Flexibility versus Rigidity," 35.

Conclusion

1. As mentioned in the Introduction, the fundamental premise of Deniz Kandiyoti's article, "Bargaining with Patriarchy," broadly inspired me to conceptualize women's actions in the courts in this way.

2. Tucker, "Revisiting Reform," 15–16.

3. For Tucker's findings on this issue in the Ottoman period, see *In the House*, chap. 4.

Glossary

1. The apostrophes in *mahr mu'ajjal* and *mahr mu'ajjal* signify different Arabic letters. The " ' " denotes an 'ayn, and the " ' " denotes a hamza.

꽃

Bibliography

Archives

Al-Aqsa Library, Jerusalem
    Jerusalem Shari'a Court, boxes 98–104/*sijillat* (registers) 434–479, 1926–1939
Central Zionist Archives, Jerusalem
    Record Group A255: Norman and Helen Bentwich Personal Papers
    Record Group S25/22717: Department of Education Correspondence
Israel State Archives, Jerusalem
    (All Record Groups below date from the British Mandate government)
    Record Group 8, Department of Education
    Record Group 10, Department of Health
    Record Group 23, District Commissioner's Office, Jerusalem
    Record Group 75, Muslim Shari'a Courts
Middle East Centre Archive, St. Antony's College, University of Oxford
    Humphrey Bowman Collection
    H. M. Wilson, "School Year in Palestine, 1938–1939." (unpublished manuscript)
National Archives, Public Record Office, London
    CO 733, Palestine Original Correspondence
    CO 742, Palestine Government Gazettes

Interviews (all interviews were conducted by the author)

2006 Interviews

Bushra, June 27, 2006, Beit Hanina, Jerusalem
Haji Kowthar, June 6, 2006, Wadi Joz, Jerusalem
Hamda, May 29, 2006, Old City, Jerusalem
Hekmat, July 24, 2006, Beit Sahour (near Bethlehem), Palestine
Im Khalid, June 22, 2006, Wadi Joz, Jerusalem
Jehad, June 29, 2006, Jerusalem

Khader Salameh, May 31, 2006, Haram al-Sharif, Jerusalem
Khalid, freelance journalist, June 5, 2006, Old City, Jerusalem
Layla and Werda, July 12, 2006, Kharbatha Beny Haris (near Ramallah), Palestine
Nader, June 3, 2006, Old City, Jerusalem
Raghda and Ruwaida, June 6, 2006, Wadi Joz, Jerusalem
Shaykh Tamimi, Chief Islamic Justice, July 13, 2006, Abu Dis, Palestine
Suad, May 29, 2006, Old City, Jerusalem

2014 Interviews

Aisha and Amal, January 2014, Birzeit University, Palestine
Wafa Al-Arj (Ministry of Women's Affairs legal adviser), January 2014, Ramallah, Palestine
Muhammad Mahar Aswadi, Mufti, January 2014, al-Khalil (Hebron), Palestine
Somoud Damiri, Shari'a Court Judge, January 2014, Ramallah, Palestine
Kholoud Al-Faqih, Shari'a Court Judge, January 2014, Birzeit, Palestine
Hana, January 2014, Birzeit University, Palestine
Lawyer, Women's Centre for Legal Action and Counselling, January 2014, Ramallah, Palestine
Nadira, January 2014, Birzeit University, Palestine
Naser, lawyer at al-Haq, January 2014, Ramallah, Palestine
Rahmad, Shard, and Shada, January 2014, Birzeit University, Palestine
Sabrine, Sahl, and Asma, January 2014, Birzeit University, Palestine
Shaima, January 2014, Birzeit University, Palestine

Government Documents

Criminal Code Ordinance Articles 182–183. *Palestine Gazette*. September 28, 1936, 1010.
"Literacy Rate of Persons (15 Years and over) in Palestine by Age Groups and Sex, 1995, 1997, 2000–2016." Ramallah: Palestinian Central Bureau of Statistics. http://www.pcbs.gov.ps/Portals/_Rainbow/Documents/Education-1994-2016-11E1.htm.
Ottoman Law of Family Rights of 1917, *Dustur* (Arabic translation). Vol. 9, 1332 to 1333 and 1335 to 1336. Istanbul: Awqaf Matba'si, 1928.
"Palestinian Children—Issues and Statistics Annual Report." Ramallah: Palestinian Central Bureau of Statistics, April 2013.
"Percentage Distribution of Persons (15 Years and over) by Educational Attainment, Region and Sex, 1995, 1997, 2000–2016." Ramallah: Palestinian

Central Bureau of Statistics. http://www.pcbs.gov.ps/Portals/_Rainbow/Docu ments/Education-1994-2016-10E.htm.

Published Sources

Abadan-Unat, Nermin. "The Impact of Legal and Educational Reforms on Turkish Women." In *Women in Middle Eastern History: Shifting Boundaries in Sex and Gender.* Edited by Nikki Keddie and Beth Baron. New Haven: Yale University Press, 1991, 177–94.

Abd al-Rehim, Abd al-Rehim Abd al-Rahman. "The Family and Gender Laws in Egypt during the Ottoman Period." In *Women, the Family and Divorce Laws in Islamic History.* Edited by Amira El Azhary Sonbol. Syracuse: Syracuse University Press, 1996, 96–111.

Agmon, Iris. *Family and Court: Legal Culture and Modernity in Late Ottoman Palestine.* Syracuse: Syracuse University Press, 2006.

Agnes, Flavia. "Patriarchy, Sexuality, and Property: The Impact of Colonial State Policies on Gender Relations in India." In *Family, Gender, and Law in a Globalizing Middle East and South Asia.* Edited by Kenneth Cuno and Manisha Desai. Syracuse: Syracuse University Press, 2009, 19–42.

Ahmed, Leila. *Women and Gender in Islam: The Historical Roots of a Modern Debate.* New Haven: Yale University Press, 1992.

Anderson, J. N. D. *Law Reform in the Muslim World.* London: University of London, Athlone Press, 1976.

An-Na'im, Abdullahi, ed. *Islamic Family Law in a Changing World: A Global Resource Book.* London: Zed Books, 2002.

Antoun, Richard. "The Islamic Court, the Islamic Judge, and the Accommodation of Traditions: A Jordanian Case Study." *International Journal of Middle East Studies* 12 (1980): 455–67.

Badran, Margot. *Feminists, Islam and Nation: Gender and the Making of Modern Egypt.* Princeton: Princeton University Press, 1995.

Baldensperger, P. J. "Birth, Marriage and Death among the Fellahin of Palestine." In *Palestine Exploration Fund Quarterly Statement for 1894.* London: PEF Society, 1894, 127–44. Wikisource, https://en.wikisource.org/w/index .php?title=Palestine_Exploration_Fund_Quarterly_Statement_for_1894 /Birth,_Marriage,_and_Death_among_the_Fellahin_of_Palestine&oldid =5212400.

Bentwich, Norman. *My Seventy-Seven Years: An Account of My Life and Times, 1883–1960.* London: Routledge and Kegan Paul, 1962.

Al-Botmeh, Reem. "A Review of Palestinian Legislation from a Women's Rights Perspective." UNDP, Sept. 2011.

Brownson, Elizabeth. "Colonialism, Nationalism, and the Politics of Teaching History in Mandate Palestine." *Journal of Palestine Studies* 43, no. 3 (Spring 2014): 9–25.

———. "Enacting Imperial Control: Midwifery Regulation in Mandate Palestine." *Journal of Palestine Studies* 46, no. 3 (Spring 2017): 27–42.

———. "Legislating Gender in Mandate Palestine: Colonial Laws on Midwifery, Employment, and Marriage." In *Britain in the Islamic World*. Edited by Justin Olmstead. Palgrave, forthcoming.

———. "Reforms or Restrictions? The Ottoman Muslim Family Law Code and Women's Marital Status in Mandate Palestine." In *Middle Eastern Societies 1918–1939: Challenges, Changes, and Transitions*. Edited by Ebru Boyar and Kate Fleet. Leiden: Brill, 2018, 239–58.

Charrad, Mounira. "Family Law Reforms in the Arab World: Tunisia and Morocco." Report for the United Nations Department of Economic and Social Affairs, May 2012.

———. *States and Women's Rights: The Making of Postcolonial Tunisia, Algeria and Morocco*. Berkeley: University of California Press, 2001.

Chatterjee, Partha. *The Nation and Its Fragments: Colonial and Postcolonial Histories*. Princeton: Princeton University Press, 1993.

Cohen, David W., Stephan F. Miescher, and Luise White. "Introduction: Voices, Words, and African History." In *African Words, African Voices: Critical Practices in Oral History*. Edited by David W. Cohen, Stephan F. Miescher, and Luise White. Bloomington: Indiana University Press, 2001, 1–30.

Coulson, Noel. *A History of Islamic Law*. Edinburgh: Edinburgh University Press, 1964.

Cuno, Kenneth M. "Disobedient Wives and Neglectful Husbands: Marital Relations and the First Phase of Family Law Reform in Egypt." In *Family, Gender, and Law in a Globalizing Middle East and South Asia*. Edited by Kenneth Cuno and Manisha Desai. Syracuse: Syracuse University Press, 2009, 3–18.

———. *Modernizing Marriage: Family, Ideology, and Law in Nineteenth- and Early Twentieth-Century Egypt*. Syracuse: Syracuse University Press, 2015.

Davis, Rochelle. *Palestinian Village Histories: Geographies of the Displaced*. Stanford: Stanford University Press, 2011.

Doumani, Beshara, ed. *Family History in the Middle East: Household, Property and Gender*. Albany: State University of New York Press, 2003.

————. *Family Life in the Ottoman Mediterranean: A Social History*. Cambridge: Cambridge University Press, 2017.

————. *Rediscovering Palestine: Merchants and Peasants in Jabal Nablus, 1700–1900*. Berkeley: University of California Press, 1995.

Edgar, Adrienne. "Bolshevism, Patriarchy, and the Nation: The Soviet 'Emancipation' of Muslim Women in Pan-Islamic Perspective." *Slavic Review* 65, no. 2 (Summer 2006): 252–72.

Eisenman, Robert H. *Islamic Law in Palestine and Israel: A History of the Survival of Tanzimat and Shari'a in the British Mandate and the Jewish State*. Leiden: Brill, 1978.

Elsadda, Hoda. "Women's Rights Activism in Post–Jan 25 Egypt: Combatting the Shadow of the First Lady Syndrome in the Arab World." *Middle East Law and Governance* 3 (2011): 84–93.

Esposito, John. *Women in Muslim Family Law*. 2nd ed. Syracuse: Syracuse University Press, 2001.

Farsoun, Samih K. *Culture and Customs of the Palestinians*. London: Greenwood Press, 2004.

Fleischmann, Ellen. *The Nation and Its "New" Women": The Palestinian Women's Movement, 1920–1948*. Berkeley: University of California Press, 2003.

Fluehr-Lobban, Carolyn. *Islamic Law and Society in the Sudan*. London: Routledge, 2013.

Gerber, Haim. "Social and Economic Position of Women in an Ottoman City, Bursa, 1600–1700." *International Journal of Middle East Studies* 12, no. 3 (1980): 231–44.

Gluck, Sherna. "What's So Special about Women?" In *Women's Oral History: The Frontiers Reader*. Edited by Susan Armitage, Patricia Hart, and Karen Weathermon. Lincoln: University of Nebraska Press, 2002: 3–20.

Graham-Brown, Sarah. "Education." In *Encyclopedia of the Palestinians*. Edited by Philip Mattar. New York: Facts on File, 2000, 103–11.

————. *Palestinians and Their Society 1880–1946*. London: Quartet Books, 1980.

Granqvist, Hilma. *Birth and Childhood among the Arabs: Studies in a Muhammadan Village in Palestine*. Helsingfors: Söderström, 1947.

————. *Marriage Conditions in a Palestinian Village*. Helsingfors: Societas Scientiarum Fennica, 1931.

————. *Marriage Conditions in a Palestinian Village II*. Helsingfors: Societas Scientiarum Fennica, 1935.

Greenberg, Ela. *Preparing the Mothers of Tomorrow: Education and Islam in Mandate Palestine*. Austin: University of Texas Press, 2010.

Haddad, E. N. "The Guest-House in Palestine." *Journal of the Palestine Oriental Society* 2, no.4 (1922): 279–83.

Hadid, Diaa. "Palestinians Chip Away at Male Divorce Monopoly." Associated Press, August 31, 2012.

Hallaq, Wael. *A History of Islamic Legal Theories: An Introduction to Sunni usul al-fiqh*. Cambridge: Cambridge University Press, 1999.

———. "Was the Gate of Ijtihad Closed?" *International Journal of Middle East Studies* 16, no. 1 (1984): 3–41.

Hammami, Rema. "Attitudes towards Legal Reform of Personal Status Law in Palestine." In *Women's Rights and Islamic Family Law: Perspectives on Reform*. Edited by Lynn Welchman. London: Zed Books, 2004, 125–43.

———. "Reflections: Deniz Kandiyoti." *Development and Change* 37 no. 6 (2006): 1347–54.

Hammami, Rema, and Penny Johnson. "Change and Conservation: Family Law Reform in Court Practice and Public Perceptions in the Occupied Palestinian Territory." Birzeit University, AWRAD, and UNDP, December 2013.

Hanna, Nelly. "Marriage among Merchant Families in Seventeenth-Century Cairo." In *Women, the Family and Divorce Laws in Islamic History*. Edited by Amira El Azhary Sonbol. Syracuse: Syracuse University Press, 1996, 143–54.

Hans Wehr Dictionary of Modern Written Arabic, The. Edited by J. Milton Cowan. Ithaca: Spoken Language Services, 1994.

Heiberg, Marianne. "Education." In *Palestinian Society in Gaza, West Bank and Arab Jerusalem: A Survey of Living Conditions*. Edited by Marianne Heiberg and Geir Ovensen. Oslo: FAFO Report 151, 1993.

Hussin, Iza. *The Politics of Islamic Law: Local Elites, Colonial Authority, and the Making of the Muslim State*. Chicago: University of Chicago Press, 2016.

Jad, Islah. "Between Religion and Secularism: Islamist Women of Hamas." In *On Shifting Ground: Muslim Women in the Global Era*. Edited by Fereshteh Nouraie-Simone. New York: Feminist Press, 2014, 256–93.

Jennings, Ronald C. "Women in Early 17th Century Ottoman Judicial Records—The Shari'a Court of Anatolian Kayseri." *Journal of the Economic and Social History of the Orient* 18, no. 1 (1975): 53–114.

Judge, The. Directed by Erika Cohn. IVTS and Idle Wild Films, 2018. Streaming.

Kanaaneh, Rhoda. *Birthing the Nation: Strategies of Palestinian Women in Israel*. Berkeley: University of California Press, 2002.

Kandiyoti, Deniz. "Bargaining with Patriarchy." *Gender and Society* 2, no. 3 (September 1988): 274–90.

———. "Gender, Power and Contestation: Rethinking Bargaining with Patriarchy." In *Feminist Visions of Development*. Edited by Cecile Jackson and Ruth Pearson. London: Routledge, 1988, 135–51.

Khalidi, Rashid. *The Iron Cage: The Story of the Palestinian Struggle for Statehood*. Boston: Beacon Press, 2006.

Layish, Aharon. *Women and Islamic Law in a Non-Muslim State*. Jerusalem: Israel Universities Press, 1975.

Lazreg, Marina. *The Eloquence of Silence: Algerian Women in Question*. New York: Routledge, 1994.

Likhovski, Assaf. *Law and Identity in Mandate Palestine*. Chapel Hill: University of North Carolina Press, 2006.

Lis, Jonathan, et al. "Israeli Ministerial Committee Okays Bill Raising Marriage Age to 18." *Haaretz*, March 5, 2012. http://www.haaretz.com/news/israel/israeli -ministerial-committee-okays-bill-raising-marriage-age-to-18-1.416489.

Meriwether, Margaret. "The Rights of Children and the Responsibilities of Women: Women as Wasis in Ottoman Aleppo, 1770–1840." In *Women, the Family and Divorce Laws in Islamic History*. Edited by Amira El Azhary Sonbol. Syracuse: Syracuse University Press, 1996, 219–35.

———. "Women and Waqf Revisited: The Case of Aleppo, 1770–1840." In *Women in the Ottoman Empire*. Edited by Madeline Zilfi. Leiden: Brill, 1997, 128–52.

Messick, Brinkely. *The Calligraphic State: Textual Domination and History in a Muslim Society*. Berkeley: University of California Press, 1996.

Mir-Hosseini, Ziba. *Marriage on Trial: A Study of Islamic Family Law in Iran and Morocco*. London: I. B. Tauris, 1993.

Moors, Annelies. "Debating Islamic Family Law: Legal Texts and Social Practices." In *Social History of Women and Gender in the Modern Middle East*. Edited by Judith Tucker and Margaret Meriwether. Boulder: Westview Press, 1999, 141–75.

———. *Women, Property and Islam: Palestinian Experiences, 1920–1990*. Cambridge: Cambridge University Press, 1995.

Morris, Benny. *The Birth of the Palestinian Refugee Problem Revisited*. Cambridge: Cambridge University Press, 2003.

Mundy, Martha, and Richard Saumarez Smith. "'Al-Mahr Zaituna': Property and Family in the Hills Facing Palestine, 1880–1940." In *Family History in the*

Middle East: Household, Property, and Gender. Edited by Beshara Doumani. Albany: State University of New York Press, 2003, 119–50.

Nasir, Jamal J. *The Status of Women under Islamic Law and under Modern Islamic Legislation*. London: Graham and Trotman, 1990.

Nathan, Robert, et al. *Palestine: Problem and Promise*. Washington, DC: American Council on Public Affairs, 1946.

Peirce, Leslie. *Morality Tales: Law and Gender in the Ottoman Courts of Aintab*. Berkeley: University of California Press, 2005.

Peleg, Ilan, and Dov Waxman. *Israel's Palestinians: The Conflict Within*. Cambridge: Cambridge University Press, 2011.

Rapoport, Yossef. *Marriage, Money and Divorce in Medieval Islamic Society*. Cambridge: Cambridge University Press, 2005.

Rouhana, Hoda. "Practices in the Shari'a Court of Appeal in Israel; Gendered Reading of Arbitration Decisions." *Women Living under Muslim Laws*, Dossier 25 (October 2003). http://www.wluml.org/node/462.

———. "Muslim Family Law in Israel: The Role of the State and Citizenship of Palestinian Women." *Women Living under Muslim Laws*, Dossier 27 (December 2005). http://www.wluml.org/node/501.

Samuel, Herbert. *Memoirs*. London: Cresset Press, 1945.

Sayigh, Rosemary. "Review of Palestinian Village Histories: Geographies of the Displaced by Rochelle Davis." *Journal of Palestine Studies* 41, no. 2 (Winter 2012): 118–21.

Segev, Tom. *One Palestine Complete: Jews and Arabs under the British Mandate*. New York: Holt, 2001.

Seikaly, Sherene. *Men of Capital: Scarcity and Economy in Mandate Palestine*. Stanford: Stanford University Press, 2016.

Shadid, Mohammad. "The Muslim Brotherhood Movement in the West Bank and Gaza." *Third World Quarterly* 10, no. 2 (April 1988): 658–82.

Shehada, Nahda. "Flexibility versus Rigidity in the Practice of Islamic Family Law." *Political and Legal Anthropology Review* 32, no. 1 (2009): 28–46.

———. "House of Obedience: Social Norms, Individual Agency, and Historical Contingency." *Journal of Middle East Women's Studies* 5, no. 1 (Winter 2009): 24–49.

———. *Justice without Drama: Enacting Family Law in Gaza City Shari'a Court*. Maastricht: Shaker Publishing, 2005.

Shepherd, Naomi. *Ploughing Sand: British Rule in Palestine*. New Brunswick: Rutgers University Press, 1999.

Smith, Charles D. *Palestine and the Arab-Israeli Conflict.* 8th ed. Boston: Bedford/
    St. Martin's Press, 2013.

Sonbol, Amira El Azhary. *Women of Jordan: Islam, Labor and the Law.* Syracuse:
    Syracuse University Press, 2003.

Stockdale, Nancy. *Colonial Encounters among English and Palestinian Women,
    1800–1948.* Gainesville: University Press of Florida, 2007.

Strobel, Margaret. "Doing Oral History as an Outsider." In *Women's Oral History:
    The Frontiers Reader.* Edited by Susan Armitage, Patricia Hart, and Karen
    Weathermon. Lincoln: University of Nebraska Press, 2002, 43–50.

Swedenburg, Ted. *Memories of Revolt: The 1936–1939 Rebellion and the Palestinian
    National Past.* Fayetteville: University of Arkansas Press, 2003.

Thompson, Elizabeth. *Colonial Citizens: Republican Rights, Paternal Privilege, and
    Gender in French Syria and Lebanon.* New York: Columbia University Press,
    2000.

Toledano, Ehud. *Slavery and Abolition in the Ottoman Middle East.* Seattle: Uni-
    versity of Washington Press, 1997.

Tucker, Judith. *In the House of Law: Gender and Islamic Law in Ottoman Syria and
    Palestine.* Berkeley: University of California Press, 1998.

———. "Revisiting Reform: Women and the Ottoman Law of Family Rights,
    1917." *Arab Studies Journal* 4, no. 2 (Fall 1996): 4–17.

———. *Women, Family, and Gender in Islamic Law.* Cambridge: Cambridge Uni-
    versity Press, 2008.

Tuqan, Fadwa. *A Mountainous Journey: A Poet's Autobiography.* Translated by
    Olive Kenny. Edited by Salma Khadra Jayyusi. Saint Paul: Graywolf Press,
    1990.

Wasserstein, Bernard. *The British in Palestine: The Mandatory Government and
    the Arab-Jewish Conflict, 1917–1929.* London: Royal Historical Society, 1978.

Welchman, Lynn. "The Bedouin Judge, the Mufti, and the Chief Islamic Justice:
    Competing Legal Regimes in the Occupied Palestinian Territories." *Journal
    of Palestine Studies* 38, no. 2 (Winter 2009): 6–23.

———. *Beyond the Code: Muslim Family Law and the Shari'a Judiciary in the Pales-
    tinian West Bank.* Boston: Kluwer Law International, 2000.

———. "The Development of Islamic Family Law in the Legal System of Jor-
    dan." *International and Comparative Law Quarterly* 37, no. 4 (October 1988):
    868–86.

———. "A Husband's Authority: Emerging Formulations in Muslim Family Laws."
    International Journal of Law, Policy, and the Family 25, no. 1 (2000): 1–23.

————. *Islamic Family Law: Text and Practice in Palestine.* Jerusalem: Women's Centre for Legal Aid and Counseling, 1999.

Wilson, C. T. *Peasant Life in the Holy Land.* London: John Murray, 1906.

Women's Centre for Legal Aid and Counselling. "Our Work: Service Unit" and "Documentation and Advocacy Unit." http://www.wclac.org/english/etemplate .php?id=1184.

Woodsmall, Ruth. *Moslem Women Enter a New World.* New York: Roundtable Press, 1936.

Working Group on the Status of Palestinian Women in Israel. "NGO Report: The Status of Palestinian Women Citizens of Israel." (Submitted to CEDAW committee.) Nazareth: n.p., 1997. http://studylib.net/doc/8242292 /the-working-group-on-the-status-of-palestinian-women-in-israel/.

Yamani, Mai. "Introduction." In *Feminism and Islam: Legal and Literary Perspectives.* Edited by Mai Yamani. New York: New York University Press, 1996, 1–29.

Index

Photos, figures, and tables are indicated by italicized page numbers.

Elizabeth Brownson is associate professor of history at the University of Wisconsin–Parkside. She completed her MA and PhD at the University of California, Santa Barbara, where she received a Fulbright-Hays dissertation fellowship. Her research focuses on Palestinian Muslim women's status in family courts since the British Mandate period and Muslim family law reform today. Brownson is the author of two articles in the *Journal of Palestine Studies* and a chapter in *Middle Eastern Societies, 1918–1939: Challenges, Changes and Transitions.*